Emotional Witness

My seven-year journey as an aid worker into
the heart of Honduras

Ellen Lippman Finn

Ellen Lippman Finn

COPYRIGHT AND LICENSE INFORMATION

Cover Art: Juan Marcos Bixcol Sosof
Cover Design: Fresh Designs,Michelle Fairbanks, mfairbanks.carbonmade.
com
Interior Design: Deena Rae; E-BookBuilders
Coach, Creative Consultant and Editor: Caroline Allen,
artofstorytellingonline.com
Proofreader: Lauren Wing

PRINT ISBN: 978-0-692-97221-2

LIBRARY OF CONGRESS:
1. Memoir 2. Self Help 3. Latin America 4. Political 5. Travel
First Edition

Dedication

This is lovingly dedicated to the memory of Anne, my sounding board, colleague, and friend during our years working together in Honduras.

Acknowledgments

There are so many wonderful people to thank for their support, which came in so many ways: financial, emotional, technical, creative. I was brand new to writing and needed lots of information about the process, as well as instruction on how to write a memoir. What surprised me most was how many people expressed their faith in me to carry out this giant endeavor.

Although friends had encouraged me for years to write about my experience, I didn't have the energy or inclination. What I did have in abundance was trepidation and an intense need to tell my story.

Thanks to Chris Bjornsen for the initial kickoff! It was you, Chris, who said it could be done more easily by dictating and having someone transcribe it. This was encouraging. I always preferred talking to writing. In the initial stages you so generously offered to be the ears and keyboard for recording.

An enormous thanks goes to Caroline Allen at Art of Storytelling, my rock, guide, and teacher during this entire process. You taught me how to write, how to express myself, but above all, you taught me how to let my voice come out fully, in spite of fears and decades of repression. I am also grateful for your extraordinary faith in me, your encouragement, as well as your enthusiasm. You validated my tears and helped me laugh during this process.

Thank you Dan McCarron, aka Vicarious Man, for listening to me *kvetch*, whine, and express my ever-changing moods and attitudes. You never let me give up.

Linda Bannerman, the best counselor in the entire world, what would I have done without you? You helped me learn and helped me leave. You saved my soul during the escape and resettling process. Your amazing wisdom and counsel got me through the hardest period of my entire life.

Donna Plantholt, you angel. Thank you for all of your support and guidance during "the best of times and the worst of times."

Laura van Dernoot Lipsky, you were a fantastic support, guiding me in my last years in Copán. Your book *Trauma Stewardship* became my bible. I read it at least ten times. I'd open it up anywhere and find gems of wisdom on management consulting, personal care, and international aid systems. Our conversations were tremendously insightful and practical.

So many friends supported this effort. Donna Russell and Lisa Cooper, the queens of email. I can't believe how many conversations we had about this project and how enthusiastic, insightful, and supportive you both were. Your humor, ideas, and love sustained me.

Kimmest Nicholas, my most comprehensive friend, much of this book is written to you.

Louise Wisechild, a brave and fantastic writer, you were one of my role models, guiding me through some of the writing process, as well as the "side effects." I was so naive, and you were there to help me learn.

To all of my friends, to the fabulous supporters of *Buenos Vecinos* too numerous to list, thank you. Your faith in my abilities, encouragement, and financial support has been immeasurable.

I want to thank the fabulous donors who were by my side, giving me financial support and emotional boosts. Some came into my life for short periods; others remained for many years and continue to this day to support my work. We accomplished so much as a team, didn't we?

f

I was so moved by the artwork of thirteen-year-old Juan Marcos. I just had to take your painting off my wall and put it on my book cover.

Thank you to the wonderful cover designer, Michelle Fairbanks at Fresh Design. Thank you interior designer Deena Rae at E-BookBuilders.com for your excellent work. Lauren Wing, proofreader, thank you. I know proofing my writing was not an easy assignment, but you did a great job. To Elizabeth Mehlin at Mehlin Conservation, thank you for working your restoration magic on Juan Marcos' painting, so that we could use it to grace the cover.

A special message to the late, incredibly brave Berta Cáceres, who was an amazing environmental activist, fighting until her premature death, murdered in her home, allegedly by North American forces: I admire you so much and, to this day, hold you so dear in my heart—an Indigenous woman fighting against so many odds. You remain my inspiration!

Finally, I want to include a love-filled acknowledgment to the fabulous children of Honduras. It is for you that I wrote this book. You will *always* be in my heart!

I used to be glued to an old TV show called *The Millionaire*. Michael Anthony delivered checks for one million dollars from an anonymous benefactor to a different recipient each week, and the program followed the life of the recipient. All of my friends used to fantasize about being the person who received the million dollars. I used to dream about being Michael Anthony passing out the money.

Introduction

The head teacher called me from the remote village of Hacienda San Juan asking if I would come visit his school. It was in terrible need. Too small to seat all of the children, the school had little furniture and few supplies or teaching materials. I said I would be glad to if the village arranged the transportation.

A few days later, the village leader called with traveling instructions. "Just take the *busito* (bus) to Santa Rita where you will catch the smaller *busito* to Cabañas, and we'll meet you there."

No problem. I was bringing boxes of school supplies—teaching materials and toys—and it seemed like a journey that wouldn't be too complicated.

At 6:00 a.m. on the day, I hopped on the *busito*. According to the driver, it was supposed to take off any minute. We waited for a long time in the blazing sun. As time passed, the crowded bus was packed even more as the driver and assistant pushed passengers up through the doors, saying, "There's still room." It was true: there were still about six inches between my head and the bus's ceiling. Why not put another passenger there?

Mercifully, after half an hour, the bus took off. Even though most of the windows were rusted shut, a breeze occasionally passed through and gave me a moment of life. My face poured with sweat. My clothes were drenched. The temperature kept increasing; I was sure I was losing weight. I thought of all the diet schemes in the

US. Dr. Atkins had nothing on us—we could drop five pounds in a matter of minutes.

After about twenty-five minutes of bumping along the rutted main road, we arrived in Cabañas. I caught the small connecting *busito* that could comfortably hold twelve people. I counted twenty-seven and a live chicken. A woman was facing me, teetering on a ledge. She placed her sweating hand on my knee to brace herself. We were bonding—oven sisters. The smell of sweat permeated the bus. I was sure that the bus had no shocks and axles. It was miraculous that we were able to travel up the mountain.

The seat I shared with three others tilted to the left. Every time we hit a bump, which was continually, the three of us grabbed on to whatever was available to keep from sliding off. The clanking, grating, and moaning noises frightened me, but I looked around and no one else seemed to be worried. They also didn't seem to be bothered by the black smoke belching from the exhaust pipe. We couldn't close the few windows that would open or we'd suffocate from the heat. I was debating which would be the worst cause of death.

* * *

When we finally arrived in Cabañas, about fifteen minutes later, three smiling men and a few teachers were waiting. They greeted me with warm handshakes and guided me to a truck that they said would take us up the mountain. *Dang, I thought we had arrived.*

The truck was old and very used, with bald tires, broken door and window handles, and a shattered front windshield. We all climbed in. It started almost the first time the driver tried.

We creaked along, and every time we turned right, my door swung open to reveal the edge of a very deep ravine. There were four of us in the front seat, so we had to grab the door and hold on, or at least one of us would be tumbling down that cliff.

After an hour and a half up a curvy, bumpy road, we stopped. We all jumped out. I was so relieved to finally arrive. But, to my disappointment, we were still not there. We were at the junction where the horses were waiting for us! *Horses?* I had been on a horse only once when I was ten, and it was a pony that took us in a circle with a nice grown-up leading us.

One of the men presented my horse to me. *Should I pet his nose? Would he bite my hand if I did?* I looked up at it, awestruck, wondering how I'd get up there onto the saddle. After a few attempts of trying to put my foot in the stirrup, I finally managed to mount, but not without the help of one of the villagers. I was nearly sixty-five years old! This was not a regular activity for me. As I centered myself on this giant beast, I tried to make casual small talk to cover my terror.

"What is the horse's name?" I asked in what I hoped sounded like a casual manner.

"*Relámpago* (Lightning)," he said, smiling back at me.

I started to pray. Panicked, I asked my new friend if he wouldn't mind taking the reins and walking us a bit.

As we climbed through the treacherous mountain paths, surrounded by heavy brush and trees with low-slung branches, I wondered what would happen if I failed to duck at some point. We marched single file, terribly close to the edge of the giant ravine, horses' hooves slipping, the constant sound of stones tumbling downward. *How sure-footed is my horse?* I wondered. *Are all horses sure-footed or are some clumsier than others?* I was about to meet my death. *How would they get my broken body back to the States? Maybe it would be most convenient to bury me here, below, piling some leaves on top of me?*

After half an hour, we arrived at an exquisite meadow covered with a carpet of colorful wildflowers and with a breathtaking view of mountains. I could see acres ahead in all directions. The scent in the air had changed from dried leaves and pine to a flowery sweetness. My guide let go of the reins at that point. More important than the view, however, was the flat land. I was finally safe!

Or so I thought.

Within seconds, *Relámpago* had come to a dead halt. (*Go, horsie, go!*) I didn't know what to do. I looked up and to my horror, a gigantic bull was coming towards me and my trusty steed. He

m

stopped in front of us, backed up about an inch from my leg, and to my complete revulsion started to cascade excrement.

I didn't dare move a muscle or I would have been covered! I had no idea bulls could defecate for so long. Trying not to choke on the smell, I started praying again. *Please, don't let me arrive at the school covered in pounds of liquid excrement.* I didn't dare breathe, yet I couldn't help laughing hysterically on the inside, seeing in my mind the image of this situation. After what seemed like an endless amount of time but was probably five minutes, the cascade ended. I had come through the situation clean as a whistle (except for being covered in dirt, fleas, and horse sweat). More prayers, this time of gratitude and a promise to be a better person.

We moved on. After the meadow came more treacherous path, again with the horrific sounds of stones plummeting hundreds of feet downward, my horse occasionally stumbling, and me gasping out loud.

Finally, we arrived at the community and the school. What a beautiful sight! It was a lovely wooded area, with a scent of dirt and pine, and it made me feel on top of the world.

In front of the one-room adobe school, gorgeous children were gathered, laughing, smiling, and singing. Parents stood nearby, smiling. It touched me to my core. I wanted to dismount immediately and run over to them, but unfortunately my legs had frozen in the horseback riding position. I didn't have a clue how to dismount, nor could I physically move because of the pain in my leg joints. I jokingly told the community, "I'll just stay on the horse, thank you."

A kind man helped me down. I plopped my rump into his arms. I feared that I was permanently bow-legged. I walked towards the children in that manner and everyone laughed. Introductions were made. They invited me to take a tour of the school, which meant going inside and looking at the five-by-five-meter room. We talked about their needs and hopes for their new community. They simply wanted basic items like a blackboard, furniture, school supplies, and teaching materials. The lack was very apparent. Their hope was to have another room someday for a kindergarten.

After talking and playing with the kids for about an hour, I was invited to a lovely meal, which included chicken soup: the traditional celebration dish. Although it smelled wonderful and I was ravenous, I felt tremendously guilty for consuming a precious chicken.

We sat in the schoolroom, where boards were placed on cut tree trunks to serve as a table. Horrifyingly emaciated dogs desperately searched for food, hunched under the table with their tails tucked under them. I sneaked them chicken bones. Children were watching us through the school window. It pained me to eat when I knew they were so hungry, but this was the custom: adults and guests ate first. Children would eat tortillas and salt later. I later sneaked some food to the children, too.

I was filled with so many emotions that day: above all, appreciation for all that the villagers had done for us. I felt sadness for their impoverished living conditions, overcome by witnessing the desperate dogs and the malnourished children, and exhausted from such a long, tiring, and eventful day. Nevertheless, I felt hopeful and excited, knowing that we'd be able to pitch in and help this community.

I explained to our hosts that I would be in touch with the teachers and village leader. Before we left, we brought in the school supplies, some teaching materials, and toys that we had unloaded earlier from the horses. The children eagerly and happily helped carry the items, and I was filled with a great deal of joy watching them.

It had truly been a great day, and I was feeling incredibly privileged and happy to be a part of this heartwarming and wonderful eye-opening experience, until suddenly it occurred to me: *we had to go back!*

Chapter 1

It all began in 2006 when I was living in Seattle. I was in need of a vacation and wanted something a little more interesting than staying in the US. On a musician's income, there were not many options. On the internet, I randomly came across an ad for a homestay/language-immersion program: "Live with a family and study Spanish in Honduras, Central America." The idea grabbed me, and I rushed to the phone to call Kristin, whose information was given in the ad. After a long conversation, I was convinced this was for me. She gave me the phone number of the woman, Nelly, in Honduras.

I communicated with Nelly by phone using my less-than-excellent Spanish skills. "Me come, happy, thank you." After speaking to her, the idea excited me even more. I set up a week trip.

When I heard Nelly's final comment, "We are waiting for you with open arms," I burst into tears. When, if ever, had I heard such openness and welcoming words? This was a hint of what I had always felt about Latin Americans: warm, open, and relating in an emotionally open manner.

A month or so later, the date came to take off. The eighteen-hour trip passed quickly. I remember the shock of sitting in the air and clouds, then landing in Houston where people in the waiting area were short, brown, and speaking another language. I was in the Land of Oz!

After a few hours of waiting, we reboarded. I already felt I was in Honduras. A few more hours passed and an enormous wave of excitement came over me. I could feel my giant smile throughout the landing process, customs, and immigration. I practically skipped from the airport to the bus station, then boarded a three-hour bumpy, curvy ride in a "luxury" bus where the bathroom door kept swinging open, offering us an offensive smell that was coupled with the nauseating aroma of exhaust. I tried to not throw up.

I took in the sights almost as if I needed to memorize each house, hill, and town. I had seen pictures of the Honduran countryside, but nothing could compare with reality. So green. Red roofs. Banana trees. It took my breath away.

As I leapt off the bus at the station, I looked around for my house parents and spotted Nelly and Tunino immediately. Nelly had a huge smile and literally open arms. She was tiny, no more than four foot eight. A beautiful woman, with light-brown skin, flowing thick hair, well dressed, probably in her early forties. Tunino was short, round-faced, and jolly. A laborer of some kind, I suspected, because of his worn and dirty work clothes. He obviously had taken off from work to come pick me up. They both hugged me, and the embrace coupled with their big smiles made me feel like I was coming home.

With arms around me, they ushered me into Tunino's beat-up truck. We jammed into the torn, tilted-forward, broken front seat, and we were on our way. The trip lasted five minutes. I took in everything. Brightly colored but worn, decaying houses; gorgeous flowering plants and trees; barefoot, raggedy kids playing soccer in each street that we drove through; tiny, broken-down *tiendas* (booths where produce was sold). Women were carrying their products to the market, balancing three or four large burlap bags, as well as carrying items on their heads, children in tow. I took in the combination of sweet flower fragrances, exhaust from cars, burning plastic, and Nelly's perfume.

At the house, Tunino helped me make the steep jump from the truck and grabbed my suitcase. We went through a broken gate and past a little iron workshop. He was a solderer, it turned out. I

2

met the kids: Emilio, the youngest boy with the big smile; Lexie, the older girl, a beauty like her mom; and Eddie, the skinniest teen I had ever seen. Eddie was a soccer fanatic. Apparently, all Honduran boys are soccer fanatics.

We walked through their windowless, high-gloss, purple living room/dining room combination. All of the rooms were set up around a small grass courtyard. Every room faced outside. There was no indoor connection to another room, so to go from the kitchen, to the stairs, to the bathroom, we crossed a small "yard."

They pointed out the bathroom beneath cement stairs. We would all use it. Sometimes there were as many as nine family members living in the house, they said. I made a special point of figuring out a time to wake up very early so that I could get to the bathroom without a long wait. My older bladder was not in top shape.

We climbed the cement stairs. I set my bag down as they showed me my room. It was an addition to the house and was constructed out of old wooden slats. There was a bed, a broken stool, and a fan that barely worked. There was a blanket if I needed it, but the weather was very hot, and they told me the room cooked during the day. They doubted I would use it.

I would start my morning classes with Nelly the next day, but first, a meal. I was in luck. Nelly was a fantastic cook. There was plenty of delicious food. I had been prepared for meals of corn and beans, but to my delight she put a large, broken plastic plate in front of me filled with fried plantains; scrambled eggs with chilies; beans; a local, homemade, rubbery cheese; and, of course, plenty of tortillas. I cleaned my plate.

After sitting and talking with the family—which was limited because only the children spoke (broken) English and I spoke very little Spanish—I told them I was exhausted and had to go to bed. They hugged me goodnight, and I climbed up the banister-less cement stairs, making a special note to be careful if I had to descend in the night to the bathroom.

I went into my blazing oven of a room and lay on the bed. Pouring with sweat, I fell asleep. For a while. The sheets were a challenge, balling up under my legs. The fan that barely blew hot air was squeaking. What was worse, I had the horrendous realization that I had to go to the bathroom. After an intense debate with my bladder, my bladder finally won.

Reluctantly and with great caution, I got out of bed, turned on the light—hoping not to see any newly arrived cockroaches—and began the precarious descent to the bathroom. I proudly made it down the steps, now wide awake.

The next challenge was to cross the tiny, two-meter square patch of grass with frogs startling me, leaping across my feet. They were all sizes. *Are they poisonous? Do frogs bite?*

Finally, I arrived at the cement-walled bathroom under the stairs. I flipped on the light and four or five giant cockroaches scattered at full speed. I wasn't sure which of us was more scared. Once again, another debate with my bladder: *Can I sit down without cockroaches running across my feet? Can I stop my "flow" if I need to get up suddenly and run?* My bladder won again and I sat, hyper-vigilant, as I searched for more visitors. Thank goodness the spiders seemed to want to stay in place in their corners.

I took care of business and hurried back upstairs, but by then I was wide awake, heart pounding. Although I got back into bed, I didn't sleep, imagining that there were many more "roommate" critters that I couldn't see. I was too excited to sleep anyway, thinking about my day to come, so I just lay there until dawn was officially announced by a neighboring bird call.

* * *

My private language classes started at 8:00 a.m. with Nelly. She held them in the mornings because by afternoon it was so hot that I could barely remember my name. They were fun and interesting, and even though I learned quickly, it often felt discouragingly slow. I began to use my new language skills outside of the house, but not with total success. Once, I was explaining to some neighbors that I was feeling embarrassed by my Spanish. I didn't realize that

I was actually saying I was pregnant. I was continually amazed that people were always patient and polite. Many North Americans are so impatient. I had a lot more to learn than just language.

My homestay contract was for one week, but I stayed for two. I just wasn't ready to leave. It was absolutely wondrous! Blazing hot, my attic room like an oven, cockroaches the size of Cleveland. Street noise and some kind of weird bird call that woke me up every morning at 3:30. Outdoor plumbing with frogs jumping over my feet as I peed. Okay, so it wasn't perfect. But I was so excited to be there, so in love. I had this incredible feeling of "coming home" for the first time since I was seven years old!

Soon, I was meeting Nelly's and Turino's friends, neighbors, and other family members. We took day trips into the mountains. Although my Spanish was improving and my sentences were getting longer, I realized something very important: not speaking the language forced me to speak with my heart. Heart to heart. I didn't know their politics, nor values, nor religion; we just connected heart to heart! How life-changing that experience was for me, coming from North America where there is so much ego and need to compete, or to have, or to achieve. I felt connected, and relaxed, and happy for the first time in a very long time.

Much to my dismay, the time came for me to leave. After many hugs and tears inside the house, we filed into the street as Tunino pulled up his ol' groaning truck to take me to the bus station. Neighbors and friends gathered outside to see me off, and my new family was standing around me, crying. I was crying. My heart was breaking. I believed I would never be back again. It was too far away, too complicated to get there, too expensive. *What would I even do if I lived here?* There was no work, no opportunity for me, and I certainly didn't want to take any work away from the locals.

* * *

After a long trip, I arrived "home," but something inside of me said so clearly, *This is no longer home.* It was where I lived, but it wasn't home. As days and weeks passed, I kept telling myself that I'd never go back to Honduras, repeating the reasons: too remote, too expensive, and what would I do there, anyway?

For three months, I told myself that there were other places to see besides Honduras. I sank into sadness, disconnection, and, at times, depression. I had a decent life, but at that point I was just going through the motions.

Somewhere along the line, I experienced a sudden shift. In what felt like a millisecond, I decided to sell my belongings, quit my bands, stop teaching music, and stop composing. I started planning my trip back. At sixty, I felt so different from most of my peers. Even though I didn't really have any specific plan other than possibly teaching English, I felt alive, and excited, and so sure of myself. Once I made my decision, everything fell into place quickly and easily. Sometimes when we make a change, it can feel like a series of small shifts, but this felt like I was being shot through a pneumatic tube! Opportunities appeared immediately.

For example, one of the churches where I was playing and composing responded to my news by taking up a collection among the large chorus and band. As I was preparing to leave, they handed me a huge envelope stuffed with cash. "Do something good with this," they said.

Other folks jumped in. There was a send-off fundraiser. I had decided to help Honduran schools that were struggling. Even though I had not yet witnessed the horrid conditions of the schools in the mountains, Kristin had described her experiences there, which provided me with an inkling of what was to come. I wanted to do my part.

Plans were carried out rapidly. I sold most of my belongings and my car, and put the rest in storage or at friends' houses. I called Nelly and told her I was coming back. Screams of delight came from the other end of the line. Of course I could stay with them, she told me.

Saying goodbye wasn't easy, especially to my close friends. We didn't know what this would look like: months, years? Would I be back in a week if I didn't like it? It broke my heart to be apart from them, my lifeblood.

My closest friend drove me to the airport. Silence most of the way. Silence and fear, excitement, sadness—every possible emotion. I can't forget going through the final gate and looking back at her, both of us crying. *What the hell am I doing?*

Chapter 2

Before I arrived back in Copán, Kristin—who had been a teacher there—had told me that I must see the rural schools. They were like nothing she had ever seen: decrepit, without teaching materials or furniture, and often in potentially dangerous condition, with roofs falling in, posts decaying, and large holes in the cement floors. She told me they were dark, dingy, dirty, and smelled often of rat feces and urine.

Upon my return, I was eager to go see a rural school, but I was told to never go alone, and I wasn't able to make a connection right away to get a ride. I didn't know why I shouldn't go alone and was a bit afraid to ask.

Two months into my return, through a casual conversation, I met a neighbor, Armando, who said he knew a couple of the villages very well and would be happy to go with me. Excited to finally find an escort, I made a date to hike to Carisalito.

Armando met me at my house at 6:00 a.m., so that we could leave before it got too hot. He looked at my sandals and told me to change into sturdier shoes. I didn't have a pair, I told him, so my sandals would have to suffice.

As we started the hike up a steep road, I understood why. The dirt road was so rocky and muddy on that day that we could only get to the village on foot. The ascent started when we left the pavement and cement-block houses behind. The dirt and stone road was dotted on both sides with houses made of sticks, tin, and plastic tarps, all in wretched condition. The smell of smoke from open-air firepits outside of the houses wafted in the air. Each house had a half-dozen skinny children outside playing with rubber tires, sticks, or whatever they could find. Some children were just sitting there in the dirt doing nothing. Toddlers were abundant and filthy, dressed in filled, weighted-down diapers. Some were naked, walking barefoot in areas where there were chickens and emaciated dogs and their accompanying excrement. Whole families would stare at me as we passed. I would wave and smile and, to my delight, would get an immediate smile back from the adults and older kids. Often, the tiny ones would run away, sometimes crying.

The views as we climbed became more breathtaking: rolling green hills peppered with large trees. People who lived on the precipice had million-dollar views and no food.

Armando introduced me to folks along the way, and sometimes we'd stop and chat as much as my broken Spanish would allow. I would always comment on how gorgeous it was where they lived. "How wonderful you can see the moon (or sunrise) from your house."

Folks were friendly, and I felt so grateful that they were so responsive to me. Shortly into our climb, we came to the house of an elderly man who invited us to come and sit for a bit. He dusted off the log for me to sit on and offered us coffee. Armando said it would be rude to decline. I drank the almost colorless, lukewarm coffee, glad to be sitting. After this little respite, we said our *hasta luegos* and went on our way. This kind of hospitality continued as we walked. I had such a feeling of connection and love, not just to the people but also to the land. I belonged there. Once again, I felt like I was coming home.

After an hour of hiking, sweating, heavy panting, and aching knees, we arrived at the summit where the village of Carisalito stood. Houses were hard to spot, scattered into the brush and trees. There was no village center, but I saw a communal building, a church, and a school just as we entered. All three were made of brick but very decayed from years of use—bricks missing, tin roofs damaged and rusted, steps broken. Everything was covered in splattered mud.

Armando took me a little further to the school. At first I didn't recognize it as a school—just a yellowish cement wall, dirty, stained, chipped—however, it seemed strong enough to last a few more years.

As we went behind the wall to enter, however, I realized that the wall was one of two, not one of four. The two walls were held together by a tin roof full of rusted holes and cement posts. I found it incongruous that the wall facing the road actually had a door. It was hanging off the rusted hinges sideways. Chipped paint, crumbling bricks, no working bathroom for the eighty-some students.

The kids were beautiful: brown skin, almond eyes, shiny black hair, and gorgeous smiles in spite of their missing or rotted teeth. They greeted me with a very loud, *"Buenos días."* I loved them immediately. They sat on the floor or at broken, slanted desks with destroyed tabletops. Some used an old, jagged board on a couple of rocks as tables. They sat in their ragged, dirty clothes with no notebooks or pencils. No blackboard.

A teacher was showing kids how to write by drawing letters in the air. She saw us and came over. Armando introduced us. As I went to shake her hand, I tripped over a huge pothole in the floor. Everyone laughed. The teacher grabbed my hands to prevent my fall, and I stood and did a little arms upward victory sign. The kids laughed again.

After chatting with the teacher, I walked around the room and talked with many of the children, saying simple things like "How are you today?" They laughed at my accent and watched my every move.

I asked a little boy if he liked school. He told me his name was Carlito. He was six. He told me especially liked reading. "One day I'd like to see a book because I know my letters."

See a book? It took me a few seconds to recover. I made a mental note to buy books for them.

They showed me how simple math was taught by using bottle caps or seeds and leaves, often on the floor. "If Juanito has four seeds and gives two to Maria, how many does Juanito have left?"

The two classrooms were dark with trees on one side and a building on the other. It was cold and dark in the winter when the wind howled through the holes in the walls, they told me, but I knew it was the lack of four walls that caused the chill.

Kids went to school in spite of being sick, hungry, or exhausted from picking coffee or doing farm chores at 4:00 a.m. before classes started. Although the government was mandated to provide a healthy snack, it rarely arrived. The teacher told me that often if the bags of beans or corn did show up, the food was destroyed by bugs or rancid. Many of the kids were emaciated, with broken, decayed teeth. The teacher told me that they were often dizzy or even fainted from hunger.

I was told that kids usually walked to school shoeless, over rocks, dirt paths, under fences, across creeks, or sometimes accompanied by a bigger sibling or a raggedy, emaciated mother toting a baby on her back and a couple of other filthy tiny ones at her side. The teacher mentioned that TOMS, a shoe company, donated canvas shoes to them each year, but due to the harsh terrain, the shoes wore out in less than three weeks.

After chatting for about half an hour, I thanked them for their hospitality and told them I would let them get back to work. They thanked me for coming. As we said our *hasta luegos*, I asked the teachers to make me a list of their needs and drop it by my house, and that I would be glad to help out.

I was compelled to do something immediately to pitch in. I thought obsessively all the way home and for the following days. I asked Armando where I would be able to buy school supplies and teaching materials, and he gave me several good options.

The first step seemed easy since I had received the donation from the church in the US. I had ready cash and was eagerly anticipating my return to the school with boxes of school supplies.

I came back within a couple of days, this time hiring a driver and a four-wheel drive that was filled with cartons stuffed with pencils, notebooks, erasers, and all sorts of teaching materials such as math flash cards, art materials, coloring books, glue, and paints. The basics. Upon arrival, most of the children rushed out from behind the school wall to help us unload. The sound of laughter and excited chatter was like listening to music. It lifted my heart.

I took some photos of the kids and teachers eagerly opening the boxes and pulling out the treasures one by one, screeching with delight, holding them with awe, examining them, discussing them, showing them to each other. My favorite, and I think the children's favorite, was a plastic pencil sharpener in the shape of a giant nose. You put the pencil in the nostril to sharpen it. As I demonstrated this, the kids howled with laughter and each begged for a chance to sharpen a pencil. Balloons were being blown up. Items were being lined up on the only, slanted, table in the room. The rest was unloaded onto the floor.

I felt like Santa Claus. I was hooked! This was definitely my new direction.

I saw my future unfold as a series of Santa-like activities, redistributing resources from richer people in other countries to the kids in the mountain villages. I had never felt so clear, focused, and joyous about anything in my life.

I was lighter and quicker in step as we walked down to the truck, but I was pouring sweat because the sun was now nearly at noon position and it was hot. I remember wanting to empty the collected sweat out of my bra but didn't know how to do this with Armando walking so near. I was filled with racing thoughts about where, how, and with whom I could start this new direction.

During the next few days, I visited a couple of more schools, essentially doing the same thing. What joyous work and what a privilege it was for me to be able to do this. I would always return home, rip my sweaty clothes off, and rush towards my second shower of the day to cool off. Immediately afterwards, I would sit down and write notes about my next steps, followed by emails to friends describing my impressions and needs.

My first wake-up call came about a week later with the arrival of a teacher from Carisalito. Over coffee, she handed me the list of the school's needs, but to my shock, it was three pages long. Pressure, guilt, and worry overwhelmed me. *What have I promised?* I had money for school supplies, but there was no way I had enough money to buy walls, a fence, a gate, desks, a table, a new roof, bathrooms, and a sink. And that was just the beginning; the list went way beyond even this.

It was challenging to contain my overwhelming emotions in a sea of need. I felt sadness, pressure, and a tremendous sense of guilt. Coming from North American middle class, I had so much. Although as a musician in the US, my income was below the poverty level, I still had access to friends, credit cards, loans, and the possibility of better paying work. I had items that I could sell, such as furniture and musical equipment. I had a tremendous education and, early in life, the support of a country that made education relatively easy. I had a mindset that offered me opportunity and success.

I remembered the comment six-year-old Carlito had made about how he'd "like to see a book one day." The disparity knocked me out. I studied the list, not knowing what to do.

* * *

Two months earlier, the flight from Seattle to Honduras to start my new life had been filled with utter magic. After the tearful goodbye to my friend, I changed flights in Texas and saw this new population of brown-skinned, Spanish-speaking people in the waiting area and knew my new life was beginning. I struck up conversations with my seat neighbors, anyone who would talk to me. "Where do you live?" "Where are you going?" "Where have you been?" The flight crew spoke Spanish; the food was Central American. When the pilot said, "*Bienvenidos a Honduras* (Welcome to Honduras)," I thought for a moment with a chuckle that they were talking to me personally. I stepped off the plane into this tiny three-gate airport and knew I was home. At customs, I had to stifle the urge to tell everyone in line that I was moving to Honduras. Everything that happened from then on was an "I can't believe I'm actually here" moment.

When the bus pulled into the terminal, I spotted them: Nelly and a crew of family and friends. We embraced, kissed, and spoke words of welcome. My heart doubled in size.

On the trip again in Tunino's old truck, the lines of laundry crossing the gardens of several houses seemed to me Chinese lanterns and flags signaling my arrival. At the house, we set my bags down and immediately cold juice and copious amounts of food appeared. We ate, talked, and touched each other as if this might not have been real. I was exhausted, but I had studied Spanish online during the three months back in the States, and to my pleasure, I was able to talk in full sentences. I had many verbs in the present tense under control. *I want. I go. I think.* It was exhilarating.

They took me to what was then renamed "my room." It was great to be back. I unpacked and was pleased that I remembered important items like my flashlight and bug repellent. After saying goodnight, followed by more hugs, I went to my creaky bed, turned on the creaky fan, checked for cockroaches and other unwanted roommates, and fell asleep. For about an hour. My body was so tired but my mind could not stop. I was actually in Honduras. I would be living there. I lay in bed grinning.

I was extremely pleased that I only had to go to the bathroom one time during the night, this time prepared for frogs with my trusty flashlight. It seemed to me that the same spiders were still there, housed in their special corners. This time, no cockroaches, at least that I could see.

The next morning, I awoke to the familiar bird call, wondering if I had slept at all. I bounded down the stairs, first to the bathroom, and then for breakfast and to talk with family members. A couple of guests were there, students from a nearby Spanish school who were doing homestays with Nelly's family. One was from the US and the other from Quebec. We all spoke broken Spanish while Nelly served us eggs and beans, tortillas, and rich coffee, while constantly correcting our grammar. At 8:00 a.m., they went off to their classes, and I took off to reconnect with the town. Neighbors welcomed me back and asked me how long I would be staying.

"Indefinitely," I replied with a proud grin.

Much of the time I was in wonder and disbelief that I was actually in Honduras. I kept talking to my US friends in my head. I made mental notes to tell them about this or that. I so wanted my best friends to be with me, but at the same time I didn't want to dilute the experience. New friends and invitations came easily, but the difficult part was speaking broken Spanish all day. My brain grew exhausted, not only from learning Spanish and being forced to speak it all day, but also from being new to the area and culture. It was mental overload, yet something wonderful was happening. When we couldn't speak one another's language, we were forced to use our eyes and our faces and our bodies. Communication was way more intimate. We did not think intellectually, nor judge opinions, nor take offense. Like during my first visit, we communicated heart to heart.

Within a few days, I went to the local Spanish school to sign up for classes for two hours a day. I needed a different teacher than Nelly this time. I had grown too accustomed to her voice and inflections and needed to hear other speakers. Besides, I loved making new connections. I met wonderful new teachers, and Nelly also taught at the school, so I was delighted to run into her regularly. It was like having an "old friend" in my new school environment.

I was learning quickly. The teachers were relaxed and accepting, and the method was fun. The immersion method was extremely helpful, but I also had no fear. It was hard to feel inhibition or fear and enjoy it immensely at the same time. Enjoyment always won out. My musical training had also given me lots of practice with skills in listening and repeating. I knew that the process would not be linear, and I didn't expect to see daily improvement. It was a process with peaks and valleys. I did have days or moments of discouragement, of course, but nothing debilitating. I was learning not just the language but also quite a bit about the culture, political system, and geography. Talking with folks on the street and at Nelly's house reinforced my lessons and sped up the process. This all contributed to me quickly feeling connected to my new town and lifestyle.

Before I left the US, I applied for and was offered a job in Honduras teaching English at the local bilingual school. Although I had serious reservations about the job, I accepted by email. I really didn't want to be a teacher and had no real classroom teaching practice, but I was hoping it might be a good experience and open other opportunities.

Not long after I arrived, I went to the school to set a start date.

It was a large brick complex of buildings, modern and in great shape. I had even more reservations when I saw the school population. Unlike the portrayal in the brochure and online, it served more middle-class kids and very few low-income students on scholarship.

I began to work there but didn't enjoy it. It wasn't the best use of my skills or interests, nor did I want to speak English all day. Within two months, I quit, deciding to teach English privately. This would also give me more time to visit village schools. News about an English teacher in town traveled fast. I received many requests for lessons and decided to set up classes in students' houses. This provided me with a little income that did not deprive any local from a job opportunity, and I felt I had something useful to contribute. It was more fun. I could be more myself and set my own agenda.

My next plan was to find a private living space. I had been with Nelly, her family, and the other boarders for months. I dreaded telling Nelly. She saw me as family and therefore would not understand my desire to live apart. I was also concerned about taking away some of the family's income when I no longer paid rent, even though Nelly had given me a huge discount.

I finally mustered up the courage to talk with her. At first, she was horrified. *What had she done wrong? Why would I want to leave her (four-room, one bathroom, nine-person) household?* It took quite a while to convince her that nothing was wrong and that I still loved her, we'd still be very much in touch, and that she was my reason for returning to Honduras. It was a difficult cultural concept for Hondurans to understand. *Why would someone want to live alone?* Things were tense for a while as I began the search, so I shared very little of the process with her, but I also didn't want to startle her with the news when I found a place.

I started by asking tuk-tuk drivers if they knew of anyone with a place to rent. Almost everyone had a brother-in-law, who had a cousin, who had an uncle, who had a place. Drivers would take me around, hang out while I checked out rental places, and drive me home.

One house in particular was comical. It was a sweet, furnished, three-room house in a great location, with only one problem: the landlords and their four kids lived in the house in back, and the

17

only access to their house was through what would have been mine. They said the family hardly went out, though, so they wouldn't be a bother. I could just picture their teenage kids coming home at ten at night through my house while I was taking a shower.

Almost every dwelling was idiosyncratic in some way. It would have everything but a bathroom, or it wouldn't have a kitchen sink, or it was on top of a church, or next to a canteen. The process was fun, though. I met lots of interesting, friendly people, and I had the opportunity to snoop in local houses.

Within a couple weeks, I ran into Jerry, an acquaintance. He told me about a fantastic woman who had a great little apartment up the hill from the town center. I was definitely interested. He walked me over to this lovely, two-story, mango-colored house with a giant garden on the side and back. It was a *posada* (small guest house), so folks were able to walk inside without invitation. We walked through the front door and through a living room made of colorfully painted cement blocks, through an outside dining area with homemade wooden tables, then into an enchanting garden. It had every tropical plant imaginable, as well as mango, coconut, and banana trees. There were birds everywhere.

A hearty, stout grandmother with her gray hair pulled back appeared. Jerry presented me to Doña Elena. It was love at first sight. Under one arm, she held small logs for her stove fire; under the other, she held a live chicken. One hand carried a machete and the other a cell phone. She was accompanied by what was perhaps the biggest dog in Honduras, Ixcel: part Rottweiler, part German shepherd, and possibly part bear. Ixcel walked towards me and nuzzled her head under my hand. We became instant best friends. Elena set down her cargo and the four of us (three humans, one bear) went into the living room to talk.

As I explained my recent arrival and that I had a job, Ixcel put her giant head in my lap. I ignored the drool. Jerry left to allow us to talk in more detail, and Elena took me on a tour, up the side cement stairs, Ixcel plowing along with us, nearly throwing me over the wrought-iron railing with every leap.

Opening the door to the apartment, I was delighted to see

that it was perfect. Two small rooms. The bedroom, painted an ugly green, looked out back onto the garden and some of the rental rooms, as well as the patio where folks ate. The front room overlooked the residential broken-cobblestone street. Not much traffic. Small, colorful one-story houses attached to one another on the other side. The other window was arched with a wooden frame and faced down the street towards the town center and the mountains beyond that. The kitchen had a tiny stove and half-size fridge and was attached to the "living room space," which was actually two plastic chairs and a small table. A tiny balcony facing the street couldn't hold more than two people standing sideways and a Rottweiler. I loved that it was furnished and came with tableware, sheets, and towels. This was perfect for getting me started. The rent was $200, including electricity, internet, water, and garbage. I could afford that!

Elena and I decided that I could move in right away. I gave her a giant hug with my first month's rent and left to make moving arrangements. Then came the hard part: telling Nelly. I went back to her house, we sat on the sofa, and I tried to explain. She tried to buck up but did not take the news well. She acted as if it was a breakup of a relationship. She kept trying to understand why I was leaving her "for Elena" and asking what she did wrong. She was sad and angry but kept her regal composure. I tried to reassure her that I needed a place to have an office and privacy to work. She offered to throw a renter out and give me that space. Guilt overwhelmed me. Within a few days, I left, doing the best I could to thank her, expressing my love and promising continued friendship. My guilt continued.

Moving in meant bringing two suitcases. Easy enough. The tuk-tuk brought me up the street, nine blocks from Nelly's, which was referred to as "the other side of town." Elena and Ixcel were waiting for me and escorted me upstairs. Elena handed me the key. It was official: I had an apartment. On some level it felt monumental to me. I was no longer a visitor, staying with friends. I was living in Copán.

During the day, I'd come downstairs for a coffee and cookie. Often Elena and I would sit and shell beans or husk corn and talk.

Those moments were so special. When I saw her from my window bringing out the tubs for the corn, I knew that was my cue, and I'd scoot down to help.

I loved my arched window that opened onto the garden and faced down the street. It was very common to see entire families sitting on the curbs in the evenings. I often noticed them looking up at my window as if they were watching some kind of gringa TV show. I'd wave and they would unabashedly wave back. Privacy was not something treasured in Copán.

Villagers who would come to Elena's door downstairs—shy, skinny girls in plain homemade dresses. They'd walk miles, often in shredded rubber sandals, to come into town, stop at houses, and sell limes, squash, or whatever was in season. Elena would buy what she needed. I'd run downstairs and buy bags of anything they sold, wanting to support these hard-working young *muchachas*. I'd give the bags away to neighbors who didn't have food.

My apartment was right at the end of a "middle-income" street and about one hundred yards away from the beginning of the dirt road up the mountain where folks lived in stick houses, slept on dirt floors, and often didn't have enough to eat. As I got to know my neighbors better, I would often stop over for coffee and bring produce.

I missed my "former life" friends terribly, but not the country, and not even the amenities (except for a bathtub and hot water). At least I could communicate with my American friends by email and Skype. What I missed more than anything I could have imagined was playing music with others. I pined to play jazz. It had been such a huge part of my life and suddenly there was a void. It felt like the end of a long-term relationship, and no one there would have been able to understand. I tried to seek out other musical opportunities in town, but nothing existed except for passing cars that blasted reggaeton music, a sort of simple, ugly, boring type of hip-hop.

Because of the economy and repression and depression of rural Honduras, music was not a priority. There was hardly any live music with the exception of Friday nights when an eight-piece marimba band played at an upscale hotel. I went regularly, sat on a bench sipping wine, and talked to the guys during break. I always left a tip, which I know delighted them. They didn't receive many.

One night, I told the leader at break that I was a bass player, too. He invited me to sit in. How could I say no? I didn't know the songs, and the acoustic stand-up bass was in bad shape and had only three strings, but I could pretty much guess the chord changes as I listened to them, and I fit in pretty well. They were shocked at first, never having seen a woman play bass, and they periodically looked up at me, smiling. I was beaming. It was so great to touch a bass again, no matter what kind of condition it was in, or what kind of music I was playing. It became a fun regular Friday night occurrence for a few months until the hotel ran out of money to pay them.

There were periods of culture shock and there was a lot to get used to. Things in the house broke down constantly from age or being of poor quality. I'd open the oven door and it would fall off in my hands. The shower leaked. I opened a window and the screen fell off. Everything was broken, but there was nothing that couldn't be fixed with duct tape, except for the roads.

Potholes were the size of craters, and often there was fallout from the mudslides, or fallen trees, or rocks, or broken-down vehicles. The heat in summer months was unbearable. Torrential rains. Dry spells. No potable water, constant loss of electricity, and therefore no internet and water. Endless delays for just about everything, giant cockroaches, and spiders the size of coasters. Stores were often out of items. Gas stations out of gasoline, lumber yards out of lumber, grocery stores out of most items except ketchup and mayonnaise. My bed was made of slats of wood with a lumpy four-inch mattress on top.

Despite all of this, I was happy. I felt home for the first time since I was seven years old.

The contrast to my life in the US was enormous, and the longer I was in Honduras, the more my awareness grew. Folks in Honduras lived and suffered in ways that were unimaginable to most Westerners. We took so much for granted in North America: potable water, healthy available food, safe housing, indoor plumbing, available health care, entertainment and conveniences at our whim, opportunities for good education, government checks and balances, a more honest voting system. We did not face corruption as severe as what my new Honduran friends would tell me. I began to hear more and more accounts of governmental dishonesty. I was well aware that I could leave the country at my whim. I had taken so much for granted over the years, and I was spoiled. It was a constant shock as I realized the differences in freedoms and privilege, but it was also a healthy wake-up call.

Teaching private English classes was somewhat fun, but it felt temporary. It wasn't something I wanted or expected to continue long term. I taught individuals and small groups; some learned English for work and others just for their personal interest. Sometimes it would be a group of family members.

One of my favorites was a twice-a-week class where I taught service terminology to local hotel staff. As part of the lessons, we would act out customer/hotel staff scenarios. I would have some students act as tourists, asking questions about the rooms or local activities, while the others acted as support staff. My students were shy but eventually started to come out of their shells. We started with key phrases like, "Yes, we have your reservation," but eventually the jokes started. An acting hotel guest would start making up statements like "My toilet is plugged," or "My stomach doesn't feel good. Is there a doctor nearby?" One staff member asked me what the translation was for "obnoxious guests" and we all laughed.

What really thrilled me—the work I was meant to do—was helping the schools in the rural villages. After Carisalito, I kept going into the rural villages with the monies I had received from the States and delivering supplies and toys to the schools. I adored the kids and connected so easily and so quickly with the teachers. They had so many challenges: extremely overcrowded classrooms, lack of teaching materials, broken-down schoolrooms, and frequently no pay. This was where I wanted to be. It was so clear.

Originally, I had two reasons for going to Honduras: to find heart and acceptance, and to help out with the education of marginalized Indigenous kids. So often in the US, I felt shut down for who I was, repeatedly being told that I was too emotional, too enthusiastic, too spontaneous. Here, those were the very attributes that others loved.

Meanwhile, I was still visiting different schools. I took photos and sent them to my friends and to the church that gave me the original donation. The photos depicted the need but also the joy of the children when they received something as simple as a full-sized pencil. My enthusiasm was boundless. I couldn't wait for each visit into a different village.

I was still working on the list from the Carisalito school. Able to buy supplies immediately, I got busy raising money for the bigger projects. After a while, we were able to buy a gate for the school, repair the walls, paint, and eventually—about a year later—we added the other two walls.

At every school, I loved getting to know the teachers and listening to their stories about schools, politics, international aid. There was nothing better than holding my arms around a few wiggling kids while we did this. I sent more photos. Folks sent more money. I visited more schools. Sent more photos. Received more money. Took on bigger projects like doing small repairs, buying furniture, taking kids on field trips. My role grew.

It was around this time that I hired my first employee. I spotted Marel for the very first time from my balcony while he was moving in across the street with his wife and two children. I had been watching the construction of his house over the last months and was curious to see who my new neighbors would be.

The next day, I saw Marel leaning against his old blue truck in the street and took the opportunity to scoot downstairs. He was a young, handsome man; solidly built; about thirty; black, curly hair; and beautiful, dark-brown skin. He gave me a very open, responsive smile as he saw me crossing the street.

We introduced ourselves and began to talk. I explained my work. This interested him a great deal. He said he had a strong desire to help out people and was always looking for a way to do this more. He wanted to be a pastor one day. He told me if I ever needed a truck and driver to call him and he would give me a great rate.

I did call him soon afterwards to help me bring supplies to a mountain village. I needed a four-wheel drive. I found him to be savvy and helpful, with great ideas on how to minimize expenses. He was terrific with the children at the schools and always attentive to my needs, so I continued to call him for jobs. He spoke English, which would later turn out to be an asset for visiting donors. We developed a great rhythm working together.

At first, I hired him on contract, but he demonstrated so many skills and such an eagerness to work that eventually I hired him as a regular part-time worker.

Now that I had a contract worker, I figured I should call myself something. I decided to officially name our work Project School Supplies. A new life and identity were born.

Chapter 3

I grew up in upstate New York in an immigrant ghetto. My grandparents were Polish immigrants escaping pogroms, who only spoke Yiddish. My parents were "Americanized" and spoke English as well as Yiddish. I lived my first seven years running from house to house, each with its different smells, different language, different foods, different way of life. I was always singing songs with my friends. We didn't know they were "French songs" or "Italian songs"; we just sang different words. I was a mischievous child and remember getting scolded by each of my friend's mothers in a different language. Life was normal and happy.

When I was eight, we moved to the suburbs. Everything changed. Everyone was the same color and a similar nationality. Life lost its spontaneity, its flavor. I was more worried about fitting in with people I really didn't want to belong to. It was a middle-class neighborhood. It felt snobby. Kids were concerned about how they looked and what was "proper." I led two lives: the life of a suburban child, but inside I was a stranger in a strange land. I had lost my tribe.

I had handicapped parents. My father had advanced diabetes, and my mother had a brain tumor that left her hemiplegic. I knew what it was like to not have parental involvement in my schooling. Sometimes I was embarrassed in public when I would go somewhere with my mother and she appeared drunk, a side effect of the tumor. My friends had "normal" parents. Sometimes in school I would receive special treatment because of my "family problems." I was not punished for acting out, such as when I gambled in the last row of my French class. "Problems," the principal would whisper to the teacher. I learned quickly that I was "unfortunate" but also that I could get away with impunity because of it.

We were Jewish, and I learned very early on about the pogroms in Russia that my grandparents experienced, as well as the horrors of concentration camps. I saw the difference between my own way of thinking and the reactions of my non-Jewish friends. They seemed much happier to me, carefree. They didn't hear horror stories when they were five. They didn't know persecution.

My first job at age thirteen was in the ghetto, working in a head start program with black children. I learned about their living conditions and many of their economic struggles. I became a teenager in the sixties. The race riots further opened my eyes to the imbalance. Even though I had been brought up with challenges, I began to realize, I was still, indeed, privileged.

I learned about feminism (before the word arose), and then later through the media, the discrimination against gays and lesbians. My brother had way more advantages than I did, such as freedom from household duties, career support, more attention from others, more respect. People expected him to go to university. People expected me to get married.

After what felt like an endless adolescence, I studied psychology at university, which interested me deeply and led to a great career. I spent twenty-five years as a counselor, thoroughly enjoying my work. I thought this would continue to be my future. Until one day, at nearly age fifty, I went into a music store and picked up an electric bass. I had studied piano and violin as a kid but stopped during my teenage years. I was shocked to find a sudden interest again thirty years later.

I asked the salesman to show me how to play an electric bass. He went to a corner, hooked the bass into an amp, and showed me how to play a blues scale. What seemed like half an hour later was in reality three hours when he finally came over and said, "Sorry ma'am, but we have to close."

I said, "Pack it up. I'll buy this and the amp!"

It was my goal to play one song in a blues band one day. I found a great teacher within a day or two and told him that I would only practice twenty minutes per day, but it would be consistent. I explained that I had a great career as a counselor/therapist and this would only be a hobby. He said he was fine with that and every student had to follow their own path.

Within two months, I was practicing two hours a day, and as the weeks passed I found myself even more immersed. Within six months, I quit my day job as a counselor in the women's program at a local college. I relied on my paltry savings, occasional gigs, and the kindness of my friends, with the hope that I would find more stable work in the field of music.

I decided to go back to college to study music at Seattle Central Community College. I was addicted. I couldn't remember feeling so excited about anything in my life! As I studied under a fantastic teacher, Brian Kirk, my career expanded rapidly. My first band was with some of the boys from my class, hotshot students from the inner city. Five fourteen-year-old African-American boys and me, an old white lady.

I was extremely successful in my music career, with opportunities to play with great people, excellent musicians, and at wonderful gigs. I played at wonderful venues such as concert halls, nursing homes, biker bars, and a myriad of other locations. As this career expanded, so did my composing. My hands were giving out from excessive playing, and I compensated by starting to concentrate on writing music. I published a piano book and had many fortunate opportunities to compose for local musicals and some films. In all, I spent fifteen years enjoying my second career. It had its ups and downs, but I felt I had found my niche.

What I didn't expect was that more extreme changes were to come.

Chapter 4

Walking to Copán's town center from my house took forty-five minutes to an hour; I only lived seven blocks up the hill!

Copán has a population of 5,000. The houses are colorfully painted, have red tin or clay roofs, and the roads are cobblestoned. As I passed the houses on my commute, I'd hear the slap of tortillas being made at breakfast, lunch, and supper time. I'd smell the cooking of beans, sometimes chicken. If I left my house early, I could take in the wonderful aroma of freshly made Honduran coffee. (I always expected Juan Valdez to come out of a side alley with his horse.)

Folks would want to stop and chat. I knew some of the people on my walk; others just wanted to say hello or practice English. Sometimes people would want to talk about a potential project for their school, community, or family. Other times they'd thank me for a project that we had done. I loved it when kids came up with a hug and a smile. "*Hola* Doña Elena," they'd call, and skip along with me for a while.

Neighborhood dogs and strays greeted me too, coming up for a sniff. I'd return a pat or two on their heads, sometimes offering kibble that I carried in my bag for street dogs or aggressive dogs.

One of my favorite stops was in front of the teacher Cristobal's house. For the first month, I thought he had only one sister. Then

I met two more. They all looked alike and were close in age. All four of them had dark-brown skin and round faces and were a bit chubbier than most folks. Cristobal was a serious and quiet fellow but enjoyed talking when encouraged. I used to love to try and make him laugh.

Cristobal and I would spend hours talking about the education system, the challenges the teacher faced, and the horrendous conditions of most schools. He was very dedicated to teaching.

Cristobal's upbringing was interesting and somewhat unusual. He grew up in a small village. His father was a farmer. Cristobal originally had twelve brothers, but two of them died when he was young. It was unclear why—I suspected the effects of starvation. He was too young to understand, and his parents would never talk about it. He attended school only to third grade because in his village there were no other opportunities beyond that point. He went to work, helping his father in the fields and learning welding so that he could bring in cash to help his still-large family.

When he turned twenty-one, he returned to the fourth grade. He sat in the classes with his ten-year-old companions and continued until graduation, still holding down a job, as well. He finished high school and went on to start university when he was offered a job as a teacher. (Teachers in Honduras don't need degrees. Often they have no education beyond high school.) While teaching, he continued to advance his studies in a weekend program.

I admired him so much, and as time went on we became friends. When I was in a position to help, I began to support his work at the grade school where he taught.

We continued to talk after work hours, our conversations often centered on the education system. I learned a lot from him.

The sidewalks in Copán were narrow, only walkable by one person at a time, and uneven or broken. I usually chose to walk the torn-up cobblestone streets instead. Some of the ruts were so deep that you could practically bury a car in them. Both routes brought potential danger if you weren't watching where you were going.

There were not many cars, mostly tuk-tuks and some old pickup trucks that would go slowly by, with motors roaring, gasping through their final days. The fine aroma of black smoke often filled the air, leaving me enveloped in a giant, black cloud. Only the municipal staff, *narcotraficantes* (drug traffickers), and a few rich farmers had luxury trucks, always spotlessly clean and adorned with shiny silver trim. Bling.

Farmers from villages rode into town on horseback, delivering firewood or picking up supplies. I used to love to listen to the clip-clop sounds as they'd come down the road and pass me. The men would tip their hats, a tradition I really enjoyed, while the horses left their "calling cards" in the streets. Besides the scent of fresh manure, I had to be alert or I'd find myself sliding down into town.

Once, I stepped off a curb onto the street. There was fresh, wet cement on the street, with no warning sign. I went tumbling, cracking my knee, hands, and head as I fell. Fortunately, kind folks rushed from every direction to help me up and set me down on a curb. One man came running out of a restaurant with a cup of coffee. (I decided if I ever felt lonely and needed attention, I would fake a fall in the town center.)

When I'd arrive in the center of town, first I came to the park. It was filled with flowering trees of all colors, and plants among the cement benches. Early in the morning, women would be sweeping and cleaning up the bountiful rubbish from the night before. Street dogs would be waking up, each with their regular sleeping spots, stretching, looking around for a morsel of food. When they saw me, they would always perk up and head my way. I came to know all these dogs well.

One of my favorites was Eduardo Pineda. He was a black-and-white, medium-sized dog with a wonderful, polite disposition. He must have been owned at one time because he was so well mannered. I first met him when I came upon a four-year-old girl petting him.

"He's homeless and nameless," I told the girl. "Can you think of a name for him?"

She thought for a while. "Eduardo Pineda!" she exclaimed. (I assumed this was her father's name.)

The name stuck. I so wanted to adopt him, but my dog, Pam, was very tough on dog visitors. I kept trying to find a good home for Eduardo Pineda, but, alas, no luck.

When I arrived at the park every morning at 7:30, I'd feed Eduardo Pineda before he was booted out of the park by the municipal staff. Dogs were considered to be in the same category as rats: dirty, diseased, and sometimes dangerous.

I ran into so many people at the park, especially teachers, some of whom worked and lived locally, others from the villages. I knew them all. I liked them all. I admired how they worked against so much adversity and were still upbeat. Besides the teachers, I would run into villagers from the entire municipality, all eager to shake my hand and say hello. Hugs often came from the women.

Central Park was also my "office," a place where I met with people seeking aid. It became a well-known joke.

"Can we meet in your office, Elena?" There were slightly curved cement benches that held six or seven people. The people at our meetings were often seated in a line, which was not conducive to easy conversation, but we made it work. Sometimes folks would squat in front of the benches.

Villagers from far away would call in advance, and we would set up a meeting time in the park. They'd pile off a broken-down, rusted truck, crammed in like sardines, with the bed of the truck almost touching the ground from the weight. I'd see them coming and I could feel my energy shift, warmed with affection.

I loved the faces of the farmers: hearty, weathered, leathery, eyes twinkling. I was at home when I was with them. There was always someone selling coffee or tortillas and I'd buy a snack for us. We'd sit on the curved bench and munch as we discussed their situations. Often they requested help for their schools, including supplies, teaching materials, repairs, and bathrooms (many schools did not have a bathroom or washing sink). Sometimes folks would request a classroom or even a school. I would take notes. As I became more well known, people lined up waiting to talk with me; sometimes four or five people would wait to have a chance to chat.

Occasionally, a teacher and I would go shopping after the meeting. The stores were less than a block away, so we'd march over. I would pull out the equivalent of maybe twenty-five or thirty dollars and they could select what they wanted. Storekeepers loved me because I was always bringing customers.

The town center was about four square blocks of restaurants, small hotels, and tiny *pulperías* (little stores that sold basic food items like canned goods, milk, and endless supplies of ketchup and mayonnaise).

I knew the storekeepers, the restaurant owners, the ice cream vendor. Inside the market, I had even more contacts. I'd never had an experience of knowing so many people in one place. It made me feel great at times and at other times self-conscious. There was no anonymity. Folks would literally know what I had for dinner the previous night and wouldn't hesitate to talk about it.

After the meetings, I would usually take a tuk-tuk back up the steep hill. I was usually pretty tired and wanted to go straight home without more chatting. The long walk up that hill, especially in the summer with skyrocketing temperatures, was a deterrent, as well.

For the first time in my life, I enjoyed my commute to and from work.

Chapter 5

I received a call from a leader of the community of Las Mesas. They'd heard about "the woman who helps" and wanted to know if I could come visit their school. The roof had collapsed. I told him I couldn't promise anything, but I'd be happy to come visit, and we could talk about options.

Las Mesas was located in the mountains and only accessible by four-wheel drive—or better yet, a *burro*. Even with good transportation, it was a tough climb.

Copán is a municipality on the west border of Honduras, about four hours from the largest city, San Pedro Sula. Most of the places that asked for my help were in three neighboring municipalities covering a hundred-mile radius. Much of this area was mountainous and without paved roads. The paved roads that were available were in wretched condition, with enormous potholes or often covered by mudslides, rock slides, or small chasms caused by harsh rains. We'd have to drive cautiously due to the possibility of fallen trees or a herd of cows around the bend. In some areas, we'd have to wait until the spring to be able to cross a river or drive safely up a muddy, curved mountain path.

Sometimes the initial meeting was in their village, and we'd go by four-wheel drive truck, horse, bus, ambulance, or a combination that also included walking. Other times we'd meet in the town center in the park and schedule a visit to the community. The directions to the villages were not always explained well and sometimes this caused an extra bit of work.

On this occasion, my friends at the local Red Cross said they could bring me up to Las Mesas, which would save us some expense. They went there all the time to give health workshops. We arranged for them to pick me up the next afternoon.

Much to my surprise, the next day an ambulance arrived. I scooted out of my house with some boxes of teaching materials for the school and hopped in, noticing that every one of my neighbors was hanging out of their windows, craning their necks to see what was happening. I waved and smiled, calling out to assure them I was okay.

We drove for forty minutes before the ambulance started "the climb." At first, it was bit bumpy, and I was pleased that I could handle the bounce. However, the bumps increased in magnitude, and the road grew rockier. We crossed streams and creeks. I was trying to disguise my dismay and impatience with casual questions and statements like, "This village is pretty far from the main road," which really meant, "When the hell are we going to get there?"

"Well, just a bit farther," was the answer, which is the Honduran answer for just about any distance question. "A little farther" or "in a little while," I feared this could mean days!

I was grateful for the metal brace bar in front of my seat as we bounced along. Unfortunately, I had Mario Andretti for a driver. He tackled the bumps so fast and hard that a couple of times I hit my head on the ceiling in spite of holding on with all my might. I tried to be upbeat and pleasant, "Oh, don't worry about it," while casually checking my head for blood.

After one and a half hours, we arrived. I was still vibrating as we dismounted in this small rural village. We were up so high, I was wondering—as I inhaled the fresh scent of pine—if I would need oxygen. Some of the residents were outside waiting— and staring, maybe because they had never seen a foreign person before. The village leader came over with a big smile, introduced himself, and we shook hands. He took me around and showed me the school, which had a badly damaged and rusted tin roof hanging down in pieces in the middle of each classroom.

I agreed with the leader that they indeed needed a roof and explained that we could provide the materials if they would provide the labor, and what I would need in advance (the measurements and a cost estimate). We talked about a timeline and who in the village would be available to help. I could see the relief and excitement in his face. He pumped my hand once again.

After about a half hour of conversation, I said we'd be in touch. I turned to go back to the ambulance to leave, excited about this new project that we would be doing together, but then came the teachers.

I didn't know we'd be meeting with the teachers. So I turned, and we introduced ourselves and chatted. They ushered me back inside the roofless school once again to sit and talk further. I asked them to tell me what supplies they lacked in the schoolroom. Looking around, I could see that they needed everything: pencils, books, teaching materials, furniture.

We unloaded the boxes of teaching materials that I had brought with me. I told them we would coordinate a more extensive shopping spree with them later on and asked them to make a priority list of items. I also explained what we were planning to furnish materials for the roof and explained the needs and expectations of the organization and how we could work well together.

They were delighted. They told me that no one ever had donated items to their school, and in fact they felt abandoned by the government. The schools in towns received a budget to buy school supplies and often had a budget for repairs, but not the rural schools. And since this school was so difficult to reach, no NGO, club, or church ever made the trip.

We shook hands and said goodbye. As we left the school, I turned to go towards the car. But wait! Other community leaders were walking towards me!

So, once again, we went inside the school, sat down, and I explained what we were going to do, how we would work together, and our procedure—pretty much repeating everything I had just stated two times. They thanked me profusely for coming, and as I turned to leave, I told them we'd be in touch soon and looked forward to working with them. I was tired and really wanted to be on my way.

But, wait again! The villagers were showing up for a meeting. Was this planned? We went *back* inside, crowded into the empty classroom, and sat on the few chairs that they had, some sitting on logs, some standing, as I explained our expectations, what we would be doing, and how we would be working together. Everyone kept staring at me in an intense way. *Is my Spanish that bad? Is it because I am "different"? Because they just 'don't talk much? Maybe they hate me?*

After another exhausting half hour, I asked if there were any questions, suggestions, ideas. Silence.

So I said, "Great to meet you all. I'm looking forward to working with you on this worthy project."

I stood up, left the building, and walked towards the ambulance. But no, we still didn't get there.

The leader behind me said, "Why don't we invite the assistant mayor? He lives nearby and would love to get to know you and be part of this project."

I dragged myself back in while pretending to still have energy and enthusiasm and sat back down (praying that I didn't have to stay the night). We waited mostly in silence for another thirty minutes. When I heard the motor, my heart skipped a beat. We went to the doorway. Maybe this would end soon.

The assistant mayor jumped out of the car with an outstretched hand and a big smile. We went in, sat back down, and talked. Trying not to whine from exhaustion, I explained what we did, what we were going to do, how we would work together—by then having polished my speech to perfection—all while hoping that I would maybe get home before midnight.

The assistant mayor said he wanted to say a few words. I managed an interested smile but had to make an effort not to scream and run to the ambulance. As I expected, a "few minutes" turned out to be a long speech about the beauty of collaboration, including his sincere gratitude. He told us that the municipality offered to pay for transport of materials, but unfortunately they could not deliver them all the way up the mountain. The villagers would have to carry these huge pieces of tin roofing on their backs.

"No problem," the men chimed in, including one enthusiastic four-year-old boy.

I thanked the assistant mayor for his support and started to say my *hasta luegos*. My heart skipped a beat. *This is it. I get to leave!*

But, no again! The village leader walked into the room carrying refreshments: a box of stale soda crackers and Coca Cola. (I knew better than to start my regular rant about the evils of Coke and how it destroys the health and finances of citizens of Third World countries.)

After about forty-five minutes of cordial festivities, I finally said, "I'm sorry. I have to rush off." This was four hours from when we had arrived!

We finally separated. As I was walking to the ambulance, I subtly kept checking from side to side to see if there would be additional attendees requiring my return—I became more hopeful with each step. I couldn't believe that I had actually made it to the vehicle.

We had to first pull about twenty-five children off the roof and hood of the ambulance before we could depart. The children ran along with us as we drove, laughing and screaming with joy. We were on our way.

When I arrived home, I thanked the driver. As I entered my house, I checked for head wounds from the trip back. All intact. Las Mesas would get a roof, and I would get some sleep!

Chapter 6

I now believe in love at first sight. This wasn't romantic love, but it was powerful.

Several times a week, a couple of boys from a nearby mountain village a couple hours from Copán would show up with their horses carrying firewood for Elena. As I came down the steps, I saw the two boys, about fifteen and eleven, unloading the cargo off their horses.

I felt as if I had been hit by a lightning bolt! I had an incredible, visceral reaction and started to shake. I went over to greet them.

When I looked at the older boy, I couldn't meet his eyes. I was so stunned by his innocent, open face and his warm smile. Never in my life had I experienced a spiritual connection like this, especially to a teenage boy. I was shocked. I felt as if we had met before. His younger brother was shyly hiding behind the horse, and that endeared me even more.

The older boy was beautiful. Wiry and strong, but very thin. He had the most open, eager face. His ratty straw hat was in shreds, barely recognizable as a hat, and his rubber boots were so full of holes that they were almost unusable. He threw out his filthy, sweating hand and pumped mine. He introduced himself as Isaias, and his younger brother was Alex. I shook his hand *con gusto* (with pleasure) and offered them water; it was about 105 degrees.

Alex was very timid. His face was hidden under his tattered baseball cap, and he was dressed in old, worn jeans and a ripped, sweat-soaked shirt. He was a muscular but very thin youngster, obviously a kid who worked in very hard labor. His hands were covered in dirty blisters. He tried to hide his sweet smile with his hand but kept peeking shyly at me.

As they were drinking the water, they thanked me. Alex was still hovering behind the horse. Isaias began to ask me questions about myself: where I was from, what was I doing in Copán. We chatted, continually smiling at each other, locking eyes, until they had to leave to get back up the mountain. They unloaded the huge pile of wood from both horses onto Elena's patio and led the horses outside the gate, mounted them, and took off.

I had told them I hoped to see them again soon and was pleased to hear Isaias say that they came by all the time and that they would ask for me. I eagerly looked forward to the next time.

Each time they arrived, Elena would call up to me, "Isai is here!" Isai was his nickname. My heart always skipped a beat. I'd come racing down the stairs like a mother waiting for her returning sons. I brought water for them. They'd be waiting with huge smiles followed by the customary pumping handshake from Isaias. Alex still stood hesitantly behind the horse, smiling brightly.

As the visits progressed, the water was replaced with ice tea or lemonade, and cookies. Alex would appear a little more and smile without hiding it. The more we talked, the more I grew to love these humble, beautiful young men. I felt a strong maternal connection to Alex, as well, but something about Isaias felt extremely special, nothing I could name. I didn't have words for this kind of special spiritual connection.

Isai told me they lived with their grandmother, that their parents had died a long time ago, when he was about four or five and Alex had just been born. An aunt who was his age, who they regarded as a sister, also lived with them. We talked about a possible visit one day, and after many meetings, a specific invitation was extended. I accepted immediately, very much looking forward to meeting the rest of the family.

The following Sunday, they came down to pick me up with a horse for me, much to my terror. I remembered the pain and fear of my last experience on a horse, on the trip to the mountain school in Hacienda San Lucas. This time, I was unnerved to see the horse had no saddle. All they used was a wooden platform to protect the horse when it carried wood. No stirrups. This was going to be extremely uncomfortable, I thought.

"Why don't we just walk?" I suggested.

Isaias laughed. "It's a long walk but much faster on horse." He put his arm around me to guide me to Chestnut.

The horse showed me all of its teeth. *Is this a common horse greeting? Is he smiling? Is he going to bite me? Do his teeth hurt?*

Isai, sensing my fear said, "Don't worry. He won't hurt you."

He won't hurt me? All he had to do was step on my toe or throw me from his back. That would definitely hurt me.

Chestnut was too tall to mount. Isai demonstrated how to hop on as he jumped up and threw his leg over. "You see? It's easy."

I was a senior citizen, way shorter than Isai, not in the same physical condition, and had only once been on a horse. I was not going to be a "hopper on."

New plan. They led me and the horse to a large rock that I could use to climb on. Unfortunately, Chestnut kept moving. Isai grabbed the reins but not enough to hold the horse perfectly still. *Could we drug the horse? Or better yet, drug me?*

Ultimately, there was no way for me to mount him gracefully. Isai said, "Just throw your leg over his back," as he tried to still the horse and keep from laughing out loud.

Again, I was in my mid-sixties; my legs were short and frankly they didn't "go like that." I couldn't get enough height to mount him even from the rock.

Eventually, Isai had to help me up by standing behind me and pushing my butt onto the horse while Alex, doubled over with laughter, held the reins. Although I was scared silly, it was the first time I had heard him laugh, and that completely won my heart.

I did not have the glamour and skill of a trained equestrian and, once mounted, I started to slide off the other side. "God help me," I screamed in English. "What the hell am I doing?"

Fortunately, the boys didn't speak English.

Eventually, though, I was placed in the center of the horse's back. The mounting had only taken half an hour. As I regained my (temporary) balance, the boys laughed and congratulated me. Chestnut and I turned and moved along slowly down the cobblestone road as the boys walked alongside, Isai holding the reins.

"Don't let go," I begged.

"Don't worry," he responded.

As we clip-clopped along very slowly, I passed some of my friends who did double takes and laughed. I tried to wave, but I was too scared to let go of the horse's neck. It took only a moment to become the laughing stock of Copán. Word got around.

After about fifteen minutes, we arrived at the deeply rutted dirt road that turned off to Llanetios. The incline. I took a breath, struggling to appreciate the beauty of the surrounding trees and rolling mountains while also trying to remain alive. I was sure there was a spiritual lesson here.

The boys were walking alongside of me, smiling and happily leading the horse as I trotted along (yes, I even trotted eventually), enjoying the incredible view. I tried not to cry out in agony over my tortured split-apart legs dangling without stirrups. The road was awful. It was gutted from rain, with large puddles and long patches of mud. A tuk-tuk would not have been able to drive through these patches, at least not in the rainy season.

Along the way, we passed tin-roofed houses separated by long distances, while domestic turkeys gobbled at us. I gobbled back, and they would gobble again, a fun conversation that continued for quite a while. Every house had chickens and dogs. The kids would come to the road to stare. I was an oddity. There weren't many foreign visitors, and certainly not many old ladies on horses. I waved, taking a huge risk in letting go of the horse. They would shyly wave back.

As we reached the mountain summit, I was treated to a gorgeous view of the emerald-green hills and valleys, and the wonderful scent of pine trees. It was much cooler up there. I could see rolling hills, but this time from above, and huge parcels of land covered with cornfields. Patches of coffee plants, deep green, were everywhere.

Bright-red coffee beans crowded each branch. Isai gave me one to chew on and taste. Not bad, but I didn't get that "Folgers taste."

Finally, we reached the house: a mud shack on the top of a muddy hill. I prepared to dismount on the road just as gracefully as I had mounted; it only took about ten minutes of planning and figuring out how to get off the giant. I decided to slide off, and Isai grabbed me in his arms, twisting my arm and waist, but the pain was nothing compared to my tortured groin.

We walked up the short but steep muddy path to their house while their four dogs greeted us with friendly wags, sniffing me constantly and jumping up, covering me with red clay paw prints. I stepped over the multitude of big and little chickens.

The house was a mud-and-stick shack, three by four meters, and leaned at a thirty-degree angle. Logs were used to hold the mud walls in place. The roof was made of broken pieces of tin and some plastic. It smelled of earth and mildew. It had a wet dirt floor, no furniture, and a pile of clothes in the corner.

I would learn that they slept on the mud floor, without blankets. I supposed they wore all their clothes to keep warm on cold mountain nights; four people crowded into this small room probably kept it warm.

Sitting on a tiny piece of log at the side of the house was their grandmother, Doña Josefa. She had a face of such infinite kindness and wisdom, the kind of face that stories are made of, with thick gray hair pulled back from her open, light-brown skin, and only a few wrinkles. Warmth and love seemed to exude from every pore. She sat erect, as if the log was her throne. Her clothes were very worn, her skirt faded, and the collar of her blouse shredded. I assumed that she was probably in her late sixties or older, but the kids told me she was "quite old," fifty-two. She smiled at me and offered her hand. I gave her a hug. We connected instantly.

She invited me to sit down. I was unsure of where until I saw Isaias bounding out from the back of the hut with another log for a chair. They brought me coffee, slightly warm, in a dirty cup, so weak that I could see through it. They apologized for not having sugar. I told them I never took sugar in my coffee. This was just the way I liked it.

Their young, bubbly aunt/sister Maria came running in from the bushes, full of energy and smiles, arms wide open. She gave me a bear hug that almost hurt and a smooch on my cheek. She said she was excited to finally meet me as the boys had talked about me all the time.

Maria was tiny. She came up to my neck and I was only five foot two. Her hair was tied back and long, but thinning with tiny bald patches, probably due to malnutrition. She wore a too-small red skirt with a broken zipper, a worn blouse, and tattered sandals. She pulled up a broken piece of plastic chair, sat down inches from me, and held my hand. She offered me more coffee.

They told me about their lives in Llanetios. Isai had only gone to school up to third grade when their mom died. He had to go to work in the fields after that, planting corn and beans. Alex finished sixth grade, which in Honduras was considered the end of grade school. (A sixth-grade education in the mountain schools is actually equivalent to a first-grade education in the US.) Due to the cost of books and school supplies, only Alex was able to graduate, thanks to financial help from others. Maria had only a couple of years of education, but she was bright. I could see it in her eyes and the way she responded.

They took me to see their corn crop, the football field, and the tiny two "competing" churches: Catholics vs. Evangelicals. The village had houses spread out, each with a bit of land to grow vegetables and support their chickens. The community looked like a postcard picture of Honduras: coffee bushes, banana trees, pine trees, rolling hills. Most houses with their red clay roofs were in somewhat decent shape compared to other villages. The two-room school housed 150 students. Its structure was solid, made of brick, but there was nothing inside except a handful of broken desks and chairs.

The community had coffee plants everywhere, as coffee did very well in the cooler mountain areas. Folks also grew bananas and grenadias, a delicious fruit if you don't mind the consistency of crunchy eyeballs. Isaias cut a hole in the grenadias with the point of his machete and we sucked the contents out, dripping crunchy, snotty-looking seeds. Deelish!

Folks cultivated leafy mustard greens, as well. Not much else. There seemed to be little interest in cultivating or eating vegetables. Isaias explained that people mostly ate corn and beans. Coca Cola was the main drink. (I believed that Coke was a main reason for children with broken or rotted teeth and it upset me greatly to think that the company was making a fortune on this.)

There was a *cancha* (football field). Hondurans were absolutely nuts about football and one could see kids playing at any given time or place, whether they were barefoot or wearing shoes, or even whether they had a ball. They would play with cans or a rolled-up ball made of any substance imaginable. More than anything in the world, "my" boys wanted a real soccer ball, but they were expensive. It would have cost about three weeks pay, and food had to be their priority.

As we ambled back to their house along the dirt road, smelling the sweetness of the flowering coffee plants, we talked more. Isaias was the guide; Alex, quiet, stared ahead or into the fields.

We arrived back at the house and chatted only for a little while longer. This was not a verbal family. Most rural folks in Honduras didn't talk much, and sometimes I found it a little painful trying to make conversation. As a former therapist, I was accustomed to asking open-ended questions to draw out the other person, but it didn't work.

"Isaias, what kinds of dreams and hopes do you have for the future?"

He thought for a while and answered, "I'd like to have a belt."

Alex chimed in. He would like a belt too. He chuckled and showed me his tattered belt, tied at the waist instead of buckled.

Finally, but too soon, it was time to go back down the mountain to get home by sundown. It would be about a two-hour walk. I was not getting back on that horse. I was informed clearly and seriously that no one wanted to be on that road after dark. I didn't want to ask what the possible consequences would be.

The boys walked me down and back into town. I was tired, but they were loaded with energy, laughing, picking plants to show me, introducing me to different types of trees, pointing out lizards. Pine and the scent of dirt wafted in the air.

When we arrived at the house, we said our *hasta luegos* and promised to see each other soon. I thanked them for a fabulous day. We had a hard time saying goodbye. They turned, waved, and proceeded to head back towards the mountain, turning around every few steps, still smiling and waving. I thought about their hour-and-a-half hike back up the mountain. How strong they were, and on such little fuel intake, only beans and corn.

I turned to walk up the steps to my apartment. I was completely stiff from all the exercise but felt really happy, connected, and filled with love. It didn't matter that my muscles were becoming so fused that I might never get up from my chair.

I saw my tiny apartment with new eyes. It seemed so luxurious: indoor bathroom with a shower, indoor kitchen, water right out of the sink (although not potable), tile floor, a bed, and even a table and chair. I felt rich in so many ways.

That day was so magical! Those folks were so happy in spite of abject poverty and huge losses; they had such generosity of spirit and open enthusiasm. They experienced such joy with no bitterness, in spite of all that had happened to them.

I continued to visit regularly, often bringing staples, basic foods such as lard, rice, cornmeal, and other items such as soap or a small towel. At one point, I brought a brand new soccer ball. The boys screamed with excitement, hugged me, danced with joy, and said about twenty thank yous.

Each visit was a piece of heaven, relaxed, filled with laughter and love. I was surrounded by gorgeous land smelling of pine, and in the winter, the sweet coffee plants.

Maria taught me (with quite a bit of patience) how to make tortillas. First, we had to grind the corn and then use a specially carved stone to grind it further. The tricky part was to roll a small bowl of the paste in wet hands and pat it into a flat, even pancake. At that point, you could drop them right onto the wood stove. Supposedly. My tortillas looked more like geographic maps with mountains. For the life of me I couldn't get them even.

Then, in spite of my excellent instructions, my tortillas stuck to my hands when I tried to drop them onto the iron top of the stove. They'd flop into a heap. Maria would try not to laugh, but I could see her body shaking as she faced the wall. I'd drop them on the floor, or into the fire, or even onto my shirt. When it was time to eat them, everyone knew which ones were mine. To this day, I am still famous in Honduras for making the most hideous tortillas.

* * *

One day, many months later, Isai showed up at my house at about 4:30 in the morning, calling up to my window. It was his birthday. I dragged my sleepy body to the porch.

"Hey there, happy birthday, sweetheart. Today is your special day! Why are you up so early?"

He looked down, trying to hide his tears. "My grandmother died in the night. I have errands to do to prepare for the funeral."

"Oh my God." I rushed down the stairs to open the gate. She had died on his birthday. My heart sank. She was the only adult family they had in their lives, and they loved her. I knew she hadn't been feeling well, but I didn't know it was that grave. I ushered him upstairs with my arms around him. I gave him a coffee as he sat at my tiny kitchen table and told me the story.

"She was sick for a few months and getting worse. There was no money for medicine." I hadn't known this. "In the last few days, she became sicker and sicker, until last night."

"Why didn't you ask me? I would have bought the medicine."

"You have already given us so much. We were too embarrassed to ask for more."

I felt sick. If I had known, I could have stepped in and maybe prevented this. I told him that he could always count on me to help and not to be embarrassed. He tried hard not to cry, but his head and body were slumped and he could barely speak. I fought back my tears, as well. He and his siblings had already lost so much at such a young age.

After a long silence, he appeared embarrassed and hesitant, but finally, stammering a bit, said, "Could you help us out with a small loan? There is no food for the funeral."

I knew that there wasn't enough food even for the family, let alone bereaved guests who would come to pay their respects. Since Doña Josefa was well known, loved, and admired, there would be many people showing up.

No food for the family, no money to bury the grandmother, and now they had to buy food to feed half a village. I gave him a rather large sum of 700 lempiras, about thirty-five US dollars. "Please, keep it. This is not a loan. If you need more, let me know."

He took the money, gave me a giant hug, and barely above a whisper said, "Thank you. You have such a big heart!"

I told him I would be up to the village as soon as I got dressed.

He continued to thank me profusely. "I do not have words to let you know how grateful I am. You are an angel, like a second mom."

I never forgot those words. My heart was breaking for these kids, who were being abandoned, yet again.

I dressed quickly after he left and grabbed a tuk-tuk to the town center. I bought cookies, coffee, sugar, and juice, and hired my friend Leonel and his tuk-tuk to take me up the mountain in the rain. The road was so muddy, wet, and rutted. I had to keep getting out to push.

By the time I arrived, I was covered to my knees in mud, sweating, my face and clothes splattered. My first sight was of about forty people sitting around the slanting mud hut, trying to find shelter from the drizzle under the small lip of the roof.

More folks steadily arrived. People were silently eating their tiny pieces of chicken and tortilla while Maria was running back and forth to the fire to serve more. She burst into tears when she saw me, dropped a pan that crashed to the ground, and came running towards me. She threw her arms around me tightly and sobbed.

Other women took over the cooking duties as we moved to a more private spot under a thatched lean-to that they used for their chickens. She continued to sob in my arms. Isaias saw us, ran over, and and joined in on the hugs, trying to hold his tears back. He was unsuccessful. They kept rolling down his cheeks.

"Who will take care of us now?" asked Maria.

The question tore my heart apart. "I will!" I shouted. "We're not blood, but we *are* family!"

I looked up and saw Alex in the distance. He was standing alone in the rain, away from the crowd, just staring into the fields, the green darkened by the gray sky. He looked so lost. He was twelve years old but looked much younger. Hatless, he hung his head, hands in his torn pockets, wet from the rain. Wearing one's best clothes was customary for a funeral. Alex's best clothes were also his worst clothes. His only clothes. Torn, ill fitting, and with permanent stains.

That day I spent as much time as I could there, among the visitors still coming in to pay their respects, mostly with my arms around the three "re-orphaned" kids. I told them that we could talk the next day about plans.

Sadly, I had to leave before dark to go home. Leaving them was painful, two teenagers and a twelve-year-old, an unstable mud house, very little food, and giant grief.

I headed home. Crying. Worried. Angry. Their lives seemed so unfair.

* * *

Sometimes in life, things go from bad to worse. In the days that followed, the rains continued, and their already dilapidated house began to crumble further, the walls caving in.

The day after the funeral, I met with the three of them to talk. They were all extremely sad and now worried about how they would survive on their own, as well as what to do about the severely deteriorating mud shack. It wouldn't last much longer. There were already gaping holes in the walls, big enough to walk through, and the roof was hardly useful. The winter rains continued to eat at the walls.

There was work to do, and not enough time for them to process their grief. They needed a house. The boys could continue working in the fields and delivering firewood for some cash, but the house issue had to be addressed. I told them I would see if I could try and raise funds to build a cement-block house. This would mean one room, only four by five meters, with a cement floor, a solid roof and a real window and door. Safe and dry. They were excited, overwhelmed with joy, and a bit stunned that I could actually pull this off.

I told them, "You will have to clear the land." It was extremely steep and covered with brush and trees.

"No problem," Isaias said. "I have a special tool." He proudly showed me his axe.

I nearly cracked up. Instead, I said, "That will be of great use, indeed."

"I have an axe and a shovel—two tools!" he said.

They would begin the next morning after chores. I went home and immediately got to work fundraising. We stayed in contact daily, and as my list of donors grew, I reported the news by phone. They updated me on their progress, as well.

The boys leveled the land in a record three weeks—by themselves. I had never seen so many blisters on hands, the size of nickels. They did an amazing job! The land was cleared, flattened, and suitable for construction. Meanwhile, through many letters and phone calls to spread the word, I had managed to raise sufficient money. The house was "a go"!

I hired a friend/builder, Manuel, to oversee the work. He gave us a great deal, as he was also concerned about the three orphans. I remember the day we showed up at their place. Manuel and I jumped out of his old, rattling truck (I tried three times to close the truck door and finally left it) and the boys ran to meet us on the road, so excited that a builder had come. They couldn't believe it. Manuel explained the procedure to the two boys and a couple of neighbors who were also pitching in. They would all work as a team over the next weeks.

It was pure joy when I visited weekly, saw the progress, and evaluated the needs, but the most joyous part was seeing Isaias and Alex leaping like young gazelles from task to task with giant grins. Manuel taught them new skills and pitched in some free labor. The boys worked long hours on top of their daily farm work.

Within six weeks, they had a warm, dry concrete house! With a roof! And a cement floor! And a window and door! When I arrived on that final day, Isai kept walking inside and then out, inside and out, demonstrating to me the possibilities and the reality of their first real house. They asked me to come in. I stepped through the doorway. There we all were, hugging and jumping and laughing, celebrating with pure joy.

Coincidentally, two days within finishing the project, during a torrential rain, the mud house completely collapsed. The timing of Mother Nature was incredible. After the rain, their former home was no longer even recognizable as a house with walls, just a heap of mud, sticks, and a little plastic.

They never let me forget how much gratitude and love they felt for me and their friends who had pitched in. For several months afterwards, Maria spent most of our visits hanging from my neck, laughing, and kissing me. Isaias expressed it with his words and hugs, Alex with a shy nod, but they never let me forget how much those days of my helping them meant to them. It was a privilege and an honor for me, and I was so humbled by this experience. It really took so little on my part to make such a big difference in the lives of three special people.

Maria continued the work of her grandmother, making clay pots to sell. There was plenty of good clay in that area, and she would fire them in her outdoor firepit. Friends and visitors from other countries often gifted them household items, and within just a few months, they each had a bed and a plastic chair. As time went on, I would bring an occasional pot or pan, sometimes mugs, blankets, or even pillows. It was tempting to shower them with everything they could possibly need, but I didn't want them to expect too much from one person.

Their "kitchen" was outside the house, a few stick posts holding up a piece of tin for a roof. Maria continued to cook there on an open fire. As they made more friends and more income through sales of their crops, firewood, and Maria's pottery, they were able to finally construct a mud-walled kitchen that included a donated cement wood-burning stove. I never did understand who donated it. Maria didn't know whether it was a friendly person or an organization, but it didn't matter. She could cook inside!

They remained in their village since they had friends and neighbors who cared for them, as well as a long tradition there, but I continued to visit them as often as I could.

Today, they are all adults (eighteen, twenty-three, and twenty-four), and they have chickens and dogs, an occasional turkey or two, and fruit and coffee trees. Recently, there have been threats of mining companies coming in and forcing people off their land. The landowners protested and won the first battle. The most recent threat was from a Canadian mining company, but they have backed off for now. Even though their lives and lifestyle are stable, the situation is precarious at best.

We became a family, and a very loving one at that. They showered me with love, and I considered myself deeply fortunate to have them in my life.

* * *

At some point around this time, I realized it was time that I had my own house, too. I needed to rent a place that would also serve as an office, offer storage space, and accommodate visitors, especially my newfound family. Elena's was lovely, but I needed more privacy and wanted my own garden. I also wanted my own dog.

I had my eye on a beautiful, newly constructed yellow house, just a block from Elena's. This meant an increase in rent up to almost $380. After a long deliberation, a dear friend convinced me that I was worth it. The electric bill would set me back an additional five dollars.

The house also had a tiny, broken-down adobe house on the property that could be used as a bodega for storing school supplies, medical supplies, and emergency food and clothing. It was perfect!

The new house had an enormous back balcony overlooking the valley, and I could see storms coming in from the west. I became the "weather girl" for my friends.

Elena was not happy with my move. Very much like when I left Nelly's house, she took it as an insult and abandonment. I assured her that I would continue to come and visit. I was only a short block away.

Moving took much longer than it did coming from Nelly's. Almost half an hour longer. My friends and neighbors helped me carry my few items down the street in caravan form, while many watched our parade from their windows.

The house had banana-colored walls inside and was furnished with yellow-cushioned bamboo chairs and a sofa. My own sofa! I had my own kitchen! I bought some pots and pans and immediately started in on the garden, buying plants and stealing cuttings from neighbors.

The house also had a front gate, which would enable me to finally seal off the endless chain of people in need coming to my apartment at all hours. Although it was a rental, it was my first house. I now had a place I liked, adopted children I adored, and a country I loved.

I was home.

Chapter 7

As my work with communities progressed, and as I got to know people more intimately, something started to change—an ideological shift began to happen. I no longer felt comfortable as an aid worker. I wanted to be more of a neighbor.

Yes, we were still replacing roofs, putting in latrines, and supplying furniture to the schools, but a more balanced interaction began to emerge. People started giving me things. Villagers would give me crops or a chicken. These were valuable gifts, a huge portion of what little they had. Kids gave me drawings. Villagers stopped relating to me as an NGO representative and more as a friend. They joked more with me. They hugged me and teased me.

Project School Supplies was no longer about doing projects. It was becoming more about helping out neighbors. I changed our name to *Buenos Vecinos* (Good Neighbors). We moved away from being donors and recipients and towards neighbors helping neighbors. Meanwhile, I was learning a great deal about what it meant to be an international aid worker.

From villages located in treacherous-to-get-to places, to managing my first contact amidst an ocean of need, to the gut-wrenching consequences of having to turn people down because of limited funds, to learning how to make a project successful by involving the community, it was an emotionally intense time, full of steep learning, some mistakes, and more than a few successes. I was continually re-evaluating what it meant to help and how to be most effective without giving up my identity as a neighbor.

* * *

Travel Conditions

On a trip to El Pinalito, a village located way up in the mountains, I decided to bring a treat that most kids there probably never had eaten: watermelons. I brought fifteen large watermelons along with the school supplies they had requested, as well as a blackboard and bookshelves.

On the day of the trip, Marel picked me up in his truck. Although the directions to the village were correct, the leader neglected to mention that the school was perched on top of the mountain (possibly on top of the entire world). We happily arrived after a few hours of difficult driving, eager to stretch our legs, only to be informed by a small welcome party that we had to take an immensely steep, winding path on foot, for "only" about a mile (in the blazing sun) and carry the items by hand.

"Oh I see," I said cheerily, internally whining even before the climb. *Easy for you,* I thought, *you're young and strong. I'm a city kid and well into my sixties!* Maybe there would be an air-conditioned café on the way where I could get an iced latte.

We unloaded the truck as boy after boy, man after man, grabbed an item. Blackboard, bookshelves, cartons of school supplies, and, of course, the damned watermelons. Marel and I grabbed two each. *Why did I want to bring watermelons?*

We marched like Sherpas up the mountain, with about six kids carrying the larger watermelons on their shoulders. Occasionally, one watermelon would escape and roll back down the hill, and the next kid following behind would capture it. At every turn, I caught amusing glimpses, like a large blackboard moving along the mountain with two sets of little human legs underneath. The views were breathtaking: green hills contrasted by an enormous blue sky. I tried to focus on that while my bra filled with puddles of sweat and my head was ready to explode from the intense heat.

This kind of journey was not unusual. There were always physical challenges and logistic surprises. To get to Los Arcos, for example, we had to cross a number of streams, occasionally too high for our truck, at which point we'd have to turn back. Once, Marel took a chance and crossed the fast current; his truck got stuck in the mud halfway. He had to wait hours for a passing truck strong enough to tow him back out. Fortunately for him, I was not with him, panicking and freaking out. After that experience, we learned to call ahead to the village to check on travel conditions.

There was always the unexpected. Sometimes the muddy inclines were so steep that folks had to meet us at the base of the hill and carry our materials on foot. Other times we were surprised by a sudden torrential rain and had to turn back. At times there were the fallen trees, electric wires down from a storm, mud avalanches during rainy seasons, fallen rocks, washed-out roads, or simply just a vomiting session from something we ate.

First Contact

Meeting in a village was not our only way of initiating a connection. Sometimes folks showed up directly at Marel's house or at mine. My new house had a large iron gate that was kept locked to prevent a constant stream of people entering. Some early mornings, there were as many as four or five people waiting to talk with me about varying requests, usually repairs to their school or supplies. There were also medical emergencies or folks looking for emergency food for their families. It was the same at Marel's house. Marel and Zoila also had a regular stream of people in need. Since Marel had recently become the pastor of his church, sometimes he and his congregation handled these matters. For example, if a parishioner was in sudden need of medical help, the congregation could pitch in.

If Marel or Zoila weren't at home, folks in need would come to me, or vice versa. One morning, I got up at my usual 4:00 a.m., looked out the window, and saw four farmers squatting by the streetlight in front of my gate, facing away from my house so as not to be intrusive. After I had my coffee and got dressed, I staggered outside and invited them in. The morning light by then was starting to show in the sky.

"We left three or so hours before sunrise to talk with Marel, but he is still asleep," said the leader, Carlos, a soft-spoken, handsome, and rugged older man.

I joked back, "He often 'sleeps in,' sometimes until as late as 4:30."

They laughed.

"Can we talk with you for a moment?" Carlos asked.

"Of course!" I opened the gate.

They took off their hats, walked single file into my house, and stood inside the front door with their heads lowered. I invited them to sit. They sat in a row on my sofa, wiggling and smiling as they nestled into the pillows. I figured this was the first real furniture they had ever sat on. If they were like most of the other rural farmers, their sofas were logs.

I poured them coffee and offered them cornbread that my friend Maribel had made the day before and sold in the street. Each shyly accepted the snack and said, "Thank you," but other than that, only Carlos spoke. I tried to engage them all in at least a couple of sentences, but they gave only one-word replies.

I always tried to crack some kind of joke to break the ice in these situations; otherwise, the energy was so serious and apologetic. I hated that, feeling the imbalance of power. The truth was that I was humbled to be with them and to be included as one of them. I felt farmers were the souls and keepers of the earth and I loved being around them. I loved looking at their weather-worn faces and hands. Unfortunately, I could also feel the power difference, demonstrated by their body language. I assumed it was because I was white, from the US, and/or the one with money. (It was ironic because as a musician in the US, my income was below the poverty line. In Honduras, I was rich, even if it was donated money.) I always hated that inequity, and if I could break it up a little with humor or cornbread to relax us all, it felt so much better. The humor was usually simple, but it worked.

As the men explained how to get to their village, they told me that they lived way up the mountain. I asked with a wink if there were bears, and not only did they all burst out laughing, they periodically kept repeating my punchline afterwards, laughing each time. (I briefly considered becoming a stand-up comedian in Honduras.)

Carlos explained that they had come on foot from a village about three hours away to talk to me about helping them put on a roof on their new, almost-finished community clinic. I said I would see what we could arrange with Marel and that we would be in touch soon to set up a visit to the site. We finished our meeting, and with more thank yous and handshakes, we said our *hasta luegos*.

Soon after, we visited the clinic. It wasn't an easy drive. The road was in terrible condition most of the way and further damaged by the rains. When we arrived, some men met us at the base of the hill to escort us up to the clinic. Marel and I donned our rubber boots. My boots were too large for me, and I practically stepped out of them with each suctioned and squishy step. A couple of times, men took my hands to help me along. I brought little toys, stickers, balloons, bubble pipes, and yoyos, and I'd hand out prizes to delighted kids on the way, which magnetized a crowd of children to me along the way.

At the top of the hill, we saw it. The men proudly took us forward. It was not the type of clinic I had envisioned. Even though I had considerably lowered my expectations of a typical US structure, I was still shocked by the small room made of wood slats. It was covered by a plastic black tarp. It had one window.

However, there *was* a cement floor inside. A homemade bed had been made of wood and rope tied together to form a strong net to lay on. There were two plastic chairs and a single shelf that held a bit of medicine, aspirin, Band-Aids, a few tiny bottles of cough syrup, and some deworming pills. I saw a bit of cotton, some syringes, and other supplies, but no equipment. There was no electricity, nor bathrooms.

We were told that because this village had voted for the Liberals, the opposing Nationalist government had told them they would not help. Although the clinic wasn't finished, it was already in use. It was staffed by a part-time nurse who came from another village a few times a week.

Carlos told us that the Department of Health had said they would send medicines after it was finished. I asked him if he believed that. He said no. They were accustomed to government promises that were never kept. They had no sources for the funding of the roof, so it didn't take more than a few minutes to make our decision. It was a worthy project, and fortunately we were in a position to help, having some cash still in our coffers. We explained to the men that they would have to carry the materials from the base of the hill and do the labor themselves. It would be a longer hike than we'd just taken since the last part of the road was not large enough to accommodate the supply truck. They were thrilled.

Everything would be arranged by Marel. We told them we would make the trip back with the first delivery to ensure all went well and take photos. We said our goodbyes and promised to deliver the materials as soon as possible. We returned home, and Marel made the purchases and delivery arrangements.

The delivery was hysterical. After slithering and sliding for miles in Marel's truck, we pulled up to the meeting point at the base of the muddy hill to see thirty-five men and older boys in work clothes and gumboots standing in the watery mist, grinning from ear-to-ear, waving at us. I felt so much joy. I couldn't explain why, but I felt so connected to these men.

The hill was a disaster. Even horses wouldn't have been able to climb through six inches of new, sopping mud. The children ran to the truck first, hoping to participate in the unloading. Each small child tried and failed to lug out a giant piece of roofing. Then it was the men's turn, each pulling out a twelve-foot piece of corrugated tin, sometimes placing it onto another man's back as he stooped and prepared for the hike up the mile incline. The children stayed by the truck, hoping to carry a piece of the tin on their backs, but to no avail.

The roofing material was rolled up into long, log-like shapes. Shorter pieces were also rolled up. What I found so stunning was the train of men weaving up the mountain carrying one long piece, with rope tying the shorter pieces perpendicular. They looked like they were carrying crucifixes on their backs, climbing their way up to Calvary.

We didn't climb with them, but we unloaded everything, giving the final bags of nails to the delighted smaller kids who finally had a chance to contribute their share of the workload.

As we left, we waved and took off happily, tooting the horn a few times. They enthusiastically waved back.

A few weeks later, the leader of the village and a couple of council members came back to Copán to thank us, telling us that the roof was on and the clinic was up and running. They invited us to visit any time.

In addition to folks coming by with requests, Marel or I would also be contacted by phone. People would introduce themselves, name their village, and tell us how they had heard about us. We would immediately tell them to hang up so we could return the call. A simple phone call could cost the same as an hour or two of their wages.

I'd suggest that we meet when it was convenient for them. Because people came from long distances, often on foot, we tried to arrange a meeting when they were already in town on other errands, to save an extra expense of a bus trip or the loss of a day's labor. I'd adjust my schedule to accommodate them.

As soon as we had the person's request for assistance, it was our policy to investigate the situation as soon as possible so that folks were not kept waiting. I had seen this way too often with other aid organizations. People could wait for weeks or months hoping for help, often to be turned down—or worse yet, to get no reply at all. Larger organizations needed more time to process a request, but I was always upset to find out that there had been no response at all. It was beyond insensitive and rude to keep desperate people waiting and hoping. As a two-person organization, we were able to move faster. No board of directors. No processing of the need or validity of a project. If it seemed like a project was too challenging for us, we would say no right away so that they could keep looking elsewhere.

I felt it was important to give out as much information as possible about how we worked, what projects we could undertake, and our expectations of the community.

If we said yes to a project, we would explain our rules: It was always a team project. It was expected that the villagers would do their part by clearing the land or helping with the labor, delivery, or purchasing of materials. For school supplies, folks would often come to town with a truck or several horses to transport the items. It was comical and not uncommon to see them leaving town with plastic chairs or a small blackboard tied to horses, and bags of supplies thrown over the saddles. The villagers almost always complied with joy no matter how heavy the burden. (I wasn't sure about the horses.)

If we had agreed to a construction project, like putting a roof on a school, they often were able to do this themselves, in which case we would just supply materials. If it was a larger, more involved construction project, like building *baños* (bathrooms) and *pilas* (cement wash sinks) for a school, we would supervise due to the complexity, as most farmers only had experience building adobe structures. If it was a large project, like building a bridge or a school, we would hire someone to take charge, but we expected the villagers' labor. It almost always went well. Another requirement was that the village leaders or teachers would write a thank-you note to the donors, and I would deliver it either by email or, occasionally, in person.

Limited Funds

The longer I worked in Honduras, the more requests we received, which of course not only meant more work, but also meant turning down many worthy projects. How does one turn down a request of "only" $175 for an operation for a child? How do we say no to replacing the stolen motor of a seventy-year-old man who used it to grind corn? This was his only means of income. These requests were small, especially in contrast to North American standards, but sometimes we simply did not have the funds.

These smaller requests added up and our income was inconsistent. I couldn't plan a budget and couldn't plan for emergencies, either. I had to set limits on not only financial resources but also my time and my energy. Marel and I had endless brainstorming sessions, hoping to find a way that we hadn't thought of yet to make a project happen. Funds were limited and the flood of requests were never-ending. I would see in my mind's eye kids huddled under a piece of tin in the rain trying to study, or sitting on dirt school floors trying to concentrate when they were so weak from hunger.

It was always painful for me to decline worthy projects, big or small. Almost all requests were worthy. Sometimes the cost or the immense complications put projects outside of our reach. For example, Nueva Alianza was a distressed community four hours into the mountains and had almost no accessible road. They needed at least a four-room school for their 250 children, but the cost was prohibitive due to the size of school, distance of the community, and poor conditions of the access roads. It would have been exhausting to find enough donors to achieve this, and we would have had to decline other smaller projects. Still, this project remained in my mind for years, but we weren't able to find a solution. It bothered me tremendously. It still does to this day.

When saying no, we always tried to do either a "consolation project" or I'd contact other organizations to seek other avenues of support for the original request. At Nueva Alianza, we helped with repairs to the walls and bought school supplies, teaching materials, and clothes for the orphans in the community. We could only deliver these during the dry season because of the road conditions. When their leaders came into town, which was rare, we sent them back with the items and building materials. Sometimes they were able to buy heavier items locally. For example, they could buy bricks from the tiny town close by and carry them by hand or on horseback, but only a few at a time due to the weight.

Donating much-needed school supplies, teaching materials, or toys for kindergartens was always a good way to support a community or school even if we had to say no to their bigger requests. These items were portable, usually easy to get hold of, easier to deliver, and always appreciated.

Saying no to projects caused me much stress and guilt, and it would overwhelm me at times. Sleep came to me less and less as the years went on. I had so much power and so little power. I hated that. I often felt that if we didn't take on a particular project, no one else would. Looking back at this, I see now it was a red flag. I was starting to feel responsible for rescuing all of Honduras. This brought depression and anger at the unfairness, the lack of balance of resources in the world, and a relentless questioning of the part I was playing. I had seen so much waste, and so much luxury in other countries. I knew millionaires who admitted that they didn't donate towards international aid but helped their already rich friends with loans or gifts. I felt such rage towards the one percent in the US who paid few taxes and had so many blinders on about other peoples' suffering. I could imagine what could be done with a million dollars of just one athlete's twenty-million-dollar salary. Maybe instead of buying personal jets, they could use this money to set up programs to relieve suffering? I was aware of my judgments but couldn't seem to change them, as much as I tried. If these people had to live for a day without water, food, and medicine, what would they be saying or doing? The imbalance broke my heart over and over.

Can I do more? Should I do more? Could I have done more? Can I do less? It brought remorse, worry, guilt. Sometimes, with luck, I'd have a solution to a problem that would come to me at 2:00 or 3:00 a.m., and I would get so excited that I'd shoot out of bed, grab my coffee, and get to work planning, designing, and writing to potential donors.

Once, I had to say no to a request from a school that didn't have furniture, and I became obsessed until I found a solution. We could refurbish the skeletons of desks and chairs that other schools had discarded. The iron parts were still good. The children could help by sanding and repainting them. I decided to support the community by hiring a local carpenter. Often carpenters in the villages had less opportunity for work than their city counterparts.

Health requests tore at my heart. The need was more personal than structural requests, and if I knew the family or the child, it was even more painful to say no.

One morning, Marel discovered Javier, one of the fathers from the village of San José Las Lágrimas, sleeping on his concrete porch. He was waiting to talk with Marel but did not want to wake him. He'd made the three-hour walk from his village. Marel had no idea what time he had arrived.

Javier, strongly built and in his late 30s, desperately needed medicine for his six-month-old son. People in San José Las Lágrimas lived in extreme poverty and without water. Their "houses" were plastic tarps, burlap bags, and sticks. The chickens, ducks, and dogs lived inside the houses and defecated on the dirt floors. There were no bathrooms; people went into the fields to relieve themselves. Filth, malnutrition, and no access to medications left many children and adults vulnerable.

Little Jorge had tuberculosis, like several others in his community. The living conditions made recovery difficult. Earlier, we'd worked on the dilapidated school there, and we came to know many residents, including Javier, a hard-working, religious, and loving father. Almost every time we were in the village, Javier asked us for help for his baby son, including medicine, milk, or trips to the hospital. We did what we could, but it never was enough. This went on for a year, with Javier desperate, crying, and begging for help. It was heart-wrenching not to be able to provide all that he needed, but we had so many similar requests from many villages. This man fought for his child like no one I had ever seen, and for that reason we chipped in quite a bit, often with our own personal money. Having to set financial limits with him was heartbreaking for all of us.

That day, when Marel saw him on the porch, we felt we could not possibly deny someone making such an effort. With our financial support plus some borrowed money from his community, the money from selling some of his animals, and other unknown efforts, he was able to collect enough money to get minimal yet effective treatment for his son. Through the astounding efforts of Javier during that year, little Jorge became healthy. It was a pleasure to visit and see little Jorjito starting to walk!

There were others from that same community that, sadly, weren't as fortunate. Little Evelin was a sweet, emaciated, almost lifeless eight-year-old who'd been diagnosed with tuberculosis. I remember the shock when I first saw her arms. I had never seen a child's arms that thin. Her hair had lost its color due to malnutrition. She often watched me with haunted eyes but rarely spoke. It took too much energy. I bought her a little stuffed animal that she clutched to her chest, looking at me with a big smile. She always wore the same torn, yellow dress that I could see was once very special, with lace and ruffles. It had transformed into something raggedy, but one could still see the beauty, like with Evelin.

We watched her health deteriorate over months as the medications stopped working. She became weaker and weaker, and her body became rail thin. Her cough worsened. We'd help her and her mom get to the hospital on occasion, but it was never enough. Evelin needed consistent care to survive. I'll never forget the horrid day when Marel called me from their village and told me that Evelin had succumbed. I was devastated. He was crying on the phone. So was I.

For a couple of weeks, all I could think about was Evelin. I found a picture of her and her mom, an older one where she was a little healthier. I bought a frame for it and brought it on our next trip to the village. I spotted Evelin's mom in the field, went over to her, and wanted to say something, but all that came out were tears. I handed her the framed picture. She looked at it and burst into tears, clutching it to her heart. She kept looking and clutching, looking and clutching, while all I could do was hug her. I tried to make words come out, but they were stuck inside of me.

Finally, I choked out, "I'm so sorry."

She replied, "Thank you for all your efforts."

I could tell she wanted to go back to her house, and I grabbed her hands. "We will stay in touch."

Over the course of a couple of years, we were able to do quite a bit to improve the living conditions of that community. With the help from various North American NGOs and the municipal government, we built a healthy school—this time with cement floors instead of dirt, walls of brick instead of adobe, and a roof that didn't leak. We also built a six-room clinic with donations from NGOs and money from crowdfunding.

One of our biggest projects was bringing clean water to the village. Thanks to the help of a North American NGO, we coordinated a forty thousand dollar water project that would ensure regular, clean water for more than eighty families.

The massive project involved bringing water down from a source thirteen kilometers away in the mountain. Men with machetes cleared the raw land in order to lay pipes—a month of grueling daily efforts. Marel told me that in addition to that exhausting work, all of the men—including himself—would have to spend at least half an hour each night pulling the ticks off their legs and private body parts.

My only comment when he told me this was, "Eeeewwww!"

Every day, a crew of twenty to fifty men cleared land, carried blocks and cement, laid bricks and pipes, and did whatever they needed to do, usually in the blazing sun. Marel's arms turned a couple of darker shades of brown.

The day they turned on the water flow, Marel and the men went to the tank and opened the valve. I wished I could have been there, but they had finished unexpectedly early in the day. Marel gave me the details.

After finishing the final touches, they marched down into the village where they went to the main spigot. As they went to open the valve for the first time, the men gathered silently, waiting. Marel started teasing the villagers by taking his time, pretended to turn the knob. They remained still and quiet until he finally opened the spigot and a gush of water—almost like from a fire hose—poured out. The villagers jumped into the powerful stream, showering and dancing, laughing and cheering.

One by one, each person took a turn in the gushing water, and women and children started to join them in a frenetic celebration of joy. Within ten minutes, news had spread to the entire community and people poured out of their houses to watch, women running over to the source with babies and small kids in tow. This was a truly spectacular and memorable experience for all.

As Marel described this, I so longed to have been there with them. After all of the hard work I'd put into the coordination and search for funds and the months of visits with the villagers, I so

69

wanted to be a part of the celebration. We were also so grateful to the organization in the US who helped us, Amigos of Honduras. I wished that they could have been present, too, for that moment. We did have an enormous celebration shortly afterwards, however, which did include opening various faucets and more showering in the outpour.

A few months later, in the same village, another project was completed thanks to a small NGO in the US. A bakery. The village was just inside the Guatemalan border, and the local government provided money for ovens, equipment, and training. Through the help of another tiny North American NGO, Marel was able to coordinate the construction of the bakery. This gave the community a means of income; they sold bread in their town and to neighboring villages. The combination of projects was a Herculean effort on the part of so many people and organizations, but it was so worth it. It required raising well over $150,000 in total to get this community healthy, productive, and on its feet.

Even a visit to assess a potential project in a village created other financial pressures. We would see a myriad of other necessities. We almost always left with a sick child and their family, taking them to a hospital or clinic. Or we'd give villagers rides back to town, saving folks time and travel costs. Necessities were in abundance. There were houses in poor repair; schools needing roof repairs, windows, or furniture; a clinic needing meds or basic equipment, such as blood pressure cuffs or thermometers. It was always an internal debate for me whether to work intensively with one community or to do less but cover more villages. Marel was always pretty amenable to whatever decisions (or vacillating decisions) I would make. Usually, we managed to do a combination of things. Every time we went to any of the eighty communities we served, we always helped out at least a little, even if it was just a matter of bringing school supplies, or a blackboard, or cases of milk and rice for the students.

Local Motivation

How did I make decisions? I wish there had been a formula, but I was never able to come up with a consistent overall plan, mainly because donations were inconsistent. Often, it was a matter of urgency. A school without a roof had priority over a school that needed a fence. Those were the easier decisions. Choosing a project was also based on how much money was in the coffers at the time, or the accessibility of potential donors.

One issue we took seriously when making a decision was the motivation of the villagers. With a large project, we would ask folks to perform smaller tasks to assess their level of commitment. This might mean getting estimates of materials or labor, measuring the land area needed to build a classroom, or providing statistics of the number of children served. Small steps. If the first steps were not completed, we would usually explain our policy and expectations again and offer another chance. If that didn't result in action, we'd usually drop the project at that time and reconsider it in the future. Without sufficient motivation, we knew the project would not go well.

One day, I was approached on the street by a woman in her mid-thirties, strong and capable-looking, with positive energy and long black hair that flew as she walked. She knew who I was, but I didn't know her. Her name was Arecely. She told me she was the head teacher of Los Quebrachos. She had wanted to speak with me for months but was too shy to approach for fear of bothering me. She asked if she could come to my house to talk. I invited her to come by the next day.

She showed up on time. She began talking immediately as she entered the gate and as we squeezed up the narrow outside stairs trying to move around the potted plants and Elena's oversized Rottweiler. These obstacles did not stop her focused train of thought. She spoke quickly and urgently, as if she had only ten minutes to state her case. I invited her to sit down, and as I was making tea, she continued her monologue. Finally, as I joined her, with tea and cookies, at my tiny kitchen table (the only sitting space in my small apartment), we talked about a roof that her school badly needed.

She brought photos but also invited me to go see the school and said she would arrange transportation. After explaining that I was interested in learning more, but that this was not a sure thing, we decided to go the next morning to have a look. She was able to borrow a truck and driver the following day, and we took the twenty-minute trip to Los Quebrachos. I was grateful that, although we traveled on a potted dirt road, it was a relatively smooth and short trip. School was not in session but there were kids hanging around the grounds, and more showed up after hearing there was a visitor in the village. It seemed that I was always somewhat of an attraction, being from another country. Often I would joke, "Not a lot of gringos here in this community," and folks would laugh.

After seeing the disaster they called a roof—but still without promising anything—I asked her to get me a quote or two. (Even though we always did our own assessments, I always liked to work with the teachers in this way. Sometimes they could get a better deal, but this also helped me measure motivation.) We returned to town and Arecely dropped me off at home. She thanked me and asked if there was hope. I said that I thought so.

She called the next day at about 8:00 a.m. and asked to come over. That kind of quick turn around was in itself a shock to me. Normally, this kind of task took days or even weeks. I invited her back to my apartment. She scooted up the stairs, sat down, declined a coffee, and presented me with three different formal quotations on paper, laying them all out over the table, explaining why there were differences in charges, what she thought was the best option, and why. She was a pistol! She told me she already had the men willing to be assembled at a moment's notice to unload the truck when it arrived, and that there were others that could start laying the tin roof immediately upon delivery.

How could I say no? Her motivation and optimism propelled me forward. We had most of the funds in our account, and it turned out that the building store could give me a short-term credit since I was a frequent and reliable customer. We bought the materials and had the warehouse deliver them a couple of days later.

Sure enough, as we drove up the hill in our own truck, we turned the bend and, much to our delight, twenty men and boys were waiting for us, some on horseback, others on foot. Women with small children or carrying babies were also there to watch. There were hand-colored signs everywhere that said "thank you!" Kids who had been playing in the schoolyard were cheering as we came into sight. It cracked me up. It felt grandiose, as if we were the cavalry coming to save a village.

I jumped out of the truck, filled with excitement, as village leaders came up to shake our hands and say thank you. I said, "No, thank *you* for giving me such a positive reception!"

The roof went up in about two weeks. It was a huge project. At the end, Arecely once again invited me, and I went there the next day. It was beeeaaauuutiful!

We continued our work with Arecely and her school over the years, doing both large and small projects. We built a small library in that community and later furnished it regularly with donated books mailed from donors in the US. Each time we delivered, kids would pour out of the classrooms screaming, run to the truck to help us unload, and then return to the classrooms in slow motion as they started reading on the way back.

Community involvement could make or break a project. In another village, we built a car bridge in collaboration with another organization from the US, with strong involvement from the villagers. This allowed the kids to cross the stream safely and get to the school in the rainy season when the water was high, as well as provide access to a road leading into town where they could sell their produce.

The village was about a half-hour ride from town, a flat but bumpy journey along the river. My favorite part was passing through the heavily wooded area, giving me a feeling of being in another climate. It was cooler and wetter here, and we had to cross the winding stream various times. The village was divided into two parts by the stream. We crossed at the most shallow point, over rocks, and continued along a dirt patch that had become a road over years of use. The vista was dotted with remote houses as we entered the village, with each one looking worse than the one before. Kids playing in the yards were filthy, each staring at us as we passed. On occasion, the small ones, naked and without the luxury of diapers, would wave back. We were told there were over 1,500 people in this pretty, woodsy village, one of the largest I had been to, but I never saw a real cluster of houses. The homes were dotted around the rolling hills, hidden by trees.

The first time I visited, we met on the school porch, about ten of us sitting on the broken cement floor. I was the only woman in the meeting for the first half hour, somewhat uncomfortably perched on the edge of the porch step, which was mostly intact. As time went on, other women with babies joined us, standing around the perimeter of our circle, listening but not contributing.

This became our regular meeting area. After many meetings, they readily agreed to be involved and organized work teams of about fifteen to twenty-five villagers daily.

We started within a few weeks of conception. It was hard manual labor. They would be standing in the stream current all day, filling tubes, hauling cement, piecing rebar together. Others would be shoveling sand and mixing it with the cement, while still others were unloading the delivery trucks and hauling heavy bags on their backs up the hill to the stream. Young boys helped, as well. I loved to watch the camaraderie. I also enjoyed the fact that we could actually watch the process of the work being done. In the US, construction was done behind large, temporary, "protective" walls with peepholes.

The bridge took several months to complete but brought much satisfaction. At the end, I asked all the men who had participated to put their handprints in the wet cement as a memorial, since many could not sign their names.

At the inauguration, the villagers put up an incredible display of flowers, plants, and balloons on the bridge. The organization that collaborated with us was invited and, fortunately, the event coordinated with the time that they would be visiting Honduras. It was an afternoon of heartfelt speeches, great food, and joy. Although we took several photographs, the best one was of everyone involved, standing on the bridge, with the men waving their cowboy hats high in the air. Pure joy!

Medical Support

The need for medical support was daunting. It seemed like everyone needed some form of medical help. We were fortunate to have a fund from a generous donor that allowed us to pay for basic exams, emergency care of smaller issues, and transportation to clinics and hospitals. We worked with a couple of doctors and a pharmacist who gave my referrals a discount. I would joke with Hilda, the owner of the pharmacy, that I spent so much money there that I wanted to leave my bank account passbook with her and she could just take out money whenever needed. She never forgot that line, and from then on she would joke, "Where's your passbook? I'm still waiting."

We often spent way more than the medical budget allowed, often from our personal pockets. How can anyone say no to a sick kid or a mother in labor with complications? Many issues were beyond what we could afford. There was supposed to be a fund in the municipal office for medical emergencies, but that usually "disappeared" somehow. The municipality, however, would give a family member a written note allowing them to beg on the streets. I'd see these incredibly sad faces of moms holding out the notes as they went from store to store, business to business, trying to save their children. Sometimes as little as fifteen dollars would save a child's life. I always said yes to those requests. As far as the larger petitions, I could always contribute something, even if it was a small amount, at least to pitch in, but often I knew that there would be little hope for their child. I would be haunted for days on end, until finally I couldn't stand it any longer. I would hunt down the carrier of the note and try and do some form of fundraising to help fulfill the request. I never regretted any of those decisions.

Crushing Need

My problem with being "the woman who helps" was that the better known I became, the more petitions came my way. After many years, this became crushing. My desire to help was contrasted with my desire to run away. By my seventh year there, I felt much of the time that I was hiding in my house trying to protect myself emotionally or going to our wild bird rescue where there was a fee to enter and therefore prohibited the entry of people in financial need. My friend Lloyd always allowed me in for free. I would sit and try to unwind by the clear creek, listening to the soothing rush of water, watching magnificent, boldly colored macaws.

I was obsessed with finding a solution to both continuing my work and protecting myself from constant requests. Their desperation became my desperation. My bird park retreats helped, but they didn't solve my problems. The days and months continued to be more intense, an escalation of demands and urgencies. Marel and Zoila tried to buffer me by not telling me about all of the people who had been contacting them for help, but even without their details, I could see they were getting burned out with compassion fatigue too. I tried to pull myself together, using all of my spiritual and counseling tools, but I couldn't stop my emotional reaction to the flood of need. My ability to step back, get perspective, and set boundaries was crumbling. I was losing the battle for a solution. Overwhelming despair set in.

Chapter 8

Everyone told me not to go through El Paraíso, *narcotraficante* country. It was extremely dangerous.

We were thinking about building a school in conjunction with the newly elected mayor of the Copán municipality, in the village of Santa Cruz de Virginia. Their existing school was uninhabitable and dangerous. The adobe was cracking at the foundations and at the ceilings. The window frames were broken shards of wood. The school was old and literally falling down.

The area was pure mud most of the year. Children were barefoot because shoes were useless. Folks were covered in mud up to their knees almost all the time, and it was caked onto their clothes.

People lived in houses made of slats of wood, often broken, with one to two inches of space between each slat, so the elements entered without problem. Women cooked outside over open firepits. Children of all ages hauled water and wood daily, the tiny ones dragging branches behind them. Folks were continually cold, wet, and covered in mud. They were subsistence farmers: always dependent on Mother Nature. Mother Nature didn't always comply.

Why did they create a village there? They liked being away from what they referred to as "the city," which was really the nearest small *pueblo*.

The newly elected mayor of the municipality called me one evening, saying he had heard about me in every village that he had gone to.

"You have to meet the gringa. The woman who helps," they'd told him.

"Will you meet with me?" he asked.

"Sure," I said, "I can scoot down to the municipal office tomorrow morning."

"What about now?"

Now? "Okay," I said, thinking 9:00 p.m. was an odd time to meet, but I was still relatively new to the culture. Perhaps this was the way things were done. "I'll take a tuk-tuk down to your office."

"Well, actually, I'm in front of your apartment. Could we come up?"

"We?"

"Yes, I'm with my vice mayor."

I looked outside, and sure enough, standing next to a brand-new, white, bling bling Hilux were two well-dressed men with shiny boots, cowboy hats, and the largest, shiny belt buckles I had ever seen. Each had several cell phones in their hands. The assistant had a gun tucked into his pants.

My first thought was, *Holy shit, do they want to kill me?* My second thought was, *All mayors in this area carry arms of some sort.*

I invited them up. I wasn't sure I had a choice. Most people didn't like the mayor. He had won the election through "questionable methods." Every neighbor on my street was either outside staring or inside peeping through their windows.

They came in and apologized for the late hour as I invited them to sit down. I gave them tea and homemade cookies. (I didn't want them to kill me on an empty stomach). They were extremely polite and complimentary. The mayor thanked me for all the good work I had been doing in his municipality. He talked about the tremendous need in this area and said I was a "blessing from God."

The vice mayor was busy answering a stream of phone calls on the mayor's cell and kept excusing himself, getting up from the table and going to my tiny balcony to talk. Each time, my eyes were drawn to his gun.

"Would you be interested in collaborating on a project together?" the mayor asked. "There is a school in Santa Cruz de Virginia in terrible shape and I am hoping to replace it before it falls down. Could you share some of the costs?"

"I would like to see it," I said.

"I can arrange that, no problem. You can go with one or two of the municipal staff any day you like," he said.

It seemed simple and a somewhat intriguing project.

It turned out to be anything but simple and way more scary than intriguing. The only way to this village was through El Paraíso. Had I known that El Paraíso was the narcotics headquarters for that area of Honduras, I never would have agreed to go.

I met Luis, the mayor's assistant in charge of transportation, early in the morning. He often made municipal deliveries of building materials and supplies to outlying villages, and he transported people for municipal tasks, as well. I brought my friend, Wilman, who was my solderer, as well. Wilman had helped us in the past with installing roofs and putting in barred windows. He was easygoing, trustworthy, and a good friend. I wanted him to evaluate a possible roof, as well as iron bars for the windows. I also wanted to have another person with me. A male friend in a macho culture would offer me a little more safety in an unknown territory. It was a fantastic decision. He turned out to be a great comfort and a humorous witness.

Luis, like all the municipal staff, was well dressed, with shiny boots and a big belt buckle. *Was this the required muni uniform?* He was equipped with cell phones and a pistol. This pistol was not concealed. He had the same swagger as the mayor and vice mayor. *Did they learn this swagger upon being elected, or did they swagger before?*

Luis was quite friendly and eager to chat, outgoing and polite. He opened the car door for me. When he got into the driver's seat, he took the pistol out of the holster and put it on the seat between his legs.

"Why are you doing that?" I asked.

"One time I shot myself in the hip, so ever since I always take it out while I'm driving."

It was all I could do to not burst out laughing. "I see. But isn't that an even more vulnerable place, where you're putting it?" My imagination rushed into a scenario of what to do if we hit a bump and he shot his balls off.

He simply laughed and started driving.

We drove for hours on bad roads, crossing streams with such strong currents that I was sure the truck would be cascading downstream at any given minute. I again planned ahead. The car had automatic locks and windows—what if I couldn't get out as we went crashing into rocks or slipped underwater? What were my options? I asked him to open my window.

We stopped in El Paraíso. Halfway there. We got out, apparently to change cars.

"We need an armored car for the rest of the way," Luis said.

Armored car? Why an armored car?

We entered a gorgeous walled-in palatial building in a compound with armed guards everywhere and a few women who were dressed extremely provocatively. My guess was they were "working ladies." Cameras were everywhere, and Wilman and I watched as every camera seemed to move in our direction every time we moved. I checked my hair. If I was to be on camera, I wanted to look my best.

Wilman and I looked at each other and quietly mumbled, "What's going on here?" I didn't know whether to burst out laughing or panic.

I was introduced around and recognized the owner of the mansion as a well-known *narcotraficante* and man of other questionable activities. Mafia. I had seen newspapers that identified him as murdering several people, but he'd never been convicted (typical in Honduras).

He thanked me for coming. "God bless you for your help."

I wondered if *narcos* really believed in God.

We were introduced to some of the ladies. I whispered to Wilman that he should get some of their phone numbers.

The *narcotraficante* invited us to lunch, but due to time constraints (thank God), we had to be on our way.

"If you need a favor," our host told me as we were leaving, "anything at all, just call me and I will take care of it."

I made a mental note to never call him.

We changed drivers at that point, to a young man, very sweet, with a gun even larger than Luis'. This car was bulletproof. *Is that a comfort?*

"Why a bulletproof Hilux truck?" I asked the new driver.

"It is dangerous. There are lots of people who want to kill us."

Us? Does this include me? Wilman? Or just the driver?

A few men climbed into the open back of the truck, unprotected except for their weapons.

The car had a small TV on the dashboard. It was showing a pure sex and violence movie. Murder and blood for about ten minutes, until I asked if we could shut it off.

The driver seemed sweet souled, and I started to chat with him.

"Why are you working with these guys?"

"It is the only job I can find, and it pays really well. My mother is sick. I need the money."

We talked more.

"I hate carrying a gun," he admitted to me. "I don't go to church anymore because I am in this situation."

"Maybe you can pray for another job?"

He smiled.

A bit further on our journey, we approached an oncoming truck filled with men. The driver calmly turned to us and said, "You may want to duck down."

My heart pounded. "I want to go home!" I cried. "Take us back!"

"We only have a few minutes left and we'll be there," he replied, and kept driving.

Sure, only one problem: we'll arrive dead!

We did arrive in about five minutes, and we did arrive alive. The moment the truck stopped, I jumped out as if it were on fire. I was glad to see people running towards us. Witnesses. Safe people without guns. The head teacher, Elias, was the first to come shake my hand. He presented us to the teachers and the community while the mud-soaked children followed us everywhere, laughing. The girls immediately grabbed my hands and arms; about eight of them hung onto my neck and every limb. Boys surrounded us.

We asked the kids to help us unload toys, and within seconds, cartons of supplies were cleared from the truck bed. Kids were oohing and ahhing with delight as they opened the boxes, touching everything, examining things they had never seen before, like pencils with decorations on them. They were awestruck. The driver and assistant remained in the truck the entire time with the windows rolled up, while Wilman and I walked around for the rest of the tour.

We talked with the head teacher about what other needs they might have. I told him we could help with some of the needs and he was extremely grateful. I knew, however, that I would not be working with the mayor on this construction project or any other. I would worry later about how I'd break the news to him. We started towards the village leader's house for coffee.

Our ascent on foot was nearly impossible, walking in pure mud in the misty rain. I couldn't make headway. The mud was so deep that it took about fifteen seconds to extricate each foot. Finally, halfway up, just as I felt like I was making progress, I slipped and fell, sliding all the way back down on my butt. Back to square one, but this time covered in mud. Everyone laughed including me, although I was certain that I'd end up with some form of diaper rash the next day.

When we arrived at the teacher's house, the women gave us coffee and started to help clean me up. Very little success. I was too far gone. We chatted for quite a while about their lifestyle there and the natural beauty of that area. One could see 360 degrees from just about anywhere in the village, such breathtaking mountain views, wild flowers, and a multitude of green everywhere.

It was getting late and the trip was long, so we thanked them for their hospitality and said our goodbyes. They thanked us profusely for coming and invited us back any time. We were always welcome. They gave us a large bag of local fruits and vegetables and walked us to the truck. It touched me that I had a woman on each side of me holding me up so I wouldn't slip again.

On my muddy behind, soaking wet, it was a cold and bumpy ride home. I worried about "bad men" along the way and didn't want to die covered with mud on my butt. However, the trip back was eventless, and—thank goodness—we didn't stop at the barricaded palace on the way back.

Upon arrival in Copán, Wilman and I said goodbye and thanked our driver. Wilman came into my house for tea and to process all that we had experienced. We talked and laughed nonstop, completely stunned by the day's events. *Was this amazing? Was he scared? Was I scared? Who are these armed Mafia people who are blessing us in God's name for going to this village?*

The next day, however, anger took over. I went to the municipality to talk with the mayor. I was invited in immediately. He gave me a warm smile. I did not have one in return.

My first words were, "How could you put us in such danger? I offered to help and this is what we had to go through? And without warning?"

Sitting behind his huge desk, he slumped like a little boy in a big swivel chair. He dismissed his armed guard from his office.

"You have my apologies," he said.

"I will not be doing this project with the municipality," I said. "But I do intend to help the school with teaching materials, supplies, and food supplement for the kids, but on my own."

"I understand," he said, looking again like a little boy being scolded by his mother. "Thank you for your willingness to help in that regard." Pleasant as ever. He didn't seem concerned or surprised, but at least he apologized and didn't shoot me.

I spent the rest of that day washing the mud from my clothes and cleaning my house, doing things that I had control over.

Chapter 9

Ten-year-old Enrique had a severely fractured leg. He needed an operation immediately, but the doctors at the hospital required his parents to pay the bill in advance and buy the necessary items for the operation, including surgical metal pins for joint repair, blood, towels, blankets, and bandages. The hospital had none of these.

While he waited in severe pain in the bleak, crowded waiting room, his parents frantically searched for people to donate blood and to help with the costs. They needed to supply Enrique's food, as well. Enrique was fortunate. Family and friends helped out quickly. This was not always the case.

The medical system in Honduras was in horrible shape. There were constant strikes by unpaid employees, and it was not uncommon to see doctors and nurses demonstrating in the streets of larger cities. Many had not been paid for as long as two years. Often, there was insufficient medicine and equipment. As with Enrique, the patient was expected to buy and bring their own items like bandages, pins, towels, and blankets. The paint was crumbling, and in fact, the walls were crumbling. Patients often had to wait outside in the rain.

The interesting thing was that there were excellent alternatives to traditional healthcare, including the use of herbs and plants from the mountains, and alternative healers.

In my early days in Copán, I slipped on a cobblestone street in the torrential rain and twisted my ankle badly. I couldn't stand up. A little girl saw me, ran over, and helped me back to my house where I called my friend Marisa who was a pharmacist. My ankle had swollen to about four times its normal size and was turning blue by the time she arrived at my house. She gave me aspirin and iced the ankle for a half hour to get some of the swelling down. She told me to go to the doctor the next morning as soon as the clinic was open.

The next day, the doctor told me it was badly sprained but not broken. I was to continue with aspirin and icing and to stay off my foot for a couple of weeks. Three weeks passed with no improvement. I couldn't put any weight on it, and it was still painful and swollen.

I asked people for advice. Just about everyone in town told me to go to Don Cundo. He was a *soba*, they said, an excellent one. I didn't know what a *soba* was but understood the root, "massage." I was leery about going to a "non-medical" healer but felt I had little choice, and so many people recommended him.

Of course, my previous experiences in the medical world included white offices, waiting rooms, endless nurse assistants, and a receptionist—all wearing completely clean and sterile clothing. A selection of appropriate magazines in the waiting rooms and non-offensive pictures on the wall. This wasn't exactly my experience at Don Cundo's.

I managed with help to get into a tuk-tuk that took me to the dirt alley leading to Cundo's house. My young driver practically carried me down through the path to the shack. There he left me. I still had to maneuver down over stones, discarded beer cans, and rubbish, trying to hop on my good leg.

Don Cundo's home was in an incredible state of decay—filthy, smoke-filled, with pieces of plastic tarps used as a ceiling. I could smell an intense combination of aromas: beans cooking over an open fire and dog poo. The steps to the one-room shack were in shambles, and as I struggled to crawl up them with nothing to hold on to, I realized that I also had to step over puppies, puppy poop, chickens, and a toddler. I thought of making a run for it, but I didn't think I could physically turn around to leave.

After making it through the obstacle course, I looked up and saw Don Cundo. A love arrow struck my heart. He was beautiful. About eighty-something, rail thin, with eyes that sparkled, and a beaming, warm smile that melted me. He took my hand, ducked under my arm to support me, and led me inside.

Dark, pieces of adobe falling from the walls, no electricity. I could barely see. It had a few broken-down beds, two with blankets. I would learn his entire family of eight slept here. Clothes were strewn everywhere.

I sat down on the bed. It sagged in the middle, and I tipped over into the sag and laughed. He helped me to sit back up. He examined my leg and manipulated my ankle a bit, smiled, and said, "This won't take long, but you may feel a twinge of pain."

Twinge of pain?? I knew what "a twinge of pain" meant in North American medical terms. It meant I'd be screaming like a banshee. He worked away, massaging and manipulating the ankle with the use of some special cream, and much to my surprise, there were actually only twinges of pain.

After about fifteen to twenty minutes, he said, "Stand up." Not, "Try and stand," not, "Let's see if you can stand," just, "Stand up."

I stood. There I was, standing. I smiled. "What did you do? Where did you learn this? How could this be fixed so quickly?"

He winked and pointed upwards to God.

I did a little jig as he chuckled

"Take it easy," Don Cundo said, smiling.

It was as if I had been faking an injury the whole time. After three weeks of constant agony, there I was walking and doing a little spin.

It was time to for me to leave, but I didn't want to leave his side. I loved him. He charged me fifty lempiras (about two dollars). I gave him one hundred and thanked him profusely. I turned to go and sprung over the chickens, dashed around the puppy poop, and walked down the broken stairs. I was smiling all the way and waving goodbye to my newfound friend, a man that not only fixed my ankle but opened my world!

Afterwards, I saw him regularly in town and we always exchanged warm greetings and handshakes. Even more than that, my heart was filled with love and an amazing sense of connection to the spiritual world.

* * *

I was deeply saddened to be informed a few days after finishing this chapter that Don Cundo passed away during the night. He was in his late eighties, but I always expected him to live forever. I'm sure his soul will.

Chapter 10

Communication was always a challenge. Direct answers seemed to be lacking. Most children were not encouraged to speak as they grew up. Asking for something was not a practice. Even those adults who requested help from us were shy, embarrassed, and gave us a convoluted message. It was a test of patience for me.

Here's an example. A teacher, Augustin, called me from Santa Cruz de Virginia, about four hours from Copán, one and a half of those hours on foot. A *niño* was very "grave."

"What do you need?"

"He's really sick."

"Yes, but what do you need?"

"He needs help."

"Transportation to the hospital?"

"No."

"Money?"

"No."

"What does he need, Augustin? How do you want me to help?"

"He has a prescription."

"So, you need the prescription filled? How much is it?"

"Not much."

"So, how do we do this?"

"Ricardo (another teacher) is coming into town."

"So he'll have the *receta* (prescription)?"

"Yes."

"When is he coming?"

"I don't know."

"Well, I can't stay home all day. I need to know when."

"Okay, I'll call him."

"Good, and find out how much the prescription is and how much the child's folks can pay."

"They are very poor."

"Yes, I'm sure, but I need them to help. I'm not a bank."

"Heh heh, I know."

Later, he called me back. "Ricardo will come at 9:00 a.m."

At 10:00, I called Ricardo. No answer. I called Augustin.

"I'll call Ricardo and find out when he's coming." He called me back and said Ricardo would come at 11:00.

I called Ricardo to confirm; I had other things to do than wait.

Ricardo called me back. He knew nothing of the prescription.

"What do you mean you don't know about this? Why am I waiting for you then?"

I called Augustin.

Augustin called Ricardo.

Ricardo called me. "Oh yes, the prescription. I forgot."

Ricardo showed up at noon.

I asked how much the prescription would cost.

He said, "350 lempiras."

"350 lempiras! Augustin told me it wouldn't cost much!"

"Yes, but it's for three kids."

"Three kids! Augustin told me it was one very ill child."

"Yes, but his brothers are sick with the same thing."

"How much money did the parents give Augustin to give to you?"

"Nothing."

I called Augustin. "Did you tell them they have to contribute?"

"They are very poor."

"Do they have beans? They can pay for part with a pound of beans."

"I'll ask."

"So, meanwhile, I have to pay the whole thing or let these kids get worse or die?"

"I guess so."

I expressed my frustration.

Augustin apologized.

I gave Ricardo my last 350 lempiras, leaving me with fifty for the week.

* * *

It started with the children. Children were seen and not heard. There was no communication within the families. Children were told what to do. There was no questioning. Children were not asked what they thought or felt.

Sometimes I asked a child what they would like to do when they grew up. No answer. The answer would not have been surprising, sadly; the girls would probably marry and get pregnant, and the boys would be farmers like their dads.

The school systems offered rote learning and nothing more. Teachers were overworked, often not paid, with huge classes. There was no room for the "special student." If a student fell behind or wasn't able to keep up, they simply lost the opportunity to make progress. There was no time for individual support.

If a student was exceptionally bright, they'd have to entertain themselves in the boredom of the class. Often kids who were capable of going further in their education dropped out due to lack of stimulation. The average sixth grader in Honduras is said to come out with a first-grade equivalent education of that offered to US students.

Another barrier was that most rural children were so malnourished that teachers didn't even have an awareness of what could be possible for them. Children were mistaken for being "dull."

When we put milk programs in the schools, teachers were amazed at the difference. Kids interacted more, learned faster, and showed more interest in their studies.

Kids were seen and not heard. It was difficult for a child to make a choice or respond to the question, "What do you want"? Silence continued through adulthood. The education system, at least in the area we served, was based on teachers writing on the blackboard (if they were lucky enough to have one) and kids copying the material. The best and worst students were often left unattended.

Chapter 11

My role in Honduras kept evolving. I became even more a part of the community, helping to connect people within the surrounding communities. This took me out of the helper/rescuer role and I became more of a neighbor and friend.

My friend Agada was a produce exporter who had a huge farm near Copán. She exported squash, sweet potatoes, and oranges. She usually donated the serviceable but misshapen vegetables to be distributed to the folks in the mountain villages.

She called me one day, saying she had more than three hundred pounds of oranges, good quality but not suitable for export—could I make use of them?

"Absolutely!" I said, and immediately called my friend Tulio who drove a tuk-tuk to come pick me up. Tulio and I had become friends early on in my time in Copán. We met when I first stepped into his tuk-tuk. He was a warm, sincere young man and eager to help, especially after he found out about the projects I did. He'd give me discounts on trips into the local areas. Sometimes we would do reverse arguments about his fee, since I felt he undercharged me. That day, he showed up within minutes and we scooted over to the farm at the edge of town to pick up several huge sacks of oranges.

Agada was there to greet us as we jumped out of the tuk-tuk and gave her a huge hug. The air was thick with the scent of warm citrus as we loaded the sacks into the tuk-tuk, the back seat, the back ledge, the front floor, and my lap. I was wedged in among oranges and plastered to my seat with the weight of them, barely able to see out of either side of the vehicle. We took off down the dirt road with fruit bouncing on my lap. Our intention was to pass them out at six villages of subsistence farmers.

I was familiar with the area and knew most of the children. They'd run to greet me when I came by, in a car, a tuk-tuk, or sometimes by foot. They were severely malnourished, with rotted teeth and hair or hair-color loss, and they often had distended bellies due to untreated parasites. They were all rail-thin; most were dressed in rags and shoeless, but some were naked.

The area was peaceful, with the only sounds coming from the river, the wind, and the laughter of children. As we passed houses near the edge of the road, we'd see women washing clothes or cooking while children played.

Tulio beeped the horn as we drove, and I yelled, "*Tenemos naranjas* (We have oranges)!"

The children ran full speed from their houses and the fields, smiling and shouting. We edged along, passing out oranges to each kid. They called to their brothers and sisters. Some ran home to get their siblings and brought them by hand to the tuk-tuk; some ran towards us with little ones bouncing on their backs. They followed along with the tuk-tuk, laughing and screaming, as we inched our way down the dirt road past each village. There were some precious moments, like when we'd see a toddler trying to hold a giant orange in his two little hands. Complete joy for every one of us!

As we drove, we came upon an older woman standing at the side of the road hoping to catch a tuk-tuk to take her to her village. We stopped and explained that we would eventually get there and we'd be happy to take her for free, if she was willing to come with us on our slow trip.

She was delighted and hopped in. She introduced herself to us. Her name was Berta, and she lived up in the mountains. She said she was used to walking from town and climbing the hill from the road but would really appreciate the lift. She was carrying a basket filled with items that she had bought in town. She was a rather large woman, maternal-looking but with great energy. Lively. Her clothes were homemade but in relatively good condition. Her shoes, though, were worn. She wore her long, greyish hair tied back in a bun. What I noticed most about her was that she had a glow about her, a beaming smile, and a face that exuded joy. She laughed easily and carried an air of dignity and love. I could tell she was probably a prominent presence in her community. She told us that she had many children, as well as twenty-three grandchildren and a few great-grandchildren. Her husband was a farmer. Sometimes she made extra money washing people's clothes in her *pila* (cement wash sink).

We explained our task for the morning and asked if she would help.

She gave a hearty laugh and said, "How wonderful!"

We put her to work! We opened a sack for her and asked her to give out one orange per kid, and she accepted her task with joy.

At that point, children were swarming around the tuk-tuk, which now inched along. Tulio, I, and now Berta were all passing out oranges. Tulio had a charming method of bouncing them off of his upper-arm muscle, and the kids would squeal with laughter as they tried to catch one. We received many thank yous.

As the children and moms thanked Berta, she answered, "You're so welcome. We are glad to give these to you."

I sensed that Berta had never had a chance to give out anything concrete before; she was having a magnificent time. It was pure joy that sunny morning for all of us.

When we eventually arrived at the path to the *señora's* village, she edged out of the tuk-tuk, grabbed her basket, and thanked us for such a wonderful experience. She said there was nothing as fulfilling as giving and quoted a passage from the bible.

We agreed and thanked her for helping us. We gave her the remaining thirty or so oranges as a gift for pitching in and said our goodbyes with hugs.

She took the sack of oranges and gave a huge wave as she turned to start climbing up the mountain towards home.

Tulio and I laughed as he turned the tuk-tuk around and gave her a few friendly beeps.

All of the school projects we did were gratifying, but for me, there was a special kind of gratification in that simple task on that beautiful morning along the river, handing out those oranges—especially with such a lovely volunteer from the community joining in. It was also special because, for me, this was not an act of charity; it was neighbors sharing abundance with neighbors.

The generosity of people who had so little moved me. One day in town, I ran into a boy from a school that I visited often. I was buying a piece of fried chicken near the park. Ramón was an extremely skinny child.

"Would you like a piece of chicken?" I asked him. "I'll buy you one."

"Yes," he answered.

We went to sit in the park to eat it.

Ramón only took a couple of bites and put the rest in his pocket.

"Don't you like chicken?" I asked.

"I want to share it with my brothers and sisters," he said.

I saw this kind of selfless generosity often.

Chapter 12

The following is a letter to my dear friend, Kim, the friend I'd cried with at the Seattle airport when I left the States for good, the friend who always listened to my joys, victories, and stories of grief and loss. It always helped me to write to her. As I witnessed so much in Honduras, I needed a witness, as well.

Yes, Kimmy, you're right: integrating cultures is always challenging. I am getting accustomed to many things, but I'm still challenged by many issues, including the unbearable heat. I'm embarrassed to let my local friends know that I take three showers a day. Am I too much of a princess?

I try to fit in, try to be okay withor even laid back about—what happens, and I try not to complain to locals. (I complain like hell to you, of course.) Here are some examples:

"Oh, the electricity is out again today. Oh, okay, I'll just shift the work I had planned to do today. I guess I'll just cook all the perishable items in my freezer."

"Oh, the lumber yard is out of lumber. Will it be out for several weeks? I see. I guess we'll just postpone the con-

struction of the school until then. I'm sure the (Northern timescale) donors won't be bothered by this."

"Oh look, a little scorpion!"

"Oh my! I've never seen a cockroach that large."

"Oh, the road is closed (again)? Okay, no problem; we can walk the final mile. The mud isn't that deep."

"I'm sure we can get those blackboards onto the horses, no problem."

"Whoops, looks like I have a little parasites in my stomach again."

I went into a restaurant for breakfast Tuesday with Yarely. We sat down and the girl brought us menus. When she came back to the table, I said, "I'll have the orange juice and the breakfast tipica."

She responded, "No hay. (We don't have that.)"

"Okay, I'll just have the eggs."

"No hay."

Yarely asked, "Well, how about just bringing me a fruit milkshake?"

"No hay."

I asked, "What do you have?"

The owner came by and said, "Sorry we don't have a cook this morning."

I felt like I needed a rimshot to end the comedy scene.

I have hardest time staying calm and patient during more dire situations. For example, I work quite a bit with the health centers. Sometimes there are kids being brought in who literally will die if they don't get to the hospital.

My friend Anne often offers to pay for the expenses, such as travel, food, medical exams, etc., but the parents often don't respond. The attending doc says something like, "This child absolutely needs to go to the hospital." The parent takes the child home instead.

We all try to understand. Maybe the parent is afraid of the big city. It can be overwhelming when one has never left the community and is illiterate. Maybe there are too many children at home to leave unattended for an extended period. Maybe the father badly needs the work, so he can't afford to leave for a day. I wrestle with this a lot! Often I hear, "It's God's will if the child dies." I hear this with pregnancy too. Anne, when she is working with the doctors at the clinic, often asks the patients, "How many children are you planning to have?" The answer often is, "However many God gives us."

As you know, Kimmy, dealing with my own judgments is one of the biggest learning tasks of my life, and with these kinds of episodes all the time, I mean, ALL THE TIME, I struggle with how much to stay out of this and how much to step in. Sometimes, actually more often than not, I feel caught between two cultures, trying to understand both.

For example, rural folks here have much more of an acceptance of death than we do. We come from an environment where we fight for life at all costs. I love the people here, and I think it's natural and normal as a friend or a neighbor to want to help, but I always struggle with "how much" or when to step in. I don't want to be a rescuer. That requires that someone must be a victim, and yet I have access to so much privilege and resources. I also don't want to create dependency, and I don't want to take over, yet how can I stand by and let a child die? This culture has already been so deeply wounded by good-meaning folks who take over what Hondurans can do for themselves, leaving the receiver feeling inept, helpless, and dependent on foreigners.

Okay, you know I can go on with my rants. I'll give you a break here (at least for the moment).

Write me back. I miss you!

Chapter 13

O ne day, I was waiting for a tuk-tuk to take me downtown and was picked up by a driver I recognized, Antonio. I got in and we were on our way when suddenly he pulled to the side of the road and, without turning around, said, "*Gracias a Dios y gracias por usted.* (Thank God and thanks because of you.)"

I said, "I understand thanking God, but why are you thanking me?"

He turned and looked at me. "Because you saved the lives of my wife and baby."

"What!!!?" I was shocked.

"Yes, we called Marel one night last week to get help for my woman who was in labor and having much difficulty. She was screaming. I didn't know what to do. He called you, and you sent him with a truck to take her to the hospital just in time! The baby was coming out crooked and there was too much blood."

I had goosebumps up and down my arms. I remembered the call. Marel told me about the emergency but didn't give me any names. I remembered racing around frantically, trying to put together the limited funds to pay for gas.

"How are the mom and baby?" I asked, hoping they were healthy. "Was it a boy or a girl?"

"A boy," Antonio said proudly. "And my woman is doing much better, *Gracias a Dios*. I want to bring them to your house, but the mother is still too weak."

"Any time, Antonio. I look forward to meeting them." I was still stunned.

Two weeks later, the family showed up in front of my house. The mother was beaming, holding a darling baby, all bundled up in a red shirt. Once again, I had chills; these two most likely would not have made it if they hadn't gotten to the hospital.

* * *

There are way too many incidents of pregnant women having difficulties with labor in this impoverished area of Honduras. We'd get this type of emergency usually a couple of times per month. Sadly, we could not always find the funds to offer hospital rides to every expectant mother who needed one.

I sometimes went with the driver during the day trips to pick up a woman in labor, always feeling that the mother would want another woman present. I was haunted for days, often weeks, if I had to say there were no funds. It broke my heart, knowing this might mean the death of the mother and baby and the future neglect of the rest of the children in the family.

Often when we were able to send transportation, the women in labor had to be carried down the mountains to the truck if the driver couldn't get the vehicle all the way to the site. Then she had to endure a long, bouncy ride over rocks and bad roads when she was already in severe pain. It was not uncommon for my assistant to have to stop and check on a passenger, or to have to wash the blood out of his truck bed later on.

Folks like Antonio could not save in advance for things like transportation or pregnancy complications; he only worked part-time as a tuk-tuk driver, and there was rarely enough money for even the basics like food.

We were limited in the number of women we could help. Sometimes I would pay for transportation out of my own pocket. Marel did this too. It cost around seventy-five dollars, the equivalent of two months' salary for most local people. The cost of an ambulance was higher. We couldn't always find a willing driver to face the danger of going into the mountains, especially at night when attacks and robberies were common. If they did agree to go, they would charge exorbitant fees.

Most women in rural Honduras had their babies at home. There were often midwives in the villages who helped. Prenatal care was non-existent because of the distance from available services, lack of resources for mothers to travel to hospitals, and the necessity to stay home and care for young children. There was also the fear and discomfort of being examined by a male doctor. The hospitals were hours away from the villages and very poorly equipped.

If a pregnant woman did choose to have her baby at a hospital and was lucky, she wouldn't have to share a hospital bed. Often, though, women in labor shared a twin-sized bed and a plastic chair, and alternated between chair and bed when they had contractions. Newborns were put in cardboard boxes on the floor, sometimes covered with a towel unless the family brought a blanket.

The mortality rate, due to complications, inadequate care, poor nutrition, ill-equipped clinics, or delayed response times was extremely high. If a patient needed blood, for example, they had to supply it themselves by bringing a family member. Many clinics didn't even have something as basic as a blood-pressure cuff.

Buenos Vecinos worked with the local government health center, *Centro de Salud,* to support a prenatal program, but when we started, pregnant women weren't able to attend due to the expense of transportation. It was often too far to walk, so we developed incentives, such as subsidizing the cost of the transportation. Thanks to the donation of another organization, we were able to offer prenatal vitamins. We also started offering incentives to the monthly prenatal group—raffle prizes like baby blankets, nursing bottles, toys, baby clothing—which tripled attendance almost immediately.

Most rural families were extremely large. The use of contraceptives was not popular, sometimes for religious reasons, but other times because men just didn't want to use any. Family planning was not common. Folks expected that at least one or two children would die, so there was safety in numbers. Unfortunately, once a baby was weaned, there were not many options for food since the families were so poor, leaving him or her at high risk of malnutrition or death. If the mother died in childbirth, this often left the care of the toddler and smaller children in the hands of the father or older children who were not capable of giving full adequate care. It was not a surprise to find a seven-year-old girl taking on the role of mother. Although there were some organizations in the nearby towns that occasionally helped out, calls for medical or nutritional assistance often came too late, if at all.

Antonio was one of the fortunate ones. His small family was healthy and happy. I saw his son again when he was four years old, and he was a happy little guy at that!

Chapter 14

The bathroom door wouldn't open. I was on a "luxury" bus, and I kept yanking the handle to get into the restroom, but it wouldn't budge. I tried to pound the door open, but nothing. Folks came back to help. The attendant came back, and yelled, "Just push."

"Obviously that isn't working," I said. He yelled something to clear the crowd and slammed his shoulder against the door like cops do in a movie. Nothing. He told us to stand back. He leaned against a seat and lifted his leg. He proceeded to kick the door in. The crowd joyously celebrated and I navigated inside the tiny one-square-meter compartment.

Only in a memoir about Honduras would going to the toilet be the opening of a chapter! Living in rural Honduras brought many such humbling—or should I say humiliating—experiences. Several seem to revolve around toilets.

I crouched and did what I could to relieve myself, but the bus was taking the turns and bumps at such a speedy rate that I was being slammed side to side against urine-penetrated walls. I was being bounced up and down as my feet kept shifting on the sticky floor. I tried to brace myself and "take care of business" at the same time. I was laughing hysterically, but thinking back now, that might have been panic, not humor. It was a "luxury bus," but I was learning that "luxury" meant different things to different people in different cultures.

Of course, I couldn't get the door open to get out! The bathroom had a tiny window and as we passed kids on the road or in front of their houses they waved to me. I waved back. *Do they know I am peeing? Do they know I am trapped in this cubicle from hell?* I feared I would die inside this cell with internal bruises and covered in stale urine. Still, nothing I did would make the door budge.

Finally, I had no choice; I had to yell for help. A few young men came back to help, but they pushed and shoved, and again as we bounced along there was no way to open the door. They called the attendant again. He yelled through the door for me to stand on the toilet while he kicked the door in. If the window had been bigger I might have made a jump and risked serious injury just to save the embarrassment. There I was, standing on the toilet trying to be brave and bracing myself for the view that some passengers would see. At least I was clothed.

The attendant kicked so hard the door blasted off its hinges and lay there broken. I had to be helped from the toilet seat to jump across to the aisle. Everyone cheered. I raised my arms in the victory pose. No one peed for the rest of the trip.

* * *

There were other humiliating experiences. A group of farmers came to my house asking for help building an outhouse for their school. There were too many of them to sit inside my house, so I suggested they go out to my large back porch while I fixed them some coffee. Hats off, they dutifully marched out back while I proceeded to the kitchen.

Unfortunately, I had forgotten that I had just washed my clothes and my underwear was hanging like colorful banners on the porch clothesline. As I walked out with coffee, I saw that these unfortunate men had respectfully taken their seats with my underpants dangling just inches above their heads. What exactly was the protocol in a situation like this? Take down the panties, ignore them, move the men inside? There was no good answer.

* * *

On another occasion, we were in a remote village and I needed to go to the bathroom. Doña Carla, the wife of the village leader who lived near the school where we were working, kindly offered her facilities. She took me to her nearby broken-down adobe house, led me to the back, and pointed down a very steep hill to her wooden-slat, tin-covered outhouse. It was leaning heavily to the right.

It had been raining quite a bit and there was no path down the treacherous, muddy hill. The area was solid mud, chicken excrement, an old shoe, and various unknown and unpleasant-looking jetsam. She walked away to give me privacy as I started my descent. To my horror, within a second I had slipped and slid all the way down on my bottom. As I slammed into the open door of the outhouse, I was covered with mud and other unpleasant substances that I chose not to identify. I reeked. As I tried to stand up, the full weight of the mixture made it hard to regain my balance. I desperately wanted to clean up, but—nature calling—relieving myself was my primary goal. The toilet itself was practically useless. It was what was called a *campesino* (country) toilet, meaning a porcelain bowl, nothing more. It required adding a pail of water to flush it. I didn't see any nearby water.

I proceeded to lower my mud-caked trousers and hover over the filthy bowl, which was filled with crawling insects. I relieved myself, desperately trying not to lose my balance.

Matters took a turn for the worse as I began my ascent back up the hill. It was just too slippery and I was too weighed down with mud and *whatever* to climb. It was demeaning, but I had to call for help.

"*Hola*," I shouted. "*Necesito ayuda* (I need help)."

Doña Carla showed up and waved, then noticed my situation and began down the hill. She waved over a couple of men who had also arrived at the scene, and the three edged their way down the muddy hill sideways to keep their balance. Doña Carla and one of the men grabbed each of my filthy arms. We all struggled to keep our balance as we made our way up the hill. I wondered what happened if someone had to "go" at night.

When we reached the summit, I thanked the men and they took off. Next on the scene were two of Doña Carla's teenage daughters who took me away (trying not to laugh) and helped clean me up in the nearby creek. They brought plastic pans to douse me. We removed the biggest chunks and most of the mud mixture, and I felt I would be at least able to make it back to the truck. The young women offered me a change of clothes but they were significantly smaller than my hulking five-foot-two frame and therefore I had to decline. I stayed in the sun for fifteen minutes to dry off and got ready for the trip home. I was miserable.

On the trip back, I reeked. Marel, laughing, put a plastic bag on my seat and made me hang my legs out the truck window to reduce the smell. The trip was excruciatingly long. Three hours later, I arrived at my house, rushed to the back porch, stripped my clothes off outside and ran to the bathroom. I showered five times. Out, out damned spots! I'm certain that Marel washed his car about that many times, as well.

Then there was the time we were building a school in a mountain community and we were offered food we couldn't refuse. The wife of the village leader offered us bowls of rice, milk, and cinnamon—sort of a warm rice pudding. They were poor and it was obvious they had no soap; the dishes were dirty with crusted food around the edges. We were also sure the milk was less than fresh. They had no refrigerator. It was considered rude to refuse food, which was often the only offering people had to give as a thank you.

As Marel and I ate the mixture, I kept smiling and said to Marel in English, "We're going to be sick, aren't we?"

Marel smiled back as he was downing his portion with feigned enjoyment and said, "Yes we are!"

Marel vomited the entire way home. My stomach stayed in tact.

* * *

A favorite pastime of mine was finding creative methods to rip my clothes. Barbed wire fences, thorned lime trees, and various flora all offered methods for shredding shirts and pants. No one seemed to even blink when I'd show up at a home with my shirt hanging open, breast hanging out (thank heavens my bra was intact) as if I had just been feeding a child, or a patch of pants hanging loose. Sometimes folks would offer a hand when we were picking ticks off our skin, a sharp contrast to my North American lifestyle where I used to worry if my hair wasn't combed.

And speaking of combs … in Union Cedral we were planning a "Children's Beauty Day," which was really a hygiene day. We selected this village because of the remoteness and lack of access to services, and because of the motivation of the pastor there. We were going to cut nails, wash hair with lice shampoo, and give haircuts to remove matted hair. We named it "Beauty Day" to give it a positive image. Kids and parents were excited.

Coordinating with the fabulous, committed teacher Cristino, we bought shampoo, scissors, hair gel, soap, towels, and mirrors. The mirrors were the best part since most kids had never seen themselves except in the reflection of the river water or sometimes in windows when they went to town. I decided to buy items to give away to each child, a hygiene package that would also include special things like hair ribbons, gel for the boys, combs, soap, and other personal items. I shopped for these items in Copán, going to my favorite booth owned by Moncho, who always gave us great prices.

It was crowded that day. I said hello to Moncho and asked for 100 combs: "*Por favor necesito cien penes.*"

Everyone laughed. I thought they were laughing at the quantity. I smiled too. "*Sí, necesito cien penes!*" I said again.

A kind woman turned to me and whispered a correction. "*Peines* (combs)," she said, enunciating the *i*.

"*Peines,*" I repeated. "What had I said?" I asked.

People laughed. Someone told me I had just said that I needed 100 penises.

* * *

One night, I woke up to being pelted with what felt like tiny, lightweight stones on my head. I was unnerved. I flipped on my nightstand light to find that they weren't stones at all but—to my horror—white, wiggly maggots. I looked up. They were falling from the ceiling tiles and had covered my hair, face, and bed.

I jumped up and let out a shriek that probably was heard in the neighboring town. After screaming and running around my house for a few minutes, I pulled myself together enough to call Manuel, the handyman who was in charge of the house repairs. It was about 11:00 at night, but I didn't care; I was crazed with disgust. He answered with a voice that obviously indicated that had been asleep and responded to my shrieking panic, saying he'd come first thing in the morning.

I screamed into the phone in horror and disgust, "You absolutely have to come now! Right now!"

My screeching must have sent a clear message because he showed up fifteen minutes later with his tool belt on over his pajamas.

I stood in the living room, pointing. "In there! In there!"

He went in casually. I watched from the living room. He looked at my bed and then up at the tiles. He seemed nonplussed. The hideous creatures were still falling onto the bed, onto *my* bed. I kept screaming. Manuel moved my bed and pulled over a bench to stand on. He took down a couple of tiles and—much to my horror—two stiff, dead rats fell onto my bed.

I screamed from the living room, "Oh my God! Oh my God! Oh my God!" I danced a frantic tarantella.

Manuel suggested I sleep in the living room that night and he'd come back first thing in the morning to clean up.

"Oh no. Oh no," I screamed. "I'll pay you any amount you want, but I'm not sleeping in this house until they are gone! I want them out." I pleaded, begged, and demanded in frantic desperation until he consented.

It took hours to clean and temporarily repair the roof. Manuel took the dead rats out in a plastic bag. He took down more tiles, and used a broom to clean out the false attic. That was all he could do for the night, but he assured me, "Everything is gone." He said he'd be back the next day to check on things and replace the ceiling tiles.

"What time?" I asked, panicked.

"In the morning."

"What time?" I needed a precise time so that I didn't have to wait around in horror all morning long.

"Seven o'clock," he answered.

"Seven o'clock Honduran time or North American time?"

He laughed and assured me he'd be there first thing in the morning.

I slept on the sofa through what was left of the night, or at least I tried, while imagining that there was a whole community of rats and maggots living (or dead) just above my head.

Manuel did show up at 7:00 a.m. He cleaned up the area above the false ceiling with a special substance, fumigated, and replaced the tiles that were missing.

Thanking him profusely, I paid him well for his services.

For months, I compulsively cleaned the bedroom, the bed, and washed the sheets, but I never slept the same, always lying in bed for the first ten minutes, eyes wide open, vigilantly watching the tiles.

* * *

One of the things I missed the most was a bathtub and hot water, the only real antidote to cleansing after a disgusting episode. I fantasized about lying in a hot bath, imagining all kinds of scented bath salts. Bathtubs did not exist in rural regions, nor did enough hot water to fill one. I had to be content to go into the bathroom, search for cockroaches and spiders, and then shower with semi-warm water (on days that we actually had water), using lots and lots of soap.

Chapter 15

B ecause of my work at the schools, I was deeply interested in the Honduran education system. As I mentioned earlier in the chapter on my commute to work, I often visited Cristobal, one of my favorite teachers.

Over time, Cristobal became a mentor to me on the subject of education. He told me how most teachers had been unpaid from anywhere between six months to two years. They continued their work for three reasons: because they cared about the children, because they were hoping to someday get reimbursed or get paid again, and because there were no other opportunities for other employment. The average salary, when they were paid, ranged from $100 to $700 monthly, depending on their education. Some teachers had no education beyond high school, and in some rural areas, young teachers who hadn't finished high school volunteered because there was no alternative for instruction.

The teachers had long and sometimes dangerous commutes. Walking long distances in isolated areas, some of the female teachers were assaulted and raped. Sometimes the men were robbed. They also faced bad road conditions, fallen live wires from storms, and narrow paths by ravines. My friend Luis had a serious motorcycle accident after hitting a rock and lay in the road for two hours until help came. We were called and were able to respond with a trip to the hospital that ultimately saved his life.

The school buildings were in bad shape. The farther from town, the more neglected the schools were. Sometimes the buildings were rendered unusable, forcing classes to be held outside. A wall or roof might be on the verge of collapse. Supporting beams for the roofs were rotted. Pieces of roof materials would fall.

Inside the classrooms was also bleak. Sometimes there were rats. It wasn't uncommon to see major ruts in the floors where kids (and visitors like me) would often trip. Many schools had no bathrooms or sinks. Often there were no blackboards or teaching materials. The walls showed peeling paint, spilled substances, and filth. Very few decorations adorned the walls except for special occasions when there would be colored crepe paper hanging from the beams. Often, windows and doors were broken. With no electricity, the rooms were frequently dark. Rain seeped through the damaged roofs.

The students were often weak from hunger and unable to concentrate. It seemed to me that most had some kind of attention deficit disorder. They came from homes that had no order and no rules. There were no "sit down with the family" meals and often no meals at all. Sometimes there were no seats or tables in the homes. Kids slept irregularly, usually going to bed when it was dark since there was no electricity. Kids arrived at school sleepy, hungry, and cold. Teachers often told me that they shared their lunches with the kids.

I admired Cristobal greatly for his spirit and love of education, and his willingness to confront challenges. His school, too, was a disaster. It looked like a bomb had hit it, with decay and rubble everywhere. On the playground, on the porches, and in the classrooms pieces of decaying brick walls were scattered everywhere. The windows that remained in the school were broken. Shattered doors had fallen off their hinges. The ancient roof leaked badly, and the smell of mold and mildew permeated the classrooms. (Fortunately, due to the lack of windows, the air could circulate.) The bathrooms and *pila* were unusable. The cement floors had giant, deep ruts the size of bathmats. Just a hint of paint remained on the damaged walls. There were insufficient desks and unusable blackboards in each classroom.

There were only two or three textbooks that were shared by the forty-seven first graders who were learning to read. I asked over and over again how folks taught reading without a blackboard or books. He told me that some teachers would copy pages from a book they had, but that would get expensive. Other teachers would draw in the sand outside the classroom. At times, some would draw in the air. This school had only two teachers and a couple of volunteers to look after more than 250 children, eighty-five of whom were in kindergarten. There were insufficient school supplies and teaching materials. The filthy walls were bare, but teachers would hang decorations from the rotted roof beams, such as bottle caps or plant seeds glued together to form a chain. The children were very malnourished and almost all were dressed in rags.

Cristobal invited Marel and me to visit his school. It was a shocking vision. Two of the classrooms were outside with children stuffed onto the large porches. The rest of the children were squeezed into small classrooms with battered teaching materials piled high on the floors in the corners. Most children were shoeless or wore almost unusable shoes.

I met eight-year-old Marco as he shuffled towards me in plastic sandals that looked six sizes too big. He couldn't run and play with the other kids unless he took off his shoes. Roberto, another boy of about eight, had a body of a five-year-old. He was born mute.

Marel was pulling out the keys of the truck and dropped two lempiras on the ground (the equivalent of about ten cents.) He picked them up and gave them to little Roberto who gave an enormous smile in return and took off for home, running full speed with one lempira in each hand to give to his mom, paying no attention to the classes that were starting.

Cristobal's commute was about an hour and a half on motorcycle over rocky terrain. Teachers, by law, were supposed to receive compensation for long commutes, but that was a thing of the past. He told me that no teachers he knew had that kind of support anymore. Rainy days were the worst. It was slippery and dangerous, and he always arrived soaking wet in spite of his plastic parka. Still, Cristobal loved his work. As I was writing this book, we spoke again. He had been paid, albeit only partially—his first paycheck in more than six months.

Chapter 16

Neighborhood kids loved to come to my house because I owned a squirt gun. After school on a hot day, they would run up to my gate screaming, "Don't come out of the house and squirt us, Doña Elena! Don't squirt us!"

I'd run out to the gate, wielding my loaded weapon. I'd open fire as they'd scream, run away, and just as quickly run back and scream and laugh some more.

One day, I decided to "trade up" and bought a squirt bazooka. I came running out of the house as always, but this time with amazing power, a force to contend with. Their faces showed shock and awe. The screams reached an all-time ear-piercing high as I chased them down the street, firing at will, kids running, neighbors laughing, drivers of cars and tuk-tuks stopping to watch. Sometimes in the frenzy, I opened fire on the onlookers, as well.

I took my arms to the villages on my school visits, too, sometimes crashing into a classroom and firing away. (Only with teachers who gave me permission.) I loved to watch the kids duck for cover under their broken desks and chairs, laughing, screaming. I was relentless. Sometimes I would corner a kid and shoot water down the back of his shirt. At recess, I'd occasionally surprise them with their own individual weapons and another onslaught would ensue.

I was absolutely crazy about the children. Being with them would lift my spirits and bring me all kinds of joy. Even the shy ones on the streets, walking with their moms, would peek at me and smile, and turn around and continue to smile, even after they passed me. I'd keep waving.

Going shopping with kids was one of my favorite pastimes. Sometimes kids would come to my house with their moms to get something from our small clothing bank. It was so satisfying to be able to replace a tattered shirt or dress. (Often I'd charge one lempira or maybe trade for a squash or bag of limes.)

The day that five-year-old Juanito and his mom came to my house, his mom brought a pound of black beans and asked if we had boy's shoes. It was blazing hot and for barefoot kids, walking on the burning pavement must have been excruciating. I found an almost-new pair of heavyweight Velcro-strapped sneakers just his size.

Juanito beamed as he took them out of his mother's hands. He sat down on the ground. He had never had shoes before and started to put one on the wrong foot. Mom gave him some help. After both were on and strapped, he just stood there without moving as if his feet were cemented to the ground. After a few more seconds, he started to walk and suddenly, weightlessly jumped in the air. He was ecstatic. So was his mom. As they left the house, I watched Juanito skipping through the gate.

We often would receive a large enough donation to take an entire school, one class at a time, shopping for uniforms. It was always a treat to see the smiles as kids would try on new clothes. We had a special place in the public market in town, where the owner would give us a big discount for buying in quantity. We would call ahead to make sure she had enough items in stock. I remember taking the kids from Los Tapescos, a tiny rural village about an hour from town. Most kids had never had the opportunity to be away from home. It was an area so poor that even the cows were gaunt, every rib showing, from lack of good soil and grass.

We picked the children up, stuffed them into the truck bed, and drove them over the bumpy, winding road into town. We ushered them in a line through the crowded market, squeezing through the noisy crowd, with the aromas of rotted fruit and fried chicken and cooked beans. We climbed over the live chickens squawking in distress and filed upstairs to Mariela's three-by-three meter cubicle. Thirty-five kids were jammed into the market stall, squeezing behind piles of clothing, with overflowing shelves of shirts, pants, and skirts. Kids would be trying on items as blouses cascaded down over their heads. Organized bedlam.

Village children were always underweight, which brought challenges when seeking clothing in tiny sizes, but Mariela came up with infinite possibilities in that clothing-stuffed cubicle. After Mariela, the teacher, the two salesgirls, and I helped the kids find the right sizes, we ushered them to the mirror. Most were seeing themselves for the first time in a mirror. They'd stare and blush, uncomfortable yet excited about seeing their own image, along with the new uniform.

Antonia, the owner, was always patient and took her work seriously. She was a young grandmother and adored children. Her daughter was a teacher in a poor village and knew well the challenges of not only the teachers but of the students. She always gave me great discounts.

There were so many times I'd walk into her booth with a child in rags. She'd bend down and say to him or her, "What can we do for you today?" The child, too shy to say a word, would look at me and I would talk about the items we wanted to buy.

With the large school group, finally each child found their new uniform. Each carried their new purchase, grinning widely as we marched out of the stall.

I asked, "Who likes ice cream?"

They all screamed, "Meeee!"

I knew that most had never eaten ice cream before, but they weren't about to say no. The *muchacha* in the ice cream booth asked them what flavors they wanted. They didn't know what a "flavor" was. They didn't know they had options.

She scooped vanilla and chocolate, thinking they might be the safest, most familiar choices. One by one, each child was handed a cone, their eyes bulging with excitement. It was an unfamiliar art to them, eating an ice cream cone in hot weather. Lots of dripping onto hands, clothes, and the floor, but they caught on quickly.

We went to the park half a block away to finish them off. After a few minutes of slurping, it was back onto the trucks to make the return trip to the village, two truckloads of very happy children.

The teacher informed me the next day that the children showed up well dressed, proud, and so happy with their uniforms, talking excitedly about the wonderful shopping event in the "city." Most had never been out of their village. None of them had ever had new clothes, ridden in a truck, or eaten ice cream.

Unfortunately, that day also brought another result. Almost all of the children got diarrhea from the ice cream and spent much of the class time in the outhouse. None of them had ever had a milk product before and their bodies reacted.

* * *

Field trips of any kind were always fun. We would coordinate with the teachers, pile the kids into trucks, and take them to places nearby such as the Mayan Ruins site or the wild bird rescue to see the exotic birds. They'd get a tour and then we'd have a picnic. We'd find rocks or cement benches in a shaded area and haul out beans and tortillas made by some of the moms who we'd commissioned. Afterwards, we'd get cake from our favorite bakery. Cake, of course, was the best part.

Kids would talk about these experiences for months. I'd always take photos and the teachers would make a mural or collage to hang on the dreary school walls. A space of brightness and joyful memories.

* * *

The children were so resourceful. Rural children had no toys, so their environment became their playground and any inanimate object was their toy. I'll never forget the image during a sudden downpour of six boys in a line underneath a big sheet of torn plastic tarp, walking down the street. It looked like a giant centipede—all you could see was plastic and legs marching along.

Bottle caps became toys, flipped in the same way Westerners flip baseball cards. A worn tire was a fabulous toy to chase down a hill, balancing it with a stick. Soccer was the passion of every Honduran male. In the villages, it was usually played with a can or plastic Coke bottle, or sometimes with a torn or deflated ball. Boys were usually barefoot. I was always amazed at how children were able to play endlessly without regular intake of food. Joy almost always overruled hunger. Thank goodness for fruit trees. Fruit appeared almost year around so there was always something to go after, such as jocotes, a small greenish fruit the size of a walnut. Mangos in season were a primary target. Kids wouldn't wait for the ripe ones. As soon as they were green and somewhat ready, kids would be on the hunt. There were oranges, bananas, and all sorts of delicious tropical fruit. They were picked by individual families and sold in town, but the kids would have first crack at eating them. One could always see children in trees tearing off the fruit from the branches and throwing them down to the smaller kids, or throwing rocks at the trees to knock down the fruit. Sometimes they'd use slingshots made out of twigs and an old piece of torn rubber.

Children loved to come over to visit. My house was like an amusement park for them. It had furniture, a fridge, pictures on the walls, and sometimes even school supplies or toys that were waiting to be delivered. They'd come in, look around, and touch things. I often had homemade cookies.

Looking at my three rooms, they'd ask me how many people lived with me, always surprised that I was just one person living in all that space.

Even teenagers would ask to come to my house to visit. Initially, I was skeptical. Why would a teenager want to come visit an ol' white lady? In the United States, I was invisible. I couldn't even get teenagers to wait on me in a store. Here, teenagers would knock at my gate and wait to be invited into the yard, wait further at my front door to be invited into the house, and wait again for me to invite them to sit down. Sometimes there would be as many as five in my house at the same time. I'd offer them something to drink, and—as is customary in Honduras—coffee or tea always included some kind of "bread," which meant a sweet bun or a cookie. They were always polite and almost never led the conversation. In fact, they often didn't talk very much.

I would ask open-ended questions that required more than a yes or no answer. We talked about their classes or my life in the US. As time went on, my teenage friends came frequently, becoming more comfortable each time, more verbally outspoken, and more forthcoming with questions. They were very curious about North American culture and had the idea that everyone up north was rich and happy. They didn't know about street people, for example, and were often spellbound as I described that lifestyle. They were surprised to know about tenements. Most of the information came through bits of television they had seen somewhere.

They wanted to know about me: if I was married before, if I liked beans, if I had children. Again, they were shocked when I said that many North Americans are single and don't have children. I often talked about how "rich" Hondurans were in so many ways. They lived on gorgeous land, they were resourceful and strong, had fulfilling experiences in church, and had families and communities— in contrast to many in the US who did not have all that. I told them I admired them.

Although it was not often directly said, I got the impression that they felt that they, or Honduras, was "inferior" to the United States. They listened intently when I would talk about how the US had more support and opportunities for education or interesting work, but it was not superior. We were all children of God, I'd tell them, using a religious reference I knew they would understand.

They loved sitting on my soft furniture and seeing my nice kitchen with an indoor sink and stove, and my numerous pots and pans. Sometimes they would ask me if I thought it would be possible that they could have these things one day. This was a common question. They'd see a real bed, with blankets and sheets, indoor plumbing with towels in the bathroom, and they'd want to know if they would be able to have those too.

They asked me about dating, marriage, and divorce. Teens rarely dated there. They'd meet someone they liked, visit with them at the family house, and then marry or live together. Weddings and divorces were too expensive, so folks just got together and stayed together or moved on. This system seemed to work. Occasionally, there would be a breakup and heartbreak, but overall there were not a lot of multiple relationships before partnering.

When conversations died down, or the *muchachos* had to leave, they always thanked me for allowing them to visit, and I'd give them an open invitation to return. They always did.

Kids of all ages came to my house asking for money. This was the norm. I understood, especially since I was in a work situation where I distributed funds for a living. This was often annoying and stressful for other foreigners because it would happen constantly, at least once a day. It was difficult for me, too, but I understood. I was richer than the locals. I would have probably done the same thing if I were in their shoes. If someone asked me, "Will you give me five lempiras?" I'd usually respond, "Give me ten and I'll give you five." They would stare at me, confused, and then laugh when I winked.

On occasion they would need money for an emergency, and I would go with them to meet with the parents and see if they truly needed help. Then, I'd have to figure out if we were in a position to help.

I often hired kids. If they wanted a bit of money, they could work in my garden, or pick up the garbage strewn in the lot next door, or sweep the bodega. Sometimes the older ones would wash Marel's truck. When I'd ask what they were going to do with the money, they always had the same response: "I'm going to give it to my mom." As time went on, the kids stopped asking for money and started asking, "Is there work, Doña Elena?"

It happened way too often that well-meaning tourists would hand out money to whomever asked, or to anyone standing on the street dressed in tattered clothing. They thought they were helping out, but this created the idea among Hondurans that rather than working, free money was available if they hung out with gringos. If this pattern continued, often locals would start to expect free money, and if it continued even further, they might feel a sense of entitlement. It bothered me tremendously. Sometimes if I offered work to a child I didn't know, they would prefer to stay on the street begging from foreigners.

What also bothered me was the number of children who did not attend school, in spite of a law that was never enforced. Lack of attendance occurred for two reasons: because the parents didn't have the eight cents to buy a pencil and notebook, and because the parents needed help with their crops, picking coffee during the season, or hauling firewood. Those who were in school had to leave towards the end of the school year to help with the harvest. They had to walk great distances to fetch water or cut, chop, and carry huge amounts of firewood on their backs. They were work horses by the time they were five. Almost every child I talked to said they would prefer to go to school.

I rarely heard a child cry, even if they were badly hurt. I never heard a child complain no matter how hungry, tired, or overworked they were. Kids as little as three would walk barefoot into town from their villages, trekking many miles on an empty stomach. They'd walk on the blazing pavement in summer and in the cold puddles in winter. I was always amazed at their strength and resilience and even more stunned by their silence.

I had a special chemistry with the children of Honduras. I loved the variety of ethnicities. There were the dark, lithe Garifunas on the coast with Carribean influence; the Mestizos, who were a mix of Indigenous and Spanish; and the lighter-skinned kids, with light-brown hair, who had European immigrant worker blood.

Most of all, I was inexorably drawn to the Maya Ch'orti'. The Ch'orti' are one of the Indigenous Maya peoples who reside in remote areas of northwestern Honduras, as well as in Guatemala and northern El Salvador.

On my first visit to a rural Maya Ch'orti' village that was not too far from Copán, I passed a field next to a school where about fifteen boys and girls of all ages were playing. They were gorgeous. I couldn't take my eyes off of them. I couldn't explain it, but the pull was strong. I wanted to photograph each one of them, but I wasn't carrying a camera. I had a feeling of familiarity, as if I had known them all my life and we were finally being reunited.

The level of poverty was appalling. Children didn't eat every day (some of the luckier ones ate tortillas and salt for supper) and the resulting malnutrition showed in their rail-thin bodies, rotting teeth, and the loss or discoloration of their hair. They were shoeless and wore ragged, dirty clothes. They slept with their families, crowded onto dirt floors, the lucky ones getting to share a blanket but almost never a pillow.

As time went on, I increased my work with the Ch'orti', focusing on about a dozen villages. They lived hand to mouth as subsistence farmers who struggled against droughts, floods, and winds. They made their own clothes, grew their own food, and sold anything left over in town. Sadly, they'd lost most of their history and culture. Hardly anyone could speak more than a word or two in Maya Ch'orti'. There were no remaining arts, crafts, or music. The large families were work-focused, and the children knew the meaning of work early in life. If they could walk, they could carry. If they could carry a pail, they could pick coffee.

If folks were home, I would visit, very content to just sit on a broken-down porch, if they had one, and play with the kids. Sometimes I'd bring marbles or balloons, or teach them how to make a funny noise with a blade of grass.

There was not much conversation. They were generally quiet, and especially quiet with me. The kids would sidle up and look at me coyly until eventually they were used to my visits and would be bolder, more outgoing. Sometimes a child would sit next to me and drape an arm around my neck. To me, that was a precious gift.

I loved visiting the schools. I would jump out of the vehicle, run into the first classroom, and yell, "*Hola!*" to the kids.

"*Hola!*" they'd cry.

"I can't hear you!" I'd yell louder.

"*Hola!*" they'd scream, turning up the volume.

"I can't hear you!" I'd cry.

"*Hola*!" I'd ask usually about three times until I got the screams I was looking for.

I'd move to the next classroom.

At some point, I'd announce that we had deliveries to unload and ask for helpers. I'd have to jump out of the way as forty screaming kids stampeded from the classrooms to pitch in. They organized themselves like ants, each finding a way to carry their weight in supplies.

I'd leave these schools delighted with memories.

Kids kept me motivated. They kept me charged up. They deserved way more than they received in this lifetime and that motivated me to always look for even more ways to get them the resources they needed.

Chapter 17

I believe that you can buy Honduras with cake. There is no better lure, bribe, method of thanking someone, or reward. It was one of my favorite methods of saying thanks.

Cake was special. It was a luxury that very few people could afford in my area—never in the mountains. Giving a cake to someone who lived in the mountain villages was a fantastic gift to everyone in the family.

Most people didn't celebrate birthdays or graduations because there were too many kids in the family and too many people in the household. It would mean celebrating at least monthly and that was a huge expenditure of money and time. Many rural folks didn't even know when their birthdays were, nor their age.

For example, I loved buying cake from our bakery and taking it to my bank. Due to many deposits, transfers, and withdrawals, I went to the bank three times a week on average, and they treated me especially well. To thank them, I would occasionally walk in carrying a cake. Eyes would pop, smiles everywhere. Even the waiting customers would be delighted. The two outdoor security guards would come in and join the other two inside, and all of them would set down their automatic weapons and dig in. (I decided that if I were ever to rob a bank, I would send someone in with cake first.)

Everyone loved it, and I loved being able to thank people for their kindness and extra work with something easy to get hold of and inexpensive for me. In a flailing economy, the bakery staff were also happy to see me.

Cakes cost about a day's wages for local townspeople. For farmers, it was closer to two or three day's wages, so consequently it was impossible to afford. There were two bakeries in town, each selling basically the same thing. White cake with lots of frosting, or sometimes, if specially ordered, chocolate cake. They tasted the same to me. They also sold rolls that were slightly sweet, which you could buy for the equivalent of a nickel.

Cakes were profusely decorated and psychedelically colored: bright orange, purple, blue, green. A snot-like substance that glowed in the dark was used for hand lettering on frosting. The choice of sayings was limited to "Congratulations," "Happy Birthday," and "Happy Day." Often, they'd draw a colorful clown or soccer ball on the top. There was always way more frosting than cake.

The bakeries were tiny, and although they could hold as many as three customers at a time, there was rarely more than one person present. People preferred to buy local bread and simple cakes (no frosting or decorations) from women who walked down from the mountains. These strong, rural baker women carried fifty pounds of hot-from-the-oven products in a basket on their heads. It was usually fresher, cheaper, and the women came directly to your house.

They'd arrive, sweating from the extraordinary effort of the walk down the mountain, carrying so much weight in the blazing heat or pouring rain. I always bought at least four or five cake-breads from Maribel, a single mom putting five kids through school. I would take the cakes to the schools, donate them to our emergency food program, or gift them to a friend or neighbor. Usually, I would buy one for myself. If it was made of corn flour, I'd devour it hot, in one sitting. It only cost one dollar.

If there was negotiating to do or favors to ask—you guessed it—I brought cake. If we needed the municipality to contribute sand or stones to a building project, we came into the meeting with cake. If I wanted to thank a business for giving us special service or prices, yes, cake.

I remember standing outside my house one day with a banana cake I had made at home. I was intending to bring it to a friend. As each tuk-tuk driver passed (I knew all of them), I would break off a piece and give it to them. I must have given out about ten pieces before I was able to deliver the remaining half to my friend. For about a week afterwards or longer, I had free tuk-tuk rides to wherever I wanted to go.

As graduation presents for the kids who were on educational grants, nothing served better. They would pick up their prize at the bakery and walk home, sometimes for as many as three hours, carrying a fancy cardboard cake box with a vibrantly decorated, frosted creation inside saying "Congratulations!" People they'd pass along the way would give them a knowing smile. Ah, cake.

My birthday was coming up one year. I think I was turning sixty-five. Marel invited me to a birthday supper with him and his family. He said he'd pick me up, which I thought was a bit strange since we only lived half a block away from each other.

On the day, I waited patiently at home. He arrived to walk me to his house. I looked down the street and saw that there were balloons hanging from his porch. His kids had decorated the house for the occasion. How special. As we got closer, I could see what looked like a "Happy Birthday" sign. I was touched by the special attention.

When we arrived at the house, a wild cheer rose up from his patio/garage area. Forty people screamed "Happy Birthday!"— neighbors, friends, and teachers from every village imaginable, some traveling hours to come to the party. I burst into tears and punched Marel a few times before I landed a huge hug and kiss on him.

His wife carried out a giant cake, decorated with every color imaginable, with glowing candles dripping colored wax onto the frosting. A huge chorus of "Happy Birthday" began, which they ended with the customary local verse, "We want cake now, and Coca Cola too." Everyone always laughed at the second verse as if they had heard it for the first time.

They told me there was a custom I didn't know. They asked me to take a direct bite into the whole cake. I did as I was told and, as was custom, my face was pushed into the cake. Laughing, I swiped frosting off my cheeks and proceeded to run around plastering my guests with fingers of frosting and delivering frosting kisses. Big cheers, big laughs, and then—the best part—eating the cake. And yes, we had Coca Cola, too.

Guests also brought presents, which meant so much to me because I knew that many of these teachers hadn't been paid in a year or two. Other folks were on very limited incomes. Because most people did not give gifts in that region, I realized what a special honor it was to receive one. The gifts were specially chosen, usually locally made crafts with the word *Honduras* somewhere on it: a small change purse, a mug with a hand-painted pastoral scene, a key chain. In return, I gave them cake to take home.

It meant a great deal to me that Marel and Zoila, in spite of how busy they were and how limited their finances were, went out of their way to make this happen. And it was so heartwarming to see my teacher friends come such great distances and with such enthusiasm to help me celebrate. I had the wonderful connection of "home" despite of being 3,500 miles away.

Parties didn't last long. After cake and Coca Cola, people left quickly. Hugs goodbye, good wishes, and they were on their way. Marel walked me back to my house, carrying the little bit of leftover cake after I had left a big chunk for his family. My arms were filled with presents and bows, and my heart was overflowing with joy.

I think cake may be the answer to the quest for world peace.

Chapter 18

In the Maya Ch'orti' village of La Laguna lived a boy named Efrain. Over the years, I came to know him well since I often worked on renovations of his school and supplied teaching materials. He was about eight when I first met him, a charming, happy, skinny boy who used to shadow me, wanting to help out.

One day, I received a call from the head teacher, Roxana, saying Efrain was sick and his mother could not afford to take him to the doctor. He was too weak to walk from his village to the town doctor, and there was no money to hire a tuk-tuk or pay for the consult. I told her that of course I'd help and asked her to coordinate the doctor visit. I would meet them at the clinic and pay the driver when they arrived. Roxana set it up.

I arrived first at the doctor's office. When they arrived, I paid the driver, greeted the mom, and as I saw Efrain try to get out of tuk-tuk, my heart dropped. He looked awful: grayish, weak, unfocused eyes. He gave me a weak smile. We helped him inside.

The doctor took him into the back for an immediate exam while I sat in the waiting room very worried. I chatted quietly with waiting patients who I knew. Some small kids were sitting on the floor doing nothing, so I took out the supply of balloons I kept in my purse and blew them up.

Fifteen minutes later, the doctor brought me into the examination room, and I sat down next to Mom. Efrain was lying on the examination table, eyes closing. The doctor said Efrain was very sick, without being sure about the diagnosis. He suspected anemia and hepatitis, but without expensive tests he couldn't be sure. I tried to pump the doctor for information, but all he could add was that it was also possibly "some sort of infection and the medicine would help."

He tried to hand a prescription to the mother, and she looked at me with overwhelming concern without taking it. I knew that with ten or so children, she couldn't afford even a part of this, let alone blood tests.

"Do not worry," I told her, taking the prescription. "We will pay for the medicine." There was a special emergency fund for children set up by a lovely benefactor from Canada. "And if the medicine doesn't work, we will pay for blood and urine tests."

She gave me an almost inaudible, "Thank you."

We thanked the doctor, took off for the pharmacy in a tuk-tuk, and bought the medicine. My heart dropped at the price: more than thirty dollars. How could a farmer who earned about three dollars per day possibly afford that? What did families do when their children were sick? I knew they used a lot of locally grown herbs, but I also knew that sometimes herbs weren't enough.

Our wonderful pharmacist, Hilda, always gave me a discount since I was a frequent customer, bringing in kids almost weekly for meds. I gratefully paid the bill, twenty-seven dollars. Outside, we hailed another tuk-tuk, and I paid the driver to take them back up the mountain.

"Goodbye," the mother said from the tuk-tuk. "And thank you."

Efrain slumped against her shoulder. He gave me a weak wave and a bit of a smile.

When I didn't hear from the teacher or the mother for a couple of weeks, I assumed Efrain had improved. However, one morning, I received a phone call from Roxana. She could barely talk through her sobs.

"Efrain has died in the night," she cried.

"What!" I shouted. "What happened? Why didn't they call me? Didn't the medicine work?" An enormous wave of shock, rage, blame, and guilt overcame me. Thoughts and emotions flooded me. *What the hell went wrong? Why didn't I follow up? Oh my God, what have I done? It was my fault! I should have followed up.* Tears and fury gagged my words.

"He was my student for five years," Roxana continued, sobbing.

I could only manage to say, "I'll meet you in the village right away and we can talk in person, and then we will go talk to the mother." I asked her to invite the village health monitor to see what extra information we could obtain and how we could prevent future situations like this one.

I grabbed my bag, ran into the street, and waved down a tuk-tuk. It only took twenty minutes to get there, but it seemed like an hour. All the while, I was overcome with remorse. In my head, I was alternately yelling at the doctor and then at the mother, the village health monitor and then at myself. *I should have known it was more serious. I should have taken a little extra time to go to their house or at least make a simple phone call. Was I so damn busy with projects that I forgot what was dear and important?*

Roxana was waiting for me on the road near the family's shack. We climbed through the thick brush as she slowly filled me in. "He didn't return to school, and after about a week, I went to his house to visit. I saw that he was still sick. The mother didn't want to do anything about it. I chose to respect her wishes."

As I listened, I kept playing over and over in my head what my mom would have done when I was little and sick. Even with my mother's personal difficulties, she would have taken me to the doctor. She would have followed up with phone calls. She would have constantly taken my temperature and given me physical affection. On the other hand, my mother had money available for exams and treatments. My mom didn't have ten children. My mom was educated. I was riddled with guilt, blame, anger, and disbelief but tried to be present and listen to Roxana.

We reached the top of the long hill to Efrain's house. The mother was home, sitting in a plastic chair in the broken-down shack made of pieces of rusted tin and sugar cane stalks. Her three youngest, who were too young to attend school, were playing outside

133

by the cooking fire. The other six children were in school. Her two adult daughters were not present.

She was quiet and almost immobile but didn't look as horribly upset as I would have expected after the death of a child. *Is she holding in her feelings? Or maybe she 'isn't feeling it in the way I would have thought?* It was eerie. We chatted for a while before I got to the "hard questions." I had seen so much avoidable death in children due to inaction of the parents, but this time it also directly included my lack of sufficient action. This all too common inability to deal with the illness until it was too late always enraged and saddened me. I had to find out if Efrain's death could have been avoided but on one level also didn't want to know.

"What happened? I thought the doctor gave you medicine and said he would be better."

"Yes, he improved but became sick again."

"Did you take him back to the doctor? I told you I would pay for extra expenses."

"He didn't want to go. Then he got sicker and his body became swollen." I was screaming in my head, *HE didn't want to go?? You're the parent!!*

"And you didn't call the doctor or me? Why?"

No answer.

I was trying to be as gentle as possible but inside I was enraged. I couldn't look at her. I didn't want her to see my anger. I played with a stick with my foot to avoid eye contact. "This must have been so hard for you," I mustered.

"Yes," she said through tears.

I couldn't pursue this further without screaming. I didn't get it. She knew he was sick and hurting. She knew doctors were available and I would pay for it all. She knew the village health monitor who coordinated situations like this. What in the world would prevent her from following through? I was angry at her, but the anger kept bouncing back onto me. *What could I have done differently?*

The health monitor arrived about half an hour into the visit. I recognized her but hadn't known she was the monitor for coordinating medical emergencies. She smiled when we greeted each other and sat down on a nearby log. She didn't greet the mother. I asked her, maybe too abruptly, "Did you know Efrain and know he was sick?"

"Yes, he was my brother."

Her brother! What? This put me over the top. All kinds of emotions and thoughts flooded my mind, but rage topped them all. I was trying to understand and couldn't. Just couldn't. *Why didn't she do anything to help her own beautiful, young brother? Why didn't they call me or Roxana? Couldn't they see him suffering and getting worse? Cultural differences? The defeat of constant poverty and seeing no options? Fear and shame of asserting themselves?* I couldn't ask any more questions. Defeat and depression enveloped me. Then came another wave of guilt. *Why hadn't I followed up on his health? I should have known. I should have done something more.* Blame kept me obsessing about this. Blaming myself, blaming them, blaming the teacher, blaming the doctor, blaming the medical system, and blaming the lack of government support for poverty projects. *Why didn't they do anything? Why didn't the doctor make a call to follow up? Why didn't the teacher go by to visit sooner?* A sweet boy was dead and I might have been able to do something to prevent it. I was riddled with judgment.

Barely able to get words out, I said, "I'm so sorry for your loss." I told them how much I'd liked Efrain. "I will help out with some groceries for the funeral." It was customary that the bereaved pay for a feast for the community and relatives, and I was sure that they didn't even have one lempira to spend. I said goodbye and told them I'd be in touch.

I felt defeated. This was a common occurrence in the villages, but this time it was so painfully personal. The tuk-tuk driver was there waiting for me to take me back, so Roxana and I shared brief, tearful hugs as we said goodbye and promised to be in touch soon. I turned towards the tuk-tuk without looking at the driver. I didn't want him to see me crying. I would have preferred to walk back down the mountain alone. It was beautiful and peaceful, and I loved being there. In a sense, it would give me more moments with Efrain, but it was too dangerous. Even though the villagers always said they would protect me, I was too defenseless at the time to take the risk.

I didn't want to leave the mountain. It would feel too final, even though I knew I would continue to come back often. I kept looking out the back window, somehow hoping to stay connected for a few more moments to Efrain. I cried all the way home.

When I finally arrived, I stepped out of the tuk-tuk, onto the pavement, through my lovely wrought-iron gate, through my lovely garden to my lovely yellow furnished house. I kept seeing the contrast of living conditions between that family and mine as I dragged myself inside and flopped down on the sofa. I remember trying to get up every so often and then dropping back down into the comfort of the yellow pillows. Everything seemed so pointless— even getting a drink of water.

Over the following days, in between judgment, blame, guilt, and bouts of depression, I searched for answers. I talked to locals, spoke with my North American friends, tried to find information through books. Nothing gave me answers or comfort. Folks there just died. Sick kids just died. That was one reason parents had so many. I apologized to Efrain over and over in my head for days, weeks, and intermittently for months.

I had to do something to make up for this. It felt urgent. I couldn't carry this pain without some kind of action, some kind of plan that would allow his death to have some purpose.

A thought popped into my mind, which became an idea, which became an action. I would set up a daily milk program at his school in his name. Kids there were so malnourished and there was no government lunch. If nothing else, I could beef up their immune systems and give them something to look forward to.

I emailed our regular supporters and explained what had happened and what I was proposing. Many people came forward with donations, including a fabulous couple who took the lion's share of the project. Within a few weeks, we received enough monies to set up a milk program, at least for the rest of that school year. Meanwhile, I kept searching for additional financial support.

As mentioned in an earlier chapter, legally the government was supposed to supply school lunches and healthy snacks, but corruption over many years had robbed the coffers. When occasional snacks did arrive, they were often riddled with bugs. At least we could provide some guaranteed daily intake of nutrition, a drink made of fortified milk and rice. The local moms would take turns preparing it for the entire school.

The milk program was set up in Efrain's name. The mother sobbed when we told her. Thanks to this young boy, almost 150 kids would have at least something healthy in their tummies at the beginning of each school day.

The program proved very successful. School attendance improved, the kids interacted in class more, and participation with teachers increased. Teachers reported interesting findings, such as "I had no idea he or she was so intelligent!" Some kids even gained weight.

Thank you, sweet Efrain!

* * *

We did something similar in the village of El Chilar when a small child starved to death. The teacher, Mari, called and said the deceased child's older sister, Arecely, who was in kindergarten, was showing the same symptoms in class, such as dizzy spells and even occasional fainting. She asked if we could help.

I called my friend who was a doctor and asked if we could bring the girl in right away to the office. She said sure, and I made immediate arrangements with the teacher and mom. That afternoon, after a series of exams and blood tests, the doctor found that Arecely had severe intestinal parasites. The parasites had increased in numbers and size over the years and were eating all incoming nutrition. She would be fine with medication. I followed up with Mari the next three days in a row. I was not going to make the same error. She told me that within a couple of days, the medication had triggered a huge purging effect and caused worms to come out of her eyes, nose, mouth, as well as her feces. In spite of this disgusting process, the results were positive, and within a few days, Arecely began to regain some strength and vitality.

The doctor told her mom at the follow-up exam about the importance of good nutrition and healthcare, for example, wearing shoes at all times, washing with soap, etc. I knew all of this would be impossible. There was not enough food or soap in the house. The child did not have shoes, nor could her family afford them.

I then discussed with the doctor about arranging a two-day clinic, going up to this village to examine every single school child and any child in the village that was sick. Moms and teachers could help with the process, weighing and measuring kids, and organizing attendance. The doctor agreed. She brought a scale, thermometers, medical supplies, and over-the-counter medicines like aspirin and analgesic creams.

We set up a classroom and lined up twenty children at a time, sitting them in plastic chairs in the makeshift porch waiting area. Moms accompanied them. After two days of examining the children and offering treatment where necessary, the teachers, doctor, and I sat and talked about the medical findings.

The doctor stunned me when she told me that *one hundred percent* of the children were malnourished to varying degrees. I'd read government statistics that reported up to fifty to sixty percent of malnutrition in the villages, but based on what I had seen in the twenty villages I'd visited, I knew it was higher. Still, the one hundred percent figure was shocking. Overwhelming.

On one hand, I knew this was not my responsibility, but on the other hand, these children were not statistics—these were my little buddies whom I adored. *How could I not do something to help out?* It was useless to go to local governments. They had heard it all before from parents, teachers, NGOs, and the answer was always the same: nothing could be done. It was (always) the fault of the previous government.

Another milk program was underway, this time with the help of another fabulous NGO from the United States that would pitch in regular monthly funds. The NGO would also provide a huge quantity of vitamins to the school, which would result in a daily vitamin for each kid for the entire school year and possibly longer, if all went well. We started in the kindergarten because it was a smaller group and it would be easier to evaluate as a pilot project in that village. We used to joke about how our goal was to produce "kinderchubbies."

Eventually, I found enough additional support to reach the grade school kids, as well. The teachers would come to Marel's house monthly to pick up their allocation of powdered fortified milk, which we bought in bulk in the city to save on cost.

One teacher said that the kids "reminded" him constantly to give out the vitamins because they wanted to grow up to be big and strong. Most parents were so thrilled to have this extra supplement, but much to my surprise, some parents asked us *not* to continue giving vitamins to their children because it gave them an appetite and there was no food in the house to give them.

Teachers often told me that after the morning classes, children did not want to return home and would stay at the school to play. When I asked why, the teachers told me what the kids had told them: "Because there is no food in the house, we may as well just stay and play."

Adin, a fantastic teacher, told me the touching story of his student Jaime. Jaime came to school one morning and told Adin that his beloved grandmother had died, but he didn't want to go to the funeral. Adin asked why; he was a bit surprised because he knew Jaime loved his grandma. Jaime said that the funeral would take place during the milk hour and he didn't want to miss it. This really hit home to me just how important the program was. I knew the program was extremely positive, but this spurred me on even more to continue to add milk programs in other schools. Adin made sure that Jaime received both opportunities: he went to the funeral and was given his milk beforehand.

We launched the program at more schools. At the height of the program, we served one thousand malnourished children per year. On good days, I thought this was wonderful. On bad days, when I had to turn down requests from other teachers or village leaders and had visions of hungry children, I became disheartened. *How does one say no to starving children?* I felt like that nursery rhyme: the old woman who lived in the shoe, had so many children, she didn't know what to do.

Ultimately, we set up the program in more than eighty villages, a drop in the world bucket. This was just one small area in one small country in a world of so many countries desperate for basics—food, water, and medicine. I thought a lot about the possibilities if everyone in more affluent countries could do just one thing to help out. Although I always tried to stay positive, there were times when I could not help thinking about how many folks didn't help us out, saying they didn't have ten dollars to contribute. I often thought about all the food that North Americans throw out in one day. The discrepancy would tear me apart. I also envisioned the local government taking more responsibility for the health and education of its children and grieved the greed and corruption that prevented this.

I learned quite a bit, albeit painfully through Efrain's death, and I was able to use that experience to help Arecely and the children of so many other communities. That was the good news. Also heartening was the fact that Arecely continued to grow healthier and so did other children in the villages.

The loss of Efrain still haunts me. As I wrote and edited this chapter, I cried each time.

Chapter 19

We were on our way to Los Tapescos, an extremely poor village an hour from Copán. The road was narrow, rocky, and at times almost impassible on the very narrow passageways over the creeks. Papaya trees had fruit hanging down like long, green breasts, and watermelon patches lined the river for acres.

As we drove, the land became drier and the farmland completely depleted, with suffering crops of corn and beans. Even the cows were emaciated. I was accustomed to this trip, but it still shocked me every time. We saw thatched roofs of adobe huts and featherless chickens as we made our way over rocks and sudden bends to start the dangerous descent into the area where the school was located. I held my breath as we skidded a couple of times, trying not to scream out like I had in the past. My screaming always made Marel laugh.

We had worked regularly with the school there—constructing bathrooms, setting up a milk program—and we regularly provided school supplies and teaching materials. Although the folks in this village worked very hard, most of the children were malnourished and without toys or adequate clothing.

On this trip, we were doing a follow-up visit. I knew the teachers and children well and was looking forward to seeing them again. We passed a vehicle coming the other direction on the narrow, rocky dirt road and had to pull over. A group of singing missionaries waved and smiled as they passed. We waved back. They obviously had come from Los Tapescos because that was the only village on this road.

We arrived at the school at recess time. The kids were sitting around, not playing in the field. I spotted the teacher, Mariela, comforting two crying children.

"What's going on?" I asked.

"Missionaries just came to visit and were teaching the children about Jesus in the classrooms. During recess, they brought out balls, jump ropes, and hula hoops and were playing with the children."

I thought, *How nice, but why the tears?*

"Upon leaving, the missionaries gathered up the toys, put them back in the truck, and left," Mariela said.

I was shocked. "Did they leave at least some of the toys?"

"No, they took everything."

I knew why the kids were crying. Most of them had never owned a single toy in their lives, and for the first time, they actually had something to play with. It hit the smaller kids the hardest, but even the older ones were sad.

Most of the boys' greatest hope was to own a soccer ball. Suddenly they were given one, and then it had been taken away. The girls were excited about jacks and jump ropes.

One of the girl, Carina, later asked me why they "went away with the toys." She thought she had acted badly and this was her punishment.

Needless to say, I was concerned. I told Mariela that I would go shopping the next day with her and we would replace the toys.

Later in town that evening, I ran into the leader of the group of missionaries at a restaurant.

"Hello," she said. "We passed you on the road from Los Tapescos." She smiled and introduced herself as part of the missionary group. There were a couple of other women with her, but she seemed to be the leader. I thought she might have been a nun, although she was dressed in layman's clothes. She was probably in her early fifties, with short, cropped, blondish-gray hair. We chatted for a moment about the community.

"I doubt there is even a single toy among those kids," I told her. "Did you know that the kids were crying when you left?"

"Oh how lovely. We really impacted them," she said.

"Yes," I answered, "but not in the way you're thinking. They were crying because you gave them toys and took them away, the only toys they had ever had. They were devastated."

She seemed concerned. "But we have so many schools to visit and to preach "the word" to. We need the toys to use in each school."

"So, you are planning to disappoint even more children?" I said. "How many are in your group?" She told me ten. "Among all of you, you couldn't come up with ten dollars a piece to buy toys that they could keep? You live in one of the richest countries in the world."

There was no real response, just silence, so I said my goodbyes and took off.

The next day, I went shopping with Mariela as promised, and then we went back to Tapescos. The kids ran out from the fields when they heard our truck; the teacher had told them what was coming. As we pulled into the school grounds after school hours, the children thronged the truck. I asked them to help me unload, and like a colony of ants, they cleaned out the truck in seconds, laughing and playing and touching, each child wanting to hold something or bring a toy into the school. They had balls, and jump ropes, jacks, hula hoops, and boxes of Legos.

Diego, who was maybe six years old, looked up at me and asked, "Do we get to keep these?"

"Absolutely," I answered, "but you have to take good care of them and put them away every day after class." He promised he would.

This was a perfect example of how good intentions didn't always create good results. These visitors were caring and certainly meant no harm, but they made many children extremely unhappy. I saw this kind of "help" way too many times over the years. Folks came down for a short visit, did not assess the needs and often did not even ask what was needed, and made assumptions. The big question was "How do we prevent problems like these?" Cultural sensitivity is a must. These groups needed to have a thorough discussion with the teacher about their intentions. Groups also needed to meet with the village leaders.

The most common excuse was that there wasn't enough time. Groups came for only a week or two. Time constraints often overshadowed the need to investigate properly. Assumptions were made that were not always correct, like "getting to play with toys is better than no toys at all." It was important to ask questions and listen carefully to the responses while being culturally sensitive to communication styles. Hondurans are often not assertive about stating what they want or don't want. This happens for many reasons. Locals are afraid of losing out if they state what's on their minds. Often they are intimidated by the donors. Recipients also don't want to endanger future donations.

Chapter 20

They asked me if I had heard what happened. I was in town and had run into Luis, the leader of the village of Nueva Estanzuela, and Adan, the leader of the area's Indigenous organization. They told me that the entire village of Nueva Estanzuela, thirty families, had been ousted from their houses and ordered off the property at 4:00 a.m. in the pouring rain by local soldiers and police. They had nowhere to go. I couldn't believe it. *Who would do such a thing, and a week before Christmas?*

I hopped into their truck and they took me a few miles down the dirt road that I had traveled many times, always pleased to be taking in the beautiful, lush green land, the river, and the surrounding mountains. Normally, it was serene and comforting.

We turned the bend and I saw one of the most stunning, overwhelming sights of my life. There, on the side of the road stood about 120 shivering, soaking people—men, women, children, dogs, and chickens, all standing in the freezing rain. Women clutched their babies. Children hung on to the skirts of their mothers.

I was horrified. I had never seen anything like it. On the side of the road were scattered household items, broken beds, and kitchenware strewn everywhere. A broken, wet baby crib. Piles of belongings, all soaking wet.

They had been kicked off the land that they had lived and worked on for more than twenty-five years. The soldiers came and banged down their doors in the dark of night. The community did not own this land or the houses, but the previous owner had let them live as if it were their own. The land had been sold to a new owner who was a pastor in a neighboring town. She had hired the soldiers to come and oust them. Four o'clock a.m. A winter morning. A week before Christmas.

I had known and worked in this community for years. These were people for whom I had a lot of affection, hard-working *campesinos* (farmers) who were trying to eke out a meager living by cultivating corn and beans. In return, the former owner gave them a small wage and an adobe house to live in. They were accustomed to poverty, but they at least had shelter.

As I stood by the truck, I couldn't decide which person to talk to first, which family to approach, what to say. I kept shaking my head. I grabbed women's hands, hugged children, shook hands with some of the men. I stood in the rain, getting soaking wet but knowing I could go home to dry off and change clothes. They no longer had a home. They no longer had dry clothes.

I talked with many of the folks. They were given notice a month or two earlier from this pastor, but they had nowhere to go. They had no money and had invested twenty-five years there. They had met with the mayor, but he was stalling on finding alternative land for them. Was it coincidental that this village voted in the most recent election for the opposing candidate? This was known to happen in many villages—political parties gave no support if a village did not vote for them. Since voting places were separated by party, everyone in the municipality knew who had voted for whom.

The wet faces of despair, the children's muddy feet, everyone's soaking clothes, it left an indelible picture in my mind.

Something else felt strange about this scenario that I couldn't identify at first, until it occurred to me: all of these children were around, but there was no sound, no laughter, no movement of feet. Silence. Just an occasional sob of a woman and the cluck of a chicken.

Trying to think straight while in shock, and while picking up and feeling their anger, sadness, and fear, I turned to Luis and Adan to ask what they needed. Tarps, so that they could make lean-tos, and water, was the first response. We took off immediately, driving back to town over the bumpy, muddy road. Neither of the men talked much in the truck, and I decided to hold my multitude of questions for another time.

We arrived in town and went to buy the supplies immediately. The owners of the building store and the water dispensary both sold me materials and five-gallon bottles of water at an especially low price and chipped in with a donation of extra supplies.

After we spent the money I had with me, we raced back to the village and started distributing the supplies and setting up shelter. The men had already pounded in posts using rocks as hammers so that they could put up the tarps. I suddenly realized that if I were going to raise funds, I would need to take photos. This thought overwhelmed me with shame and sadness. It seemed so shameful to photograph misery and distress.

I took Luis aside and, trying to hold back my tears, said, "I have to take photos. I'm really so sorry, but it's the only way I can get aid from my donors." It was heart wrenching to me that in the middle of their distress, I had to pull out the camera. It seemed so objectifying and cold. It felt ghoulish. I asked Luis to explain to the folks that I needed to send "visual proof," and as I was apologizing profusely, he began explaining this to the huddled folks.

They told me it would be okay and they would appreciate any assistance I could provide. Since I had known these families for years, it helped with trust. In the past, we had donated school supplies, taken folks with medical emergencies to the clinics and hospitals, and purchased materials to repair their roofs and *baños* (bathrooms).

We returned to town again with a plan to knock on the doors of local churches and organizations. I immediately mobilized, going from organization to organization, church to church, pleading for aid. No one said yes. I lost count of the number of doors I knocked on.

"This isn't what we do," or "We already help a village," they told me. Most of these organizations were locally run and staffed; the victims were their own people. I could feel my disappointment rise with each rejection, and also my anger. *What the hell are these folks doing here if not helping people in need? Isn't this a priority?*

I also sought out North American organizations, asking for large or small donations. Even five dollars would have fed a family for a week. I remember only one organization pitching in. Various staff members handed me cash from their pockets.

With the other groups, I encountered endless excuses until finally I gave up, my faith in humanity severely damaged. I heard later from the village leader that some organizations came and took pictures, supposedly for raising funds, but ultimately never donated a single lempira. I did see photos in their newsletters. I didn't know what they did with the donations they received.

After contacting supporters by email, I received more cash donations. My faith in humanity climbed a bit. We were able to buy more supplies, pay medical bills, and donate food and toys for the children. The first to respond was a group that we had worked with off and on for years. Their director wired me funds that same day and offered more if we needed it. I was so touched that I nearly cried.

There was also support from local neighboring villagers, and that buoyed me up quite a bit, and lightened the spirits of the survivors. People showed up from many other villages with corn and beans, even though they had little to spare. They pitched in to help construct *champas* (lean-tos with thatched roofs).

Still, I was expecting a large outpouring of local help from established organizations, churches, and individuals from town, even if the amounts were small. When this didn't happen, I grew bitterly disappointed. I wasn't able to find out how the folks from Estanzuela felt about this and was afraid the subject would be too sensitive at that time to bring it up.

I had some theories on this many months later. Possibly these other local organizations or groups did not trust me as an individual. Although they had known and worked with me for years, trust was not common in this country. It could have been seen as "just another huge need" that ultimately drained their already limited resources. It could have been my approach. I had caught the desperation of these homeless families.

One moment, my heart was opened wide by the generosity, and the next, it was slammed shut by what seemed like lack of concern. I felt both enormously disappointed in human beings and at the same time very encouraged by the beauty of the kindness of others, and I have wrestled to understand this issue ever since.

After a few weeks, I ran into the mayor of Copán in the health center, where I had taken a child with a nasty cut on her leg. I asked him what he was doing about Nueva Estanzuela.

He brushed me off. "Yes, yes, this is very serious and we hope to have meetings as soon as next month." The mayor didn't give a damn; he was not known for his compassion or even for helping rural projects, especially in communities that did not vote for his party.

"Meetings? Next month? This is an emergency. We have sick kids, no food, no work, no shelter for these folks."

Same answer.

Once again, my heart sank. For me, this wasn't just an anonymous emergency situation; these were people I had known for years and cared about. It took everything I had to curb my rage and be tactful. "What is the municipality prepared to do in the meantime?"

"I have to rush off," he replied.

My head was jammed with furious retorts, and it was all I could do to hold my temper and keep my mouth closed.

Back to the village I went, at least with money from my North American donors. Thanks to Western Union and a quick delivery of money, we were able to buy sweaters, dry firewood, water, food, and medicine. Christmas was approaching within days, their special time.

The woman who had kicked them off the land was a pastor in a nearby church. In contrast, these folks had nowhere to hold their own church. This would be a bleak Christmas for them in so many ways, so we decided to round up Christmas gifts and cookies for all the children. We showed up with red reindeer antlers (of course, no one knew what a reindeer was, but the antlers were on sale and I couldn't resist), elf hats, and a few other items. I supposed this was their first experience with a Jewish Santa Claus.

As the weeks, then months passed, there was still no new land in sight, but how incredibly resourceful these people were! They set up a makeshift camp along the side of the dirt road with temporary lean-tos and communal cooking sites, even a communal lean-to where they could hold church. The bushes were their bathrooms. Their water supply, the river and rain buckets.

We continued delivering donated supplies, and as the media covered the situation and spotlighted the villagers' needs, other individuals and groups from other parts of Honduras started stepping in with aid. The coverage also brought pressure to the local government from outraged citizens. The press wanted to interview me, possibly because they saw that I was always there when they came. In my terribly broken Spanish, I pleaded for help. I couldn't bear to watch the news that night and hear my bad Spanish.

The news did bring more help. It also brought more press. This allowed me to gradually step down from the relief work *Buenos Vecinos* had been doing there, although I stayed in constant touch. As the months progressed, I watched with amazement as the community site developed into little plastic tarp homes. Some folks found work on other farms. The months turned into a year. Finally, after endless meetings and delays, land was bought for them, literally on the other side of the road from where they had lived. They settled in immediately, built their adobe houses, planted gardens, and eventually even built a small school, which we were able to help construct.

Being kicked off land is nothing new for Indigenous farmers. Although I had read about it and heard endless painful stories, when it happened to people I knew personally and cared about, it created an internal shift for me. It became real, not just a news report.

Even as I relate this story, I am still heartbroken and disillusioned. I am still shocked by the indifference of some folks who had means to help and wouldn't. Despite this, I am also still impressed by how others who were desperately poor chipped in. I was also touched by our supporters in North America who stepped in so quickly and without as much as a question: "Just tell us what you need, Ellen."

It is such a contradiction to feel so let down at first and so supported in the end. I haven't been able to integrate this. I had assumed that most local people and organizations would have reacted as I did, quickly and positively, and I am still shocked by the organizations who took pictures with their staff at the scene, yet never gave aid.

I am also amazed by the incredible resiliency of these folks in Nueva Estanzuela. This story brings up one of the issues I continually struggle with in the area of "helping," especially concerning foreign aid. Here were the people from neighboring villages who have very little food and yet the generosity they displayed was remarkable. In contrast, there were agencies (more than thirty NGOs in the Copán area, not to mention service clubs, churches, and missionaries) that had the means but didn't step in. This issue was representative of what often happened in Honduras: the ups and downs of crisis and poverty—touching moments of gratitude and generosity versus a lack of understanding and unwillingness to help by others.

It was hard for me to sustain a mood or emotion for more than a day when there were so many stressful or touching incidents and events, large and small. All of my emotions came out for minutes at a time, both the highs and the lows, but then the barrage would need to be stuffed down by the next looming situation.

I wondered if the people who didn't help were too burned out from being bombarded by people in need. Did it become the norm, so folks just didn't step in anymore? Their emotions shut down? Their hearts? Maybe they used to come forth more, but it took too much of a toll. Yet aid is much more than financial support, it is also a morale booster and a human connection through caring, something much needed by recipients and workers alike.

I ran into Luis a couple of years after this crisis. He looked good. Relaxed. He told me with a smile that the village was getting electricity that year. All of the folks had houses, gardens, animals, and a crop. It was a long road and certainly for me a heartbreaking, shocking, but also enlightening experience. I think for them it was the norm.

Chapter 21

One early Saturday morning, my buddy Tulio and I stuffed giant plastic bags of clothing into the back of his tuk-tuk, onto the floor on the passenger side, and finally onto my lap, as well as into the driver's side floor, smashed beneath his right leg. I was hoping he wouldn't need to use his brake on short notice.

We were taking bags of children's clothing to a village up in the mountains. The village teacher was having a sale. She was selling each item for one lempira (five cents), with profits going towards the purchase of teaching materials. People who couldn't afford the one lempira could trade beans or corn, or they could volunteer at the school. I was proud that the clothes we were bringing were of high quality, lightly used, and trendy clothes from North America. I thought it was ironic that the parents didn't have enough money for food or medicine but their kids would be dressed in trendy Gap Kids clothing.

We cleared town quickly and ambled along the familiar dirt road that led for miles. I always loved the smell of the land there—earthy and fresh in the morning—and the vision of the green hills along the river, the sun streaming through. Corn was planted in every nook of land, even on the steepest of hills. In the mornings, you could always hear different birds chirping, the sound of chickens clucking, and an occasional moo from a cow.

The sale was being held in one of my favorite places, the Maya Ch'orti' village, El Chilar. I had worked there with the school doing a variety of projects over the years, and I had come to adore the children.

As we were puttering along, we passed a woman walking with her two small girls who were maybe three and four years old. They were all dressed in deteriorating rags. The girls' dresses were so tattered that they had to hold on to them while walking to keep them from falling off. Their hair was wild and probably had not been washed or combed for months or longer. They were underweight, barefoot, and dirty but had the sweetest faces you could imagine. The mom was young but already looked old and tired. She couldn't have weighed more than one hundred pounds, her bones sticking through her shredded clothing. Her bare feet were calloused and dirty, her hair also uncombed. My heart went out to them. I imagined what their living conditions were like and how I would feel if I were that mom.

As we passed, I hung out the side of the tuk-tuk and waved, and they waved back with big smiles. We kept going for almost a half-kilometer, but I was haunted by the vision. I couldn't get them out of my mind. I just had to go back.

I grabbed Tulio's shoulder and said, "Wait! Let's stop!" I jumped out of the tuk-tuk while he was still backing up and ran, calling to the woman, "We have clothes!"

When I caught up to them, the woman answered with her head bowed, "Oh, I don't have any money."

"No, these are free! Wait, I'll show you!" I ran back to the tuk-tuk and grabbed one of the huge bags while Tulio tore through another. We excitedly searched for something that would fit the girls. The first item I found was a darling sundress, brightly colored, practically new. While Tulio kept foraging, I ran up to the three-year-old, knelt on the road, put it against her tiny frame, and said to her mom, "Does this fit?"

Even before I held it up, the mom answered, "Yes it fits!"

I was sure she would have said yes to whatever I had pulled out, despite the size, for fear of losing the opportunity. The little girl's face brightened and a giant smile appeared.

The older girl started jumping up and down, screaming, "*Le queda! Le queda!* (It fits! It fits!)"

I turned to her and said, "I'm sure I have something for you too. Let's see," touched by her enthusiasm for her sister's good fortune without regard to herself.

The family and I went back to the tuk-tuk. Tulio and I dug into the bags, scattering boys' pants and baby clothes on the floor until Tulio pulled out another adorable dress, which was also practically new. It was bright yellow and green, and tied in the back.

I turned to the girl as Tulio gave me the dress. "Do you like this one?"

Both girls jumped up and down, and the mother, smiling, looked at me in way that I can't express in words. All I knew was that this moment touched my heart so intensely that I was speechless.

I went back to my bag and pulled out a couple more things for the girls. I said, "I have something for you, too, Mom." I took out a green-and-blue striped top.

She looked at it, clutched it to her chest, smiled, and said, "Thank you," in a quiet voice, the sincerity ringing through loudly.

It was so universal and so simple. We all want to care for our children. Here was an opportunity to share the abundance that was given to me with a woman who wanted to help her children in a way that she wasn't able. These three touched me in a way I couldn't explain. Woman to woman, heart to heart, soul to soul. We hardly shared words. We didn't need to.

When I looked back into the tuk-tuk, I saw my hairbrush there and pulled it out. "I found this, as well. Can you use it?"

The mother nodded shyly and took the brush.

As Tulio and I drove off, I looked back through the torn plastic rear window. The kids were bouncing and skipping, looking at each piece of clothing, laughing, and the mom was smiling back at them. I waved, and they gave me hearty waves back. Tulio slowed the tuk-tuk down, turned to me, and said, "I have a little girl."

I understood what he was saying. He was telling me that he could relate to this mom. He had a girl. He knew.

I once read that the brain chemistry of a receiver actually changes during an act of kindness, but surprisingly, so does the chemistry of the giver and the witness. I would replay this incident in my head for countless days afterwards. People often ask what some of my most gratifying experiences of working in Honduras are. This simple experience became an indelible part of my memory. I have had the good fortune of helping on so many projects, from construction to health programs, but nothing touched my heart like those ten precious minutes on that dirt road.

Chapter 22

Doña Francisca had been ninety-five years old for at least five or six years. Every time I asked her age, she told me ninety-five. I met her when a neighbor asked if we could help out an elderly couple living in extreme poverty on the hill just outside the town center. They had a piece of old rusty tin for a roof, and it leaked badly.

Normally our organization didn't support individual adults, just schools and children, but when my neighbor told me that she was ninety-five and her husband, Don Carlos, was eighty-five, I was not only eager to meet them but also wanted to help.

Marel and I took the truck as far as the rocky dirt road would allow, through a densely wooded area, then continued on foot, climbing the almost forty-five degree, muddy, rocky incline for two hundred yards. We tripped over loose rocks, occasionally jumped crevices, and slid backward. I wondered how an elderly couple were able to make this climb.

We reached the peak where we came to their rusted barbed wire gate. It took five minutes to untangle the wire and let ourselves through. Facing us was a narrow, winding path downward, where we met with several emaciated, teeth-baring, barking dogs. I always carried ammunition for these occasions: kibble. After showering them with probably the only food they had eaten that day, they ignored us and desperately chowed down.

It was a downward slide from there on a muddy path to the isolated house. I grabbed hold of a bush or Marel's arm to balance myself. The hut was made of sticks, mud, plastic tarp, burlap bags, and pieces of rusty tin for a roof. The couple was waiting for us. They were tiny. I kept thinking of them as a set of salt-and-pepper shakers. At five foot two, I towered over both of them, and probably at my weight of 120 pounds was twice the weight of Doña Francisca (or Chica, as she was affectionately called). She had a tiny voice and lacked teeth, so understanding her in Spanish, my second language, was difficult. I found out later that Marel had also had difficulty. She was dressed in a very worn dress and tattered apron, with her gray hair covered by a bandana. Her flat shoes were barely held together.

Don Carlos, a bit whiskery and bent, had the same bright eyes and eager smile as his wife. He was dressed in a suit, probably the same one he had worn for the past decade, showing the wear of age, but nevertheless neat. He wore a belt but had wrapped it twice around his skinny waist. His hair was slicked to the side by either water or sweat, I couldn't tell.

They expressed their gratitude for our visit and were quite delighted to find out we were going to replace the pieces of rusty tin that was their roof. Doña Chica offered us coffee and tortillas that she had just made, smoke overwhelming her three-by-three-meter stick-and-mud shack and filtering outside through the sugarcane posts that were their walls. It was obvious that wind and rain also poured through the spaces between the cane posts. Doña Chica threw a burnt tortilla to each of the three emaciated dogs on the dirt floor, and the cats and chickens also raced over to grab a part of what would most likely be their only meal.

As we looked outside to plan an entry for the delivery of roofing materials, I noticed there was no visible outhouse. I didn't ask them about this but assumed they simply didn't have one. There was a faucet where water from the mountain would fall directly onto the muddy ground.

I worried that the path through the trees was too narrow to accommodate long pieces of roofing tin, but Marel said the guys would find a way to bring it in. Replacing the roof would be no easy task since the current roof was overtaken by overgrown bushes and trees. Marel suggested to the couple that it was best that they go somewhere else for the day while the men worked. They happily agreed.

The following day, we bought the tin roofing and nails. Three men from the community came to work, carrying the roofing materials, puffing their way up the incline, banging them into the bushes and trees. I was reminded of the antics of the Three Stooges. We were again greeted by barking dogs, but this time they were looking for my kibble. I obliged.

Then came the treacherous descent down the narrow path. I was amazed at their good humor. They all landed safely in front of the shack, pouring sweat, looking for a space to set down these huge sheets of tin, dogs at their feet alternately begging for food and ready to attack.

The men got to work. After hours of sawing away intruding branches and pulling off rusty, broken pieces of tin while balancing themselves on narrow wood beams, they were able to finish the task. The new roof gleamed in the sun.

The couple returned in the late afternoon, so delighted to have the help, and thanked us profusely. Doña Chica offered everyone a bowl of water (since she only had one cup) and gave us eggs from her skinny chickens to take home with us. We accepted her offer reluctantly, knowing it was most of their food supply, but also knowing that turning it down would have been an insult. (We came back the next day with a food basket for them.) I knew I would see them again, and sure enough, a friendship developed as we continued our visits either at their house or mine. Doña Chica loved to come and sit in my chair. It had a pillow seat and a pillow back. Absolute luxury. She'd always bring me a few eggs, and I'd always give her some staples from my cupboard.

A couple of years later, Don Carlos passed away. We had been taking him regularly to the doctor, but finally there was no more that could be done. No one seemed to know what it was that was ailing him (not unusual in that area). Of course, it broke Doña Chica's heart. They had been sweethearts for more than seventy years. I somehow thought that neither one would ever die. They were already so old and had beaten the odds of early death.

Doña Chica and I are still good friends, and I adore her. She continues to inspire me with her pure heart, her positive attitude, her spirit, and her astounding physical competence. She still walks miles every day to go into town and climbs that mountain each time to get home. I visit her each time I return to Honduras. She recently had a birthday where she progressed from ninety-five to ninety-seven years old.

Chapter 23

As the years progressed, the concept of giving and helping became an increasingly complex subject for me. I had the good fortune to work with incredible donors from around the world, but there were times when donors were so arrogant and self-centered that I was pushed to the limits of my patience.

I received a call from a man named Avril, who described himself as wealthy and wanting to do projects with a good organization such as ours. He had heard outstanding praise for our work and said he wanted to meet with me about helping out. Although put off by his dismissive and superior attitude, I decided to at least agree to the meeting since it seemed that his heart was in the right place.

Since I had no office, we met in a tiny café that opened onto the street. He was there before I arrived. He was a short, well-dressed man from East India who lived in Canada. In his sixties, probably. He gave me a warm smile and handshake. We sat down and talked about his interests and desires.

He told me he was a successful accountant. "I'd like to do some worthwhile projects with some of the income I've made over the years," he explained. "Honduras appeals to me because I like the people." He didn't seem to have any questions for me about our work, our values, or our style of operating, which was the first red flag. But, his wealth and his plans to spend it were tempting, at least tempting enough to check this out further. I listened a little more.

I tried to explain what types of projects we did, what our goals and limitations were, and how important it was for us to respect the people we work with. His eyes wandered as I spoke. "Although we do a lot of construction projects like building, repairing, and furnishing schools," I explained, "we also provide educational support by giving scholarships, school supplies, and teaching materials. We also organize relief work such as providing milk programs for children, medical assistance, and emergency help, like helping out individuals during floods and hurricanes."

"I assure you," he said, "we're on the same page."

I still had that feeling that you get in movies when the low, discordant music starts to play. Something was wrong.

Marel and I were planning a trip to a village a few hours from Copán. They had one classroom there but needed an entire school for 250 students, as well as a retaining wall to keep the mud from sliding into the classroom. I asked Avril if he would like to come with us. It would be a long, rough ride, but probably quite worth it in terms of getting a picture of the community and their needs.

"I have already seen a village," he replied. Red flag number two.

I explained that, just like in North America, each area had its own personality and needs, and that the people were unique. "If you want to help out, you really need to meet the people and see the projects."

He reluctantly agreed but said he did not like the idea of getting up at 4:00 a.m. to make the trip.

As it turned out, he didn't like riding in the back of the truck, either. I could hear him complaining through the back window about the potholes, the curves, the lack of shocks on the truck. Nor did he like the weather or the rain or the sun when it finally came out. (Unfortunately, despite my desire, I couldn't dump him out right there on the dirt road, in the middle of nowhere. Or could I?) Although the complaints continued, I was able to close the window. Fortunately, none of the locals with him in the back could speak English and therefore couldn't understand his whining.

At one point, Avril said he was cold and literally took the hat off of a *muchacho* next to him and put it on his own head. Red flag number three. A hat cost about a day or two's labor.

Finally, we arrived at the turn off and the steep ascent. The road at that point was gutted and ruined by torrential rain from the night before. We learned later that the men from the village got up at 3:00 a.m., went to the road, and put rocks in what would be tire tracks, so that our four-by-four could make the trip to the top. I was already impressed and eager to look at the possible projects there. I loved a community with initiative and the desire to collaborate.

Avril's behavior upon arrival disgusted me even further. Fifteen more red flags! The smiling villagers, adults and children, village leaders, and dogs all ran up to the truck to greet us, hands outstretched, with eager smiles. Most were dressed in homemade clothes that were worn, and folks were covered in mud from the recent rain. Children who owned rubber boots wore them. Most, however, were barefoot with mud squishing between their toes. The scent of oranges from the local trees filled the air, and the winds from the mountaintop were turning clothes into flying capes. Everyone in the truck jumped out to return the handshakes—everyone except Avril. Instead, he took pictures with his gigantic camera. I told him to put the camera down and shake hands, that his behavior was considered rude. He reluctantly complied but shook hands tentatively because, as he said later, he was concerned about germs.

We were ushered to a shack where a mother was cooking breakfast for us: eggs, coffee, tortillas, beans, all very aromatic. Avril took pictures of the house without permission. I was embarrassed. They offered us a seat at the large, old, weathered board that was their table. A couple of semi-functional plastic stools, a couple of logs as seats, and some broken plastic dishes.

Avril said to Marel and me, "I can't eat that food because it will make me sick," and began to rise from the table.

The two of us, one either side of him, pulled him back down and said, "Sit!"

Fortunately, he couldn't speak a word of Spanish (nor did he have any interest in learning). I "translated" for him, saying to our hostess, "Avril has been sick, and even though the food smells so appealing, it is better that he not eat this time. Next visit he will eat double." Everyone laughed (except for me, as my anger was reaching a boiling point) .

Marel looked at me with a wink and smile as if to say, "Good save."

After our meal, which I loaded into my stomach, eating Avril's share as well, we thanked the woman, complimented her, and proceeded to the schoolroom to assess the situation. By that point in my career, I was accustomed to seeing unnerving scenes, but I was still stunned to see eighty-five children—some two to a seat, some standing—pressed in like sardines in a five-by-five-meter classroom. A handful of desks, broken blackboard, no teaching materials, no school supplies. Most kids who did have pencils were using stubs. No erasers. No notebooks for most. Several emaciated dogs had squeezed in as well, hoping to find crumbs. Where there are kids, there are often crumbs. Liquid mud was flowing like melted chocolate into the room. When we entered, the kids stood and yelled hello and welcome, with giant, heartwarming smiles. They won me over. I wanted to build a school there immediately.

We talked a bit, and I gave a little English lesson, mostly *hello, goodbye, please,* and *thank you.* They were eager to learn and giggled as they repeated the words among themselves, as well as to me. After the lesson, I asked if a few kids could help us unload half a truck bed of school supplies and teaching materials. The entire classroom emptied out; the kids were so eager to help, unloading, screaming, and laughing.

As always, a dozen or so emaciated dogs accompanied the activity, their tails tucked in, heads bowed, but hoping for something that might go into their empty stomachs. They were in luck because I always brought pounds of dog kibble into the communities. I emptied my bag as the dogs scrambled to down as much as possible. The kids watched curiously. I was sure there had never been kibble or even "leftovers" in their houses. Dogs were lucky if they got a tortilla thrown to them.

Avril, from afar, took pictures. I said I wanted to introduce him to the teachers. He stood where he was and waved.

Within an hour, to avoid returning in the late afternoon rain, we were ready to leave. The villagers escorted us to the truck, piled bags of freshly picked oranges into the truck bed, and shook our hands. We were on our way.

The very decision to go to a community to visit sets up hope among the potential recipients, even though I always told them many times that we were just visiting, no promises. Potential beneficiaries didn't necessarily hear you. Hope clouded the reality. Sadly, we couldn't help everyone. One way I combatted my personal guilt and their lack of resources was by bringing toys, school supplies, and teaching materials when we visited, so that the village or the school had at least something.

Villagers often talked of "being abandoned" by the government. Frequently, other visitors, such as those in service clubs and other organizations, tended to want to stay closer to the comfortable towns and stay in the nicer hotels, so they did not often work with folks in the difficult-to-get-to areas. This increased the level of hope and desperation of the villagers.

Hope, if followed by disappointment, could be excruciating for us as well, if we had to say no to a project. We just couldn't do it all, and it could be heartbreaking for everyone involved. That's why we tried to do at least a little something like buy a blackboard for a school, fix a bathroom, or set up a field trip for the students. It was sort of a consolation prize. To me, it felt like a drop in the bucket, and it tore at my heartstrings, but folks always received the offers graciously, whatever we brought.

When donors came with us for visits, we tried to explain this dynamic in advance. I had tried to say this several times to Avril. "Please don't promise anything. The very fact that we are there can set up all sorts of expectations that we cannot meet and can lead to great disappointment."

Avril said upon leaving, "I'll build you a school."

My heart sank and my future life passed before my eyes when he said it. I knew he would leave to go back to Canada and we would be stuck with the responsibility of saying he had changed his mind. How did I know this? Because it happened all the time, and coupled with his dismissive and disrespectful manner, I knew it would almost certainly play out like this.

The trip back was long and painful. Probably most painful for Marel, since he was trapped behind the steering wheel while I ranted about Avril all the way home.

A couple of days later, Avril called me and wanted to meet about what I thought was building a school. I pulled together a group of people who would be involved, including a builder, Marel, and some others.

Avril arrived, and as we talked, it was apparent that he was avoiding talking specifically about the project. He had his own agenda. He said something about taking over *Buenos Vecinos* and how "we" needed to have more of a business approach to aiding the villages.

I tried to move the subject back to the issue of the school with no luck. I finally dismissed the meeting and suggested that he and I talk later in private.

A day later, he came over to my house. My student friend Carlos was there. He was trying to go to high school. He was motivated but lacked the finances since he came from a large subsistence farming family with a handicapped father. I introduced them, and Avril said hello without even turning to look at the boy.

"Carlos and I are talking about how we can work together to pay for his schooling," I explained.

"Don't worry about it. I'll cover everything," Avril said, without even turning to look at Carlos.

Carlos was in shock, excited, smiling ear to ear, thanking him over and over again.

I knew better. "We'll need to discuss costs and delivery of funds and other pertinent issues."

"No problem, I'll take care of that," Avril said.

Carlos got up to go, offering his hand, and Avril, still without turning to look at Carlos said, "Goodbye."

I had a sick feeling. I knew full well that Avril would not follow through, especially after what I was about to say to him about not wanting to work together. I would not leave Carlos stranded with nothing but an empty promise, so I started flipping through my mental Rolodex of donors who might help us out.

After Carlos left, I searched for a tactful way to tell Avril that I didn't want to work with him. "My organization and your needs are not a good fit," I said.

"I have many years of business experience. You are ignorant about these things. How could you pass up this wonderful opportunity?"

"Thank you, but I suggest you look into some other local organization."

He left, furious.

At least I could move on and never see him again. Or so I thought. The next thing I knew, he arrived at Marel's house, offering him a job as his assistant at three times the salary I was paying him. He told Marel that I was incompetent and didn't know anything about business and offered him all sorts of promises for opportunities for his future: salary increases, benefits. Marel said no thanks, that money wasn't everything, and that he loved working with me and loved the work we did together. He also said loyalty was very important to him.

Within days, people from other local organizations were calling me saying that Avril had contacted them and had said very bad things about me. Lies. Apparently, Avril tried to make deals with these groups and was turned down by all of them.

He returned to Marel, going to his house and offering "incentives" (bribes). He became manipulative, saying that Marel would "go nowhere" with me. There were also other more invasive attempts to secure Marel, which I am not comfortable discussing specifically.

Fortunately, my reputation in the town and in the local villages was in excellent shape. No one believed Avril's stories, but it was still very hurtful and time-consuming to do damage control, having to fend off this constant bad-mouthing, slander, and manipulation. Marel stopped answering his constant phone calls. Eventually, after a couple of months of this nightmare, his attempts to take control withered and died.

I was still left to honor the promises he had made to the community and to Carlos. It wasn't my responsibility, but I couldn't bear their disappointment.

Carlos was sent to high school on a grant that I was able to get from a kind and generous donor. The school in the village was built within a year, but by other donors. My scars started to heal, but from that point on I remained skeptical of premature large promises. No one in the area around Copán ever paired up with Avril, in spite of his wealth and his "desire to help."

I want to stress that, overall, donors have been fantastic. They come from all over the world and are of all ages, colors, and nationalities. We were fortunate to have the support of service clubs, churches, small community groups, and individuals, each bringing a special way of working together. We had donations from girls' running club, a church quilting group, and lots of student groups. Each time we received a donation, no matter what size, it gave us a shot in the arm. Sometimes I was reduced to tears. This happened when I was working hard and not much financial support was coming in, and then out of the blue a wonderful surprise would arrive.

The truth was, however, that some donors needed to be educated, and that exhausted me. We were only two people and had only a couple of volunteers; donor demands often consumed too much time, with expectations that were not realistic. For example, ongoing programs were not something we could take on with only two of us.

People would come to visit for a week or two, wanting to do a project. They were in a hurry, wanting to see something completed or at least started and advanced while they were there. They didn't know the culture and were not familiar with the problems of infrastructure or local styles of operating.

Often, donors wanted to do the project themselves without the involvement of the community because they could finish faster. This undermined the confidence and respect of the recipients and took away the team spirit. It also gave the message, "We can do this better or faster than you."

Sometimes a group would come down wanting to do a project so they could feel good about themselves: "Look what we did. We helped." I am not saying it was entirely selfishly motivated, but there was a large element of it. Often out of politeness, the recipients said thank you and let the project proceed, meanwhile feeling less than. No one ever said no to a free offering.

It was common that volunteers did not ask what the community or individual needed, but rather had an agenda of their own. This often led to locals not taking good care of what had been given to them for free. It had less value than if they had worked on it themselves, or had helped raise the money, or had in some way contributed. I admit, with shame and embarrassment, that I was guilty of this too, especially at first. Eagerness to help often ended with stepping on toes.

Another problem was that many donors wanted an enormous amount of reporting before, during, and after a small project that had minimal impact. A small organization like *Buenos Vecinos* did not have the time or staff. Tasks were not as simple as they seemed. Many times, folks in the villages would not have a phone signal, or a camera for frequent photos, or would not communicate specifics.

We didn't have enough money or time to make a long trip to follow up as often as donors would like. Donor expectations were often unrealistic. I understood that they had their own expectations and wanted to be connected to the project, but it often required way more time than we had.

We were often in the middle, mediating between donors and recipients, and that became uncomfortable. There were time expectations or quality expectations that just didn't match the resources we had to work with.

We had infrastructure challenges that were hard to imagine. For example, someone suggested we make walls out of adobe because it was cheaper than bricks. But often water wasn't available to mix with the straw. Once, an expectation to finish a project quickly was met with a surprise mudslide. Broken bridges, washed-out roads, and truck repairs often curtailed deliveries. In coffee season, folks had to take advantage of the good pay that was available for only a few months and would therefore drop a project in the middle of completion. Sometimes the building supply store would be out of the supplies we needed or their delivery truck broke down.

Communication was key, but we had inadequate phone systems, sub-par electrical systems, and other aging structures. Electricity went out, which wiped out communication for anywhere between a few hours to a few days. We tried to explain in advance that there would be unexpected challenges, but people from the Western world had difficulty imagining it. It was a continual learning experience for me, doing these projects and also being a liaison between donor and recipient, and this required endless adjustments. The main concept of what I learned was to always prepare for a plan B, plan C, and sometimes more.

Chapter 24

A visitor stopped me on the street one day, asking for directions. She was mature, well dressed, and had been trying to make her way down the broken cobblestone street in high heels. While we talked, passing cars splashed us with muddy water.

"Are all the streets this bad?" she asked.

"This is one of the good ones," I replied, laughing.

She told me she was in Copán for a week's stay and was excited about her plan to help some villagers. "I want to buy washing machines for some of the poor unfortunate women who have to handwash their clothes in the river. It must be so hard for them."

She was coming from a North American perspective, like many people who wanted to help. "It may be hard to do laundry that way for us North Americans," I explained, "but not hard for the women here. They are used to it. Besides, many have daughters to help." She seemed unconvinced. I continued, "Washing clothes in the river is a tradition handed down for generations. These women are strong. It's an opportunity to get out of the house and connect with other women."

She found this hard to believe. "Who wouldn't want a free washing machine?"

There were so many things I could have said to this. *Is this woman sure all of the women have electricity to run the machines? Does she know about the power outages? Do the women have a place to put the machines in their tiny adobe houses? Do they have plumbing? How good is their water pressure if they do? Good enough to run a modern washing machine?* I decided to keep it simple.

"Donating to some but not all in the community could cause envy among the families and make community life uncomfortable, and most rural houses can't accommodate a large appliance that uses water or electricity."

"You're being negative and unhelpful," she said. "It'll help free up the women's time."

I was getting annoyed. This lack of awareness from people wanting to help the "poor" Hondurans was just too prevalent. "Free up time for what?" I snapped. "For their bridge club?" Okay, I should have been more tactful, but my patience on this issue was wearing thin.

She huffed away. I heard from a friend that she eventually abandoned the idea.

This woman was one of hundreds if not thousands of people who traveled to Honduras (and, of course, other developing countries) with a desire to help. Besides individuals, there were also organizations—NGOs, like Red Cross and Save the Children; medical teams from other countries; faith-based organizations and missionaries; businesses that came down to donate; and universities and schools that sent groups for cultural-education programs.

The purpose of this chapter is to share some of the lessons I learned doing projects in Honduras—lessons on listening, on hiring good local labor, on creating projects that work, and the lessons learned from those projects that didn't work.

With the larger charitable organizations and individuals, unfortunately, I frequently witnessed failures and unnecessary difficulties. One of the biggest issues was the lack of adequate oversight to monitor the different types of projects that were occurring at any given time. Projects were often duplicated. Some villagers received copious donations from various organizations, some none at all. But too frequently, people didn't seem to understand *how* to give, nor was there much available information on the process of donating.

Let me give a few examples. The village of La Pintada was close to town. Local tour groups would bring visitors there on horseback, in tuk-tuks, in trucks, or even on foot, and they almost always brought school supplies. It was wonderful that this village could receive such great support, but there were thirty-five other schools within the same radius that received nothing. My suggestions to the different organizations running these tours fell on deaf ears.

Here's another example. One year, a service club member who came down with his group once or twice a year informed me that they were going to build a school in the village where we had just completed one.

"What?" I blurted. "Why would you do that? They have a brand new school!" (We had built it.)

He continued to talk as if I hadn't said a word. "Yes, we want to put a school in this community, and we plan to start in the next couple of months."

"That's ridiculous. Why would you waste all that money on duplicating services?" I knew his type. He had a good heart, but he was white, privileged, from the US, and knew nothing about what it meant to be Indigenous and poor. His way of communicating was to command. He had not learned the art of listening.

I ran into him again a couple of days later, this time on the street. He stopped me to proudly tell me that they had altered their plans and now they were instead going to build a kindergarten in the village. I think he expected my approval.

"Are you kidding? Haven't you evaluated that community at all? There are only six or seven kids that go to kindergarten in that tiny community, and most do not even go regularly. Nor is there a teacher." Having worked there very intensely for many months, I knew the village and the people's needs well. "Why don't you consider building in another area where there is an *actual need*, for example, where there are hundreds of starving kids sitting on the ground, using rocks as their seats and pieces of wood as their desks? I know of many desperate communities who actually really need help, and I would be glad to fill you in."

I knew my expressed frustration was counter to my goal of educating him, but having experienced this kind of thing for many years, I was out of patience.

He, of course, ignored my advice. He was fixated on his original idea, proceeding to talk to me as if I had never been to that village, telling me the obvious. "They grow watermelons. People live in mud-and-stick huts. They really like me." (*Or your money*, I thought to myself.) "The children are so happy when I visit."

There were so many examples of service duplication. A nearby school playground was painted every year by a different group of visitors (I, myself, had witnessed five paintings), while other play areas were neglected. It was a town joke that the swings and slides had become twice their original size due to so many coats of paint.

At Christmastime, multiple agencies, unaware of one another's donations, would support the same families. Some destitute families received three or four Christmas baskets filled with food and supplies, other families, nothing.

These incidents bring up key points I want to make in this chapter, from the importance of understanding what people in Honduras really need before offering help, to really listening, to being present in the country for more than a few days, to asking local organizations their opinions, to not assuming that Hondurans want a North American lifestyle.

Many people living and working in Copán, including me, already had great inside information, such as what businesses were honest and the best caliber, who the most efficient local personnel to work with was, what specific products or services locals had to offer, what the villagers' desires and needs were, and what the geographical challenges were.

I've seen projects that were never launched or were ultimately not followed through to completion due to various factors such as dishonesty, lack of good building materials, lack of follow through on the part of the government or the villagers, use of alcohol by the contact person, and most of all, lack of good communication, lack of understanding of the culture, and unwillingness to listen on the part of the donor.

What I struggled with was that often people did not take time to ask or properly assess what was needed and what the possible ramifications were. Whose needs were we meeting, the donors' or the recipients'? The donors came with their own agendas that were not necessarily helpful for the recipients, as in the case of the washing machines.

Helpers' agendas often were based on their own cultural norms and expectations; they assumed that the recipients would fully cooperate and greatly appreciate their efforts and would respond as they would in the benefactor's country. I saw numerous projects fail within the first year, mainly because there was a cultural difference that wasn't addressed or a misunderstanding due to a lack of proper assessment of motivation on the part of the beneficiaries, lack of good communication, and/or lack of follow-up.

Often, the organizations or individuals who were providing the grants became frustrated, angry, and gave up. They'd blame "these people," meaning the locals, calling them lazy, unappreciative, or unwilling and bad workers.

Our small three-person group, *Buenos Vecinos*, was among these "helping" organizations. I believe because we were small, based in the country, and we hired only locals, we had substantial insight into how to create successful projects. I'd like to share some of these insights.

Deadlines needed to be flexible. When I first arrived, I wished I would have waited six months before charging in with projects, but like many others who come and see the poverty, I was too eager to help. It would have been wiser to know the culture and language better first.

In my initial projects, for example, I worked harder than the recipients. This set up an expectation with the people I was helping that they didn't have to do much. The harder I worked, the less they participated.

When service clubs, missionaries, or helpers came for a week or two and stayed in the main town, they could not understand the real needs of the potential beneficiaries, especially in the outlying areas. Local folks were often too polite or too shy to explain what would or wouldn't be successful, or what they really needed. It was nearly impossible to assess need in a few days, especially as an outsider. No potential beneficiary would decline free stuff, but their actions would speak louder than words. Often the required maintenance afterwards would not happen. Bridges broke down, schools were not cared for, materials were stolen.

Over time, I learned to not be so eager to set a start date. I tried to make sure that the proposed date was not coming from a personal agenda, but from the practicality of what was needed and what was possible. I learned that plans could go awry, and that just because I had an expected finish date, it didn't mean a project would be completed at that time. Stores ran out of materials. Roads washed out. Workers got sick, injured, and sometimes even murdered. Weather was unpredictable.

As time went on, my language skills and cultural understanding improved greatly, and I was able to communicate better with leaders, teachers, and members of the community. I asked more questions. Up to that point, I had relied quite a bit on Marel as my translator and cultural liaison. Gradually, I began to discard some of my North American values and to understand more deeply what people really needed. I tried to listen to what they said and especially what they didn't say. I figured out how to distinguish between when people were expressing enthusiasm and motivation to work versus rote responses to possible offers. I researched more. Had these projects been attempted before in the community? If so, where, and what happened?

I talked with people outside the community and tried to ask what support the community had already received so as not to duplicate services. Sometimes what was donated was not valuable.

A leader of a recipient organization told me that they received a shipment of donated books from a service club that had been down to visit. It was a lovely gesture, but the books were in English, or in Spanish at a college reading level. The money spent on shipping these items could have been used to buy local items, supporting local businesses and allowing local people to make the decision of what would be appropriate.

A colleague who was the head of an organization serving children told me she would often receive oversized children's clothing. Honduran children, and especially malnourished children, are much smaller than North American children. This colleague often re-donated the clothes to teenagers and adults.

I feel it would be helpful if visitors would listen to long-term residents who are aid workers. We have years of experience working on projects and valuable information regarding resources, cultural norms, and the genuine needs of the communities. We have a tremendous amount of insight and information to dispense and are willing and eager to offer this to short- and long-term visitors. We are familiar with both Western culture and Central American culture, but too often, we were not asked, not listened to, and discounted. I found that so disappointing, especially because it furthers the message that the Western world knows best and therefore they are the experts.

The most successful projects happened with helpers and liaisons living in-country, thereby creating reciprocal relationships with people in the community. The communication was better, and assessments of projects were more accurate. As a neighbor, it was easier for me to more accurately assess needs, or to give out work or assistance in some way. I felt that as a neighbor, people were more open and the connection was more balanced.

Often folks repaid the favor, making it a more reciprocal interaction. They would bring us oranges or eggs in return for a favor. It felt neighborly.

After working on a particular school project, one of the villagers, Geronimo, brought me a live chicken. He walked the three hours down the mountain carrying this chicken, along with vegetables that he was bringing into town to sell. I bumped into him in the street in the town center. He said he was glad to see me because he was on his way to my house to bring me this chicken to thank me for helping his school. I was touched. A chicken was a valuable prize and it meant a lot to me to accept this.

Thanking him profusely, I put the chicken under my arm, not quite sure if I was carrying it properly or if it was going to bite me (I am a city kid). As I walked home, people on the street commented on what a great chicken I had, and I chuckled to myself.

"What a beauty," folks said.

I wondered, what made a chicken "a beauty"? I was proud to reply that it was a gift.

There is a huge difference between being a donor, visitor, or missionary and living side by side with folks. Donors donate. Neighbors share. I was much more comfortable as a helpful neighbor than being a part of a helping organization, and as an eventual result, I changed my organization's name to *Buenos Vecinos* (Good Neighbors). It was a major turning point for me, punctuating my role as a neighbor and validating my connection in Honduras. There was no sign on our truck, but everyone knew it was us riding around in the blue truck. Even the village dogs recognized the sound of our heaving motor and would come running.

It often was a tough balance being in the middle between donor and recipient, and it required patience and understanding from both parties, as well as diplomatic communications as a project manager and cultural liaison. Unfortunately, I didn't always have the energy, wisdom, or patience. It was easier to decide how to use donations when their use was unspecified; it was wonderful for us to be able to divvy up the funds as needed without needing to consult, negotiate, or explain each step to the donor, which was time-consuming.

Most of our funds came from people who had never been to the area but trusted us with the best way to use the money. The donations were connected to their hearts, and we were the stewards. I often felt that this was the supporters' best way of helping out. My best way was by being on the ground, connecting first-hand. It was a great blend.

Years of counseling experience taught me to "do with" and not "do for," but this situation was different. It was a global issue, not a personal one. The temptation, even with my awareness, was to take over. It was a natural part of my personality, as well as North American cultural style. As I learned more about this, I also observed that many groups acted similarly. They came down to build a house or a church, for example, with little or no participation from the locals. After the initial meeting, the leadership fell into the hands of the donor's project officer who was often a visiting foreigner with the mindset, "We are doing this *for* these people."

What kind of message did this give? Were beneficiaries so incapable that they could only receive or hold down the basic labor jobs on a project rather than leading or performing more skilled tasks?

How many times did I see building, agricultural, or construction projects taking place with a white person giving the instructions and the locals doing the labor? Kids grew up witnessing this, learning that their government couldn't help, their community leaders couldn't help, their parents couldn't help, but white foreigners could. It led to a feeling of inferiority. I heard it so many times, locals saying that North Americans or Europeans were smarter.

Outsiders had knowledge to contribute, but so did the locals. Marel would hear the complaints about being "dissed" from villagers more than I would because he was Honduran and people trusted him more. They reported feeling disrespected and ignored, with the result that the beneficiaries would put in their time but not their full commitment. I had to learn and relearn this lesson continually because there were subtleties that I didn't get at first. For example, villagers would say yes to a request but not show up for their part. They wouldn't attend a meeting, or follow through with some of the tasks. Maintenance after a project on occasion would be lacking because a dependence on foreigners had been created with the assumption that they would take care of it. Trust and good communication required time. In some cases, it took months of my visiting a community before the women would come out of their houses to greet me. A week or two visit by foreigners was not sufficient to foster trust.

I knew these visitors were well meaning, but they often did not take the time or make the effort to find out what really was helpful. Organizations or individual aid workers would give handouts or donated labor and see it as generous and helpful, while local people opened their arms and were required to do very little to be a part of the project. It was common that donors thought they could do it better or faster, so they'd prefer to do it themselves. This set up a welfare mentality that over the years seriously harmed the production and initiative of Hondurans.

There was a saying in Honduras: "After Hurricane Mitch, Hondurans received so much aid that they put down their hoes and watched the sky." In 1998, the category 5 hurricane devastated the country. It was labeled the worst in the twentieth century, causing two billion dollars in damage to structures and crops, not to mention the death and disease it brought. Aid came in the form of loans, cash, and programs. This unfortunately evolved into a sense of entitlement where beneficiaries became used to receiving without having to participate.

What I learned during emergencies was that handouts could be very helpful, but they needed to include methods to transfer the responsibility back to the recipients. I saw the situation with handouts happen over and over again, and in my initial months there I fell into this situation many times myself. The first donation or gift was given without question—we sincerely wanted to help. Later came a second request, maybe for something different or possibly larger. If that was granted, then a sense of expectation began. A granted third or fourth request set up a sense of entitlement, and recipients often became angry when their requests weren't granted.

I was shocked the first time I experienced this. I had been helping a neighbor, a single grandmother who took in her daughter's children after their mom died. I heard about her and stepped in with clothing and school supplies for the children. I did this for two school semesters. One day, the grandmother sent the granddaughter to ask me to buy shoes for the kids. I told her we didn't have enough money. The grandmother stopped speaking to me.

* * *

I often saw organizations and individuals with the best of intentions making promises to build or initiate projects, but when faced with the realities and challenges of the local culture, they turned and ran.

Many local organizations, groups, and individuals told me about such abandoned projects that were promised by visiting groups from another country. Village leaders told me that they would receive offers to build a community center or help with a water project, but the potential donor wouldn't come back or even follow up with the leaders. When visitors left, that would be the end of the communication. If visitors used me as the go-between, often I was left holding the bag and had to be the one to break the news. Sometimes it was just a simple promise to stay in touch that was broken. Locals would feel this so deeply, not understanding why a friend would not follow up. Sadly, I saw many people hurt this way. Often visitors didn't realize the impact they had emotionally on the people they met. Often when I told people I was going on vacation, they frequently assumed I would never come back.

Sometimes potential recipients, having been let down so many times, stopped believing that promises and offers would actually materialize. Once we were doing a water project in San José, a village of about eight hundred people who lived in houses made of torn plastic tarps. After many meetings and phone conversations between Marel and the community, a group of thirty-five men was organized to start clearing the land on a specific day and time.

Marel arrived early on that day, eager to start, but no one showed up to work. He found the village leader, Leopoldo, and asked him what was happening. Leopoldo said that because they had been let down so many times, no one believed we would actually follow through with our commitment. He explained that the farmers decided to go to work on that scheduled start date but said they'd be available should the project actually happen. Leopoldo then blew a whistle and within minutes Marel was shocked to see almost fifty men running in from the fields, from every direction, faces lit up, carrying their hoes and machetes, ready to work. The group proceeded happily to the path where they started the twenty-day process to clear the brush and trees for waterlines.

There was a woman who offered to put a roof on a school that was being built. While her group were staying in the area, there was a careless accident in their hotel and they had to pay for damages. Upset over the hotel incident, they rescinded their offer to the community, leaving them stuck with a partially built school and nowhere to turn. We scrambled to find funds to complete the project. It wasn't uncommon to see half-built churches, partial fences, and foundations of buildings not completed.

Marel was invaluable in helping me learn. Other locals were my key to understanding. Even after all the years that I had been in Central America, I found that I still had difficulties due to language problems. Sometimes there were simple mistakes. For example, the words for *two* and *twelve* sounded similar to me. You could imagine what happened with price quotes, or meeting times, or numbers of people coming to a meeting when I made such a mistake.

A funny incident occurred while I was working on a water project. I was talking to the leaders of the community about how I wanted to put water spigots in each of the eighty houses. The word for spigots is *ramales*. I used the word *rameras* (prostitutes). I was telling them that I wanted to put a prostitute in each house. The men tried not to laugh, but I'm sure they would have been delighted.

Language confusion was unavoidable, so it was important to double-check and make sure folks understood what one another was saying. When working with an interpreter, one often assumed they would be accurate, but of course, they made mistakes and/or sometimes did not capture the tone or intent of the speaker. Occasionally, they omitted parts of conversations that were important. Often expectations were misunderstood because they were not explained clearly. Intercultural interpretation varied.

Asking that something be done "quickly," for example, is a relative term. The word "quickly" to a North American may not be the same time frame as "quickly" to a Central American. Also, it was important to explain the whys of a particular request. Sometimes the local recipients did not feel it was a priority to meet that expectation if they didn't have the reason explained clearly. Some expectations could appear foolish to locals, while on the other hand, resulting actions could appear annoying to visitors.

I remember a fellow from the US came down and wanted to buy tables for a school. A fabulous contribution! We organized a group of workers to build some in a backyard with a table saw and hand tools. Frustrated after seeing the lack of speed of the process, the visitor explained to them that they could be way more efficient if they set up a production line. Smiling, the folks said sure, but when the visitor left, they went back to their former way of working.

Marel was supervising this project, and I asked him why they reverted to their old work process. He explained that there was very little work in town. If they finished quickly, they would lose their camaraderie, and the positive feeling they had from having at least temporary employment. Since they were paid per job and not per hour, they had no incentive to complete the task quickly.

I would help out from time to time as a translator with visiting medical brigades who came for a few days offering free service and medicine. They set up makeshift clinics in the town or surrounding areas. Often they hired young, local, bilingual high-school students who were considered skilled enough to translate. These kids could translate many words correctly but not necessarily medical terms. Worse, they were young and did not act appropriately or respectfully towards the patients. I remember watching one of them eating potato chips and translating while a woman was talking about losing her third child.

There were cultural differences that were challenging, as well. Often the doctor or nurse would not introduce themselves. It was not uncommon for the male doctor to stand two inches away from a woman's body, possibly the first man besides her husband to touch her or come near her. I used to ask over and over again that the medical staff introduce themselves and the interpreter and think about the differences between the Western world and their boundaries and local customs. Because of the large numbers of patients they would want to accommodate in a day, they sometimes moved too quickly. This was common and accepted in the United States, but doctors moved slower in Honduras.

Patients often told me afterwards that they didn't talk about the main problem that brought them to the consult. I would suggest they go back and talk with the doctor. "*Tengo pena,*" they would reply, a phrase that meant they felt too shy or too uncomfortable.

Medical brigades are extremely helpful, but sometimes there was a cost. Often local folks lost their self-respect and dignity in the process and were seen as an anonymous, needy recipient. Their voices were often not heard, and the methods of aiding were many times not carried out in a culturally or individually sensitive and respectful way. I'm not saying that the service providers were unkind or boorish. They often did an amazing amount of great work in short periods, but they were often acting within North American cultural norms.

I was and still am a quick mover. I work and think fast and have a hair-trigger response at times. This was always a major learning lesson for me, to become more patient, to relax. Honduras was my test. Constantly. At times, a rapid response was required, but at other times, patience was key. I was certain that, especially in my early years, people could pick up on my impatience. In my later years, there was an impatience that came from exhaustion, overload, and burnout. Although I yelled only in my head ("Just do it!"), I was sure my frustration manifested externally on some level. My own impatience appalled me.

I was also learning about setting timelines and deadlines based on the needs of the locals, not on the needs of the donors. Initially, for funding purposes and to please the donors, I set deadlines that weren't feasible locally. For example, during coffee-picking time, I became aware that most project work came to a halt or slowed down. People could make good money picking coffee that would help them buy the year's necessities that they couldn't otherwise buy. I didn't know this when I took on my first project and later saw that I needed to alter the expected time frame for completion. Other times there were problems with infrastructure, such as washed-out roads or delivery of supplies. I often was the link between frustrated donors and the local population, having to explain that we did not have the same services available as the Westerners. This is another reason communication was so important—to assess and discuss with everyone, recipients as well as donors, what barriers or obstacles might come during the process of the project.

I learned to tell donors, when possible, that they needed to go to the site. See the damage. See the need. Before starting the work, get several estimates from different carpenters, different stores. Do research. If you're adding a roof to a school, go to another school to ask how they did it. Check out the reputation of the business people and village leaders. It takes more time, but it's worth it.

It was not uncommon that donations of money, supplies, and food ended up in the hands of people who were less than honest. Not everyone would tell you who wasn't honest, but they would tell you who was.

On occasion, I had to have conversations with well-meaning donors about less-than-reputable workers or organizations, and that put me in an uncomfortable position. I certainly didn't want to point the finger, saying that someone was dishonest. Folks needed the work. But where was my loyalty?

"In a country that has great needs, it is important to set up transparency and accountability standards," I would tell the donors. "You might want to look around further." I'd ask the benefactors if they trusted the distributor of goods, or if they took the time to check his or her reputation before contracting them.

Often the response was something vague: "We're sure we can trust him," or, "I have a good feeling about this."

I would sometimes respond, "Desperate people sometimes do desperate things. If my family was hungry and I couldn't find work, I bet I would become less than honest if I felt it was my only option."

It wasn't just about trusting locals. I would also mention that there were some well-off foreigners who ran programs locally and had very bad reputations. Trust takes time. Often aid groups and individuals didn't have enough.

Giving could be such a beautiful and pure thing, but it needed to be combined with mutual respect, accountability, and evaluated thoroughly before, during, and after any endeavor.

* * *

I observed that disastrous side effects sometimes occurred when donors imported supplies and materials. Materials didn't arrive or would get stuck in customs, where they would charge an exorbitant fee to release them.

In addition, importing items competed directly with local businesses. A flailing economy was even further damaged. I saw folks spend a fortune sending items by mail, boat, or airplane when these charges could have been used directly in the programs or to buy locally and therefore support the store owners and businesses. I witnessed the closing of school-supply stores and children's clothing stores due to competition with tourists bringing in "presents."

My friend Moncho, who had a little store selling odds and ends and school supplies, told me that when tourism increased, his business declined considerably. "They come with their suitcases filled with supplies and go directly to the communities. They don't shop at our stores. The quality of North American products is so much better. We can't compete with that," he told me.

It was important to support the communities, not just the projects. By buying within the villages whenever possible, even though there was less to choose from, it helped the economy. Hiring people from the villages to do the labor gave the locals an opportunity for work that they would not otherwise have. This kept income within the community.

This issue also applied within the country, between rural areas and town centers. Even buying little items in the communities' *tiendas* (stores) versus in town helped local families. It might have cost a few pennies more, but I much preferred to support a family than a big business.

Most Indigenous people were not hired in the towns. Due to prejudice, lack of experience in the more mainstream work, or the great distances they would have to commute, it was less common. The truth was that there were excellent carpenters, toy makers, corn-husk doll makers, and hard-working laborers in these villages. Rural children, as well, were always looking for work. Sometimes just a few coins—asking them to carry some items or help unload a building supply truck would mean a lot to them.

Everybody said yes to whatever help we offered. Even if they couldn't use it. So, we learned to give potential recipients tasks to assess their readiness for a project. When the actions and words did not match, we would listen to the actions for our answer. For example, we would ask village leaders to get project estimates or to clear and prepare the land for construction. If they didn't do these things, we wouldn't go further with the project until we could assess the issue. Sometimes it meant stopping the project altogether.

I remember one village reluctant to help us unload building materials. It was like pulling teeth to get them to finish the task. After much conversation, we learned that they did not want to continue with the project even though they initially agreed to help with labor. They changed their minds when they spoke to recipients in other areas who told them that other organizations would do everything for free. We said okay, if it was their preference to wait for another organization, we would bring the truck and collect the delivered materials. It was uncomfortable, to say the least—or should I say even scary at one point—but we took the materials back and delivered them to another community that had been begging for a kindergarten for many months. They built their school in less than five weeks.

If we had serious time pressure, sometimes we offered incentives or bonuses for projects finished on time and a job well done. It was a great motivator, and often took the time pressure off my shoulders.

It was essential to find a trustworthy local supervisor. Once, we built a home for a single mom with ten children. She had been kicked out of a house and had moved into a lean-to under an electrical transformer. During rainy season. One of the daughters was struck by lightning. It was an urgent situation.

We found a supervisor who was referred by several locals. We were told he was great—efficient, honest, hard-working, and sober. So, after our interview I contracted with him. I was pleased that he was all that was said of him. Nelson built the tiny house in about two weeks, hiring extra manpower to get the job done within the urgent time frame and within the proposed budget.

There were other times, however, early on in my time in Honduras where I did not properly assess the situation. For example, there was an excellent worker, a kind man who we hired early on.

Unfortunately, we didn't know he had a drinking problem. This caused many time delays. I asked in advance several questions about his qualifications, but not about his sobriety.

I learned to stay in close contact with project leaders, as well as the village. I couldn't assume the project would get done because workers needed the money and were motivated by the results of the project. That wasn't always true. When people came from other countries to get their own project going and only had a short time to spend, I would often see failures or incomplete tasks. It was important to stay in touch in whatever manner possible. For those helpers living in another country and trying to coordinate with locals, this was not always easy. It was essential to have an excellent, qualified coordinator.

It was even better if the benefactor could be in-country. Phone and email often worked, but nothing replaced presence. The donor can motivate people by demonstrating in person their commitment and excitement, as well as have more opportunity to get first-hand information. It also established a relationship that couldn't happen by email.

I would ask local people to evaluate a project as it was in progress. It was important to talk *with* them about how they felt. It was essential to talk *with* the teachers as the school was being built and ask the community what they thought as the process was going on. I would gain valuable information. New ideas were often generated during the course of the project, not just at the beginning. A villager, for example, in the midst of the project, might have suddenly found a contact who could save us money in transportation or sell us lumber at a better price. One schoolteacher watched a builder measure for the windows and came to me worried that the windows were too large and too low, and that children and other "visitors" in the night would be able to climb in and take things. She told us we needed to add bars on the windows, not just glass.

I thought I didn't have much ego invested in the building of two of our schools until I saw the mayor on television taking credit. I was angry for two reasons: he was corrupt and trying to further his career by lying and trying to take advantage of us, and he was not giving credit to the villagers who had done so much to make these schools happen. What also surprised me was my ego reaction. "I" wanted the credit. I felt discounted even though everyone knew it was our organization that helped build the schools with the community. This egotistical reaction surprised me. Later, we would go on TV to counter the official's claims, and I was glad we did to set the record straight, but most importantly, I learned a great deal about my ego and its needs throughout this event.

I learned that this work wasn't about how great an organization was. Local people deserved credit too. In Honduras, people thanked God first, then others, and finally their co-workers.

Organizations in Honduras put up signs everywhere, taking credit for projects. I personally thought these signs were offensive. Many locals felt this way too but wouldn't say anything for fear of offending the group offering the support. I personally thought signs were the height of arrogance and detracted from all the efforts made by local people and government.

These signs rarely acknowledged the community's contributions, but rather just highlighted the helping club or group. I would liken this to having my neighbor help me trim my banana trees and then the next day coming over with a sign for my garden with his name that said "I did this!"

I understood the dilemma. Donors needed to show tangible proof of their work in order to raise funds, but there were less offensive ways to do this such as with photos, videos, or thank-you letters from recipients.

It's important to point out that there were often people on-site who worked for free; usually way more people were involved than met the eye. Local women often supplied free food for the workers. Village council members ran errands, did negotiating with the municipal government, and organized meetings. Community leaders made lots of expensive coordination calls or trips into town. This required acknowledgment and sometimes reimbursement.

There were other NGOs that provided great services. I used to love to watch the development of these programs and the expansion of staff and services. A model that I liked very much was Urban Promise, a multinational, faith-based organization that worked with local teens in developing leadership skills. Foreign volunteers who worked there received training about Honduran culture, as well as Spanish lessons. There was close supervision. The local Honduran teens were involved in the programs, took on leadership positions, and had a voice in the decisions. This was a model that I greatly respected.

The big question is finally being asked in the universities and among the international aid communities: What is help? There is a difference between support and doing. There is a difference between reciprocal activities and setting up a rescuer/victim dynamic. Another question that I continually ponder is, "Does help need to be sustainable, and if so, what is sustainability?" We can easily measure setting up a business or a clinic as sustainable. But aren't love, encouragement, and training also forms of sustainability? A grant for a school student, for example, may not be useful if the student doesn't believe in him/herself.

My foremost question is, "Whose needs are we meeting when we help?" I had to ask myself this over and over again when I was struggling with a project: *what is my goal and why?* I learned to ask donors this question, as well. Folks meant well, but their efforts often were mixed with and clouded by their personal agendas, often hidden agendas. "Helpers" might not even be aware of their own egotistical needs, wanting to be the rescuer or the saint, which requires that someone is the victim.

Another agenda might be competition between donor clubs. Folks wanted to feel good about themselves and their group. It was a human need. Certainly, there was genuine caring, but the methods could often be, to varying degrees, self-serving and competitive.

In my case, my predominant need at first was to "fix." If something was broken, such as school latrines or a roof, this was an easy process, but I was also trying to fix the system. That wasn't an easy process. It was also an arrogant assumption, thinking that I could find a way to undo centuries of governmental corruption and bad policies, or that I could fix a mindset held by the majority of oppressed people. I'm embarrassed to say that I kept thinking, however naively, that I could find the key to start reversing the damage.

It's important for me to keep looking at how we can improve international aid. In the meantime, there is lots of trial and error in this field, and the errors often set us too far back. Rescuing sets us back into a welfare mentality. Misguided assumptions cause mistakes. Prematurely developed plans create frustration and failure. Not being aware of our own needs shifts the focus off the project and the recipients.

I still have no answers, and that's an extremely frustrating and painful situation for me, but I feel strongly that the traditional view of charity doesn't work. It sets up a dynamic of one-downmanship. It hurts the recipients and insults them. I believe everyone on earth has something to offer and that international aid workers can work as a team and as equals with the beneficiaries. For example, I learned that one of the best ways to support an impoverished region is to buy their products. Hire their workers. In some instances, carefully organized loans had tremendous impact. Above all, I learned to be a better listener.

Chapter 25

Fortunately, not all donors were difficult. Although we had long-term struggles that would sap my energy and even at times make me want to throw in the towel, the vast majority were beautiful donors, people with big hearts who had healthy concepts of aid. These people were my antidotes to the hard times.

There was a day when I thought I couldn't take one more step forward and that any simple challenge would do me in. It was a day of many demands on my time, my emotions, and our funds. It was blazing hot. A trip to the lumberyard was a waste of time. They were out of lumber. This meant that we couldn't start building the foundation of the school until who knew when. I was stood up for a meeting, which happened because of poor telephone systems and a lack of communication skills. On my way home, I saw a dog hit by a car. He cried out and took off running. My heart sank. I had seen this all too often, and this time there was nothing I could do. At least he was able to run. I desperately needed a break. Searching for comfort, I went to my kitchen cupboard hoping against hope that I might find a tasty treat to help soothe me. I opened the cupboard door. What did I see on the shelves but a huge team of ugly, giant cockroaches scattering for safety.

Heart pounding, I ran for my mega can of Raid and went after those suckers like General MacArthur. After amassing a virtual graveyard of ugly, crusty, black bodies, and permeating the air with chemical warfare, I fell to the floor and sobbed. I just couldn't take any more.

After about half an hour, I picked myself up and dragged myself to my computer to put on some soft music to accompany my crying. I noticed an email from a woman who was a regular donor. I had never met her personally; she was a friend of another supporter, yet she was always a huge emotional support.

Usually I avoided looking at emails when I was overwhelmed, fearing another demand on my emotions, limited time, and energy. This time, however, I decided to open it, and while still trickling tears, I read her email. She said she had been thinking about me and how hard life must be for me at times, and just wanted to let me know she was there for me. It was just the tonic I needed.

I read on. She was sending me five hundred dollars, no strings attached. I was overcome, flooded with gratitude. I felt connected again, understood, supported, and appreciated. I felt something besides grief and exhaustion. Sobs turned into bawling. This letter meant so much to me, I think partially because sometimes I felt forgotten. There was little support there for me in terms of being able to confide about the realities of my work. I had always been so concerned about how I could help, what next project to take on, or how to deal with a complication of a project. Often, acting in emergency mode due to a crisis, I had a strong tendency to forget about my own needs.

The donor mentioning that she was thinking about me, not just my work, and sending "free, unsolicited money" without me having to try and raise it or explain how I would use it was such a positive affirmation of confidence in me and an injection of love and energy. It melted me to the core.

It was recognition that my heart needed support too. It was also a sign of respect and trust. Integrity is everything to me, and it meant so much to have that appreciated. I used to think that recognition meant compliments and praise. I never felt like I needed much of that. Recognition that I was working hard, that there were exhausting challenges both physically and emotionally, and that

I was doing my best—that was what I needed. Understanding. I finally learned to distinguish the two definitions.

When there were sudden crises, such as when a flood hit a rural area, where stick-and-mud houses were washed down the river, as well as animals and crops, I wrote letters to our supporters and immediately the funds poured in. Some donated as little as five dollars, others way more. To see the response, no matter what the amount, filled my heart with so much love and a strong sense of connection. We weren't alone. We were supported and protected. A team. A world community. It meant everything to me!

Among the responses was that of an eight-year-old, the daughter of one of our supporters. She wrote saying that she had gone around to her neighbors and in her school to ask for pennies to help us. She gave 850 pennies to her mom, who then sent me the check. I didn't have words to describe the effect on me. I wrote her back, telling her how touched we were that she made such an incredible effort to help. I sent her some photos of people receiving the clothes and stuffed animals that we purchased with her donation.

Some folks would say they didn't have any money but wanted to help. I tried to explain that even five or ten dollars was helpful. Big amounts were not necessary. It seemed to fall on deaf ears. I was writing to people in some of the richest countries in the world, and they didn't have five dollars? To be rejected in that way was painful. I felt discounted, and I felt like the people I loved who were in tremendous need were being ignored. I tried to stay focused on the positive with gratitude for what we did receive, but it was still painful, for example, when people close to me wouldn't pitch in.

One time, I decided to organize a shoe drive. Kids walking barefoot in animal excrement were a guarantee of parasites. Walking on rocks or burning hot pavement was a guarantee of foot damage. I wrote to people asking for *only* donations of five or ten dollars for shoeless kids. We received well over one hundred responses. With a discount for quantity shopping, we were able to give out almost 150 pairs of shoes. Five dollars does matter!

Donations came in all forms. Most often it was financial support for projects, but sometimes—like the woman I described earlier—friends would send me money just for me. It was so easy to forget to treat myself. These "just-for-me" gifts were wonderful. Often I would buy something special in the city, like better quality sheets that didn't rip the moment you put them on the bed, or an expensive imported food like chocolate chips. Since my personal budget was small, a treat of a good cheese was a delight.

Sometimes donations came in the form of packages of items that were not available in Honduras, sent through an international delivery company. I used to love to see my helpers coming from down the street carrying gigantic cartons to my house. I'd let them rip open the boxes, but it was my job to look inside. I'd find things such as cool baseball caps or special toys that couldn't be bought locally, mixed in with something special for me like matzo meal or baby gourmet jelly beans. My other personal favorite was good chocolate, which usually came melted into some strangely formed puddle within the wrapping. I'd put it in the fridge and eat it when it had hardened—misshapen and unattractive, but nevertheless deelish!

Usually the kids who helped me pick up the boxes from the post office would stick around, hoping to receive some kind of treat. I always had something for them. I used to love to watch their faces as I pulled out items only found in North America. They'd look on with wonder. "What is this for?" I would explain it was a nutcracker or a cheese-slicer. My young friend Alexis would always stare in a particularly intense way, baffled by some of our strange North American customs.

Visiting friends of friends would bring us donations, as well: medical supplies and equipment, vitamins for children, and prenatals for pregnant moms. Others would stuff their suitcases with items that were expensive and hard to find in Honduras: educational wall posters, maps, children's books in Spanish. I wouldn't want items that competed with local sales, but these specialty items were great and very difficult to find locally.

One woman brought me a box of plastic eyeglasses. One set had springing eyeballs; the other set sported eyebrows, large noses, and mustaches. Both were extremely popular with the kids, who laughed hysterically as I placed them on their faces.

It always encouraged me when local people would donate. We worked for a couple of years with a local sweet potato and squash exporter named Agueda who would always allow us to pick up truckloads of culls. These were perfectly good sweet potatoes and squashes, but slightly misshapen and therefore not sellable. She would call me once a month or so and ask if I was interested, and we'd immediately shoot over to her farm. Nothing gave me more pleasure than grabbing a couple of kids along the way and hiring them to spend an hour loading up the truck.

Afterwards, we would take off into the nearby villages and hand the products out to kids. Some of the squashes were so big that the little kids had to drag them up the hills to their homes or push them from behind. Sometimes we'd load up a few bushel bags and call World Vision or Red Cross to transport them to the villages farther away. There was something primal and earthy about giving out homegrown food.

Maybe this wasn't considered a donation as much as a thank you, but I loved it when villagers came by to sell their produce or their wares and gave me extras. If I wanted to buy a pound of tomatoes, they would throw in a few extra. There was something about that generosity of spirit that touched me deeply, sharing what little they had.

A donation in any form was an expression of caring, and I loved being a part of that circle of receiving, giving, and receiving again.

Chapter 26

It was going to be a normal school supplies delivery. We had been to La Laguna at least ten times over the years; I always loved going there. On the trip up the mountain in the crisp early mornings, I could see the fog hovering over the red clay roofs of Copán. The sun would catch the fog and the trees and make everything glow.

We knew the teachers and kids well; the kids always plastered their bodies and faces to the school windows when our truck pulled up. This time, a very important connection was about to happen.

As we pulled around the bend and up to the school, we saw a group of fifteen to twenty North American teenagers painting all three classrooms, inside and out. They looked like a horde of colorful bees, each working on their own special spot. From time to time, visiting groups came to do projects, such as building a fence or painting, but I usually knew about them in advance. This group took me by surprise.

A friendly, open woman in the group came up to me, smiling, as I jumped out of the truck. She introduced herself as their teacher and guide and explained that her class was from Montreal and on winter break. They were learning about rural life in Honduras and doing a service project.

We chatted for a while, and I waved to the teens as the head teacher of La Laguna, Roxana, came out to greet me. The Montreal school had been referred by the education administration in Copán, Roxana told me, and she was delighted to have the help.

The school desperately needed painting. There were few chips of color left on the gray cinder block walls. I was glad to see some of the Laguna students helping with the work, as it was their school. I was introduced to the visiting students; all were friendly and responsive. We tried to piece together French, English, and Spanish to communicate, while our hearts did the rest. A couple of sixteen-year-old girls stood out to me, friendly and eager to talk in spite of the language barrier. They were high energy, enthusiastic young women, eager to work, eager to learn, and eager to contribute. I really enjoyed the connection.

After chatting with them, as was my custom, I moved inside to each individual classroom to greet the 150 students, class by class. They answered my screaming *buenos días* (good morning) with their own screams at the top of their lungs.

"I can't hear you!" I screamed back, as we went into our familiar call and response routine. Then I did my little "happy dance." After about ten more minutes of this, I asked for the kids' help, and they ran out to unload school supplies and powdered milk, practically knocking one another over. They emptied the truck in minutes.

Once our task was finished, we said goodbye to the kids and to the students from Montreal, who waved their dripping paintbrushes at us. As we took off, I dropped two pounds of kibble out my window for the starving dogs. They rushed to the truck and gobbled frantically.

I had to go back the next day to finish our delivery. As we pulled up, Noémie, one of the sixteen-year-old girls who impressed me the day before, waved and came forward. She was wearing a red polka-dot bandana, her face and clothes covered in green polka dots from the paint. She gave me a big, smiling greeting. Her enthusiastic energy really drew me to her. After we unloaded supplies, she came over and wanted to know more about our organization.

"I'm loving my experience here and want to contribute further," she said.

"Since you're leaving the country soon and going home, let's exchange emails," I suggested. I never expected to hear back from her. Often visitors would genuinely want to reconnect, but by the time they returned home, they'd get back into their normal lives and lose the intention to follow through. Besides, Western teenagers were usually not that interested in me or my work.

I was surprised to receive within a week a long, sincere letter from Noémie, again talking about her desire to provide more aid in some way. I wrote her back, and we started a back and forth correspondence about options for projects. Due to the distance, her actually returning here would require a long, expensive trip, almost two days of travel. I wanted to come up with several smaller, less expensive projects where she could do fundraising and we could carry the projects out locally in a relatively short time. I wrote to her with suggestions: raising money for school supplies, building a school fence, or setting up a school garden.

She replied. She wanted to build a school. I laughed. It was preposterous. Still, I thought she was a plucky, ambitious young woman; maybe she was serious. She asked good questions. *How much would it cost to build a small school or one-room schoolhouse? How much time would it take? Did I know of any areas where a small school was needed?*

I responded to all of her questions, still skeptical. Still, she impressed me with specific, well-thought-out questions. She asked me to identify an area or village that needed a small school. There was no harm in responding, I thought, even if it didn't happen, as long as no promises were made to the community.

One village immediately came to mind: very much in need of school, close to town, one that she could visit easily if she was ever able to come back our way. I did some covert research, not wanting to give undue hope to the community, and gave Noémie a basic price proposal.

It would cost about five thousand dollars for a big one-room schoolhouse to replace the broken-down adobe hut, if the locals volunteered the labor. There were about thirty-five students, all grades. She thanked me for the information, and that was the last I heard from her.

Time went by, and we continued doing projects. All the while, I wondered if Noémie would actually come through. More than

201

a month went by with no communication, so I assumed she had lost interest. Most people who visited did. I understood. She was young, busy, and this was a huge undertaking. I tried not to feel disappointed.

When the next email came, I expected an apologetic bowing out, so I was completely surprised to find out it was just the opposite. She was in the process of raising funds for the school and that was what was causing the delay in communication.

The following is part of her letter. English is Noémie's second language, however I am including her email as written because I love her energy:

> So when I saw that you could built a school, at this moment I knew it was my objective. My parent told me: Noémie, don't think too big, it is a lot of money etc. etc. But my idea was done: I wanted to raise enough money so you could be able to built the school.

> When I came back from Honduras the first time, it was really weird to go to my private school and see all the student not realizing the chance we have to be here and being able to study. We hear this often but when you see it it is different. I remember how I felt like a stranger while walking in the school. So I think it is the reason why I wanted so bad to raise that money. I think that the best way to fight against poverty is the education. To have access to education is the greatest thing.

> To raise the money, I did an event at the high school cafeteria after class. I had a lot of sponsor who provided the food and beverages and my friends of the trip in Honduras were voluntary for serving the dinner. I remember how surprised I was with the big amount of people present that night. During the week before, someone of the local journal did an interview on my event so a lot of people came. It was amazing! So with the event and some donation I raised enough money for the school.

If I remember correctly, she had raised almost one thousand dollars at that point. Our emails continued. She regularly reported the latest tally of funds raised. Her parents and family contributed, and she held an additional fundraising event.

A month went by and again I didn't hear from her. I tried to check in but received no response. Again, I thought she had overestimated the ease of fundraising. Then came an email apologizing for being too busy to write. Of course, I thought, she was in school and had a part-time job, and she was young and active outside of these activities. Again, I misjudged her.

The reason she was too busy? She'd taken on a second job to raise money for the school. She had held other fundraising events, such as a dinner. I was astounded to witness this amazing young woman raise the total amount needed within five months. I joked with Marel about hiring her as our fundraiser.

Meanwhile, during these months, Marel and I went to Santa Cruz to chat casually with the leaders of the community to see if they might be interested in building a school should the opportunity ever arise. We did not let on in any way that there was a strong possibility, for fear of letting people down.

As we saw evidence of Noémie's commitment through her reported tallies of fundraising, we met again with the leader, Oligario. He was a lifelong farmer in his sixties who offered us both hearty handshakes with his big, strong hand covered in blisters and sunspots. It felt like shaking hands with a sandpaper glove, and the warmth came through so strongly. I liked him immediately. He was an open, friendly man, a highly respected leader of the community. He told us he would talk to the members of the community to see if they would be willing to put in the labor to build a community school. He was sure they'd say yes.

We explained that we had the funds to buy the materials but not to pay for the entire labor, except for the salary of the head builder. His response was so positive; he said he'd call a meeting later that day with the entire village and explain the possibility of a school if folks would pitch in with labor. I was expecting a long wait for the reply, but he reported back to us almost immediately with lots of excitement in his voice that everyone was on board and extremely excited and grateful.

Santa Cruz de Rincón del Buey is a tiny community of maybe twenty-five families living along a riverbed. They grow watermelons as their main source of income, in addition to corn and beans for subsistence. I loved driving by and seeing acres of round watermelons in neat little rows, stopping at local stands, and talking with a farmer while buying ten or fifteen watermelons at a time to take to different schools. This brought a tidy profit to the vendor, as well.

It was Marel who discovered the original school as we drove by one day. It was a tiny, broken-down adobe hut with a caved-in tin ceiling, maybe four by four meters, directly next to the narrow dirt road. He stopped the truck in front and said to me, "Hey, this is a school!"

I answered, "It can't be. It must be some family's little hut."

"No, I see kids inside," he said as he flung open his squeaky car door. "Let's go in."

I was reluctant, not wanting to risk invading someone's private home, but as we left the truck and headed closer to the crumbling hut, we saw about thirty or so children of all ages stuffed inside this broken-down one-room schoolhouse. The aging adobe was crumbling inside as well as out. There were a handful of broken, unpainted desks, with kids sitting on some since there were only a couple of chairs, while others were standing in the corners holding their notebooks and pencils. The lucky ones had seats.

As we walked in, the kids jumped to their feet as best they could in that tiny, crowded space and greeted us with big smiles and a hearty *buenos días*. We returned the greeting and smiles and then introduced ourselves to the lovely teacher, Berta. She gave us "the tour," meaning that she pointed to the drawings that the kids had made to cover the damaged walls while we stood scrunched in the door jam. There was no blackboard. The floor was puddles of mud, dried in a couple of spots. Berta said that although it was very crowded, the children were not allowed to lean against the walls because the decayed adobe house was very dangerous, inhabited with life-threatening bugs called *chinches*. The sagging tin roof was full of holes, making rainy days challenging.

The only bright spots were the crayoned drawings on white paper hanging on the dark walls. I thought it was strange, though, that most of the drawings were in single colors. Berta explained that there were not enough crayons to make multicolored pictures. I made a mental note to buy an enormous quantity of crayons and colored construction paper for this school.

We had to be on our way, but we promised to return with supplies. We said our goodbyes, and again the kids jumped to their feet and gave us loud, hearty farewells.

In the truck, Marel and I talked. We were both thinking the same thing: how some day we might build a school here. We shared more excited thoughts and ideas as we drove on. My blood was boiling with excitement as I tried to think who could help us raise funds.

Little did we know that Noémie would enter the picture within a couple of months, sending the funds to our volunteer in Seattle who was in charge of collecting donations and depositing them into my account. This all happened way faster than I had expected. We were ready to build!

We set up a meeting with the mayor of the municipality and the village leaders, and we requested from the government a donation of sand and stone to help us build the foundation for the school. This was a common support that the municipality offered on building projects. The mayor agreed, and we were shocked and encouraged when he offered shovels and wheelbarrows to the village workers to clear the land and haul cement. (Then I remembered that it was election year. I made a mental note to have a list of requests ready again in four years.)

The land presented some challenges. The best area for building was on top of a giant hill to prevent flooding from the local stream. This meant delivery of materials would be a bit tough, but the residents assured us that they were strong and wouldn't mind the extra work.

A major storm came through as we began to assess the site, adding to the difficulties and leaving a portion of the road to the village impassable by any vehicle. Large trees were down, so we not only had to walk through half a mile of mud but also climb over felled trees. I was less than agile, but Marel and some villagers helped me through the tough spots. As I took a step, I lost one of my gumboots in the mud, resulting in my bare foot landing right into another mud puddle up to my knee. My helpers didn't laugh until they saw me laughing. Subsequent trips were easier, however, since the villagers spent many days clearing the tiny road.

Within a few days, the large municipality truck—as well as our trusty ol' pickup—arrived to deliver building supplies, having driven as far as we were able. Local men, women, and children met us at the end of the road and unloaded the trucks. They hauled cement blocks, bricks, and other materials on their backs and then climbed the muddy, slippery hill to reach the building site. I put in my share of hauling as well, but as I was in my late sixties, my share was more symbolic than significant. Some smaller kids met us at the bottom of the climb and pushed the blocks up the hill as if they were playing with a toy truck, with their little butts jutting out as they huffed and puffed, laughing all the way.

All we saw from the workers were smiles. Not a single complaint. Folks were so excited, and that in turn generated more excitement for us during the day of unloading and carrying materials. Enthusiasm filled the village. I had never seen such joyful workers. Smiling women brought the builders coffee and breads at break time, and we'd chat. I felt a special connection with Maria, Oligario's wife. They felt like grandparents to me, even though I was probably ten years their senior. They were accepting, warm, affectionate older people, always glad to see me.

The clearing of land at the top of the hill started the next day. Men worked in shifts and made excellent progress, leveling the land so that it was sturdy and able to support the construction. A form of steps was carved into the hill to make it a bit easier to climb, even though the mud was still a challenge. It was only a matter of days until the land was ready.

We visited several times a week during the entire process, bringing drinks and sweet breads to the workers. Marel met regularly with the head builder, Adelmo, to discuss what materials they would need to buy next and talk about any problems.

I wrote regularly to Noémie with updates and photos, and she continued to send back praise, enthusiasm, and a bit more money. She was lovely to work with. Never demanding, always appreciative and excited. She was so poised that I had to keep reminding myself that she was a teenager.

The building process was quick, revealing marked advancement on an almost daily basis. Kids who weren't working attached themselves to me and followed my every move, staring and smiling, asking questions. "Where are you from?" "Do you like beans?" "Where is your family?"

Within two months, we completed a six-by-eight-meter brick schoolhouse. I found a local artist who painted the outside of the school and bathroom in a jungle theme: coconut trees, monkeys, plants, and birds in beautiful, rich colors. She drew the designs on the outside walls and numbered each shape, turning the painting job for the artists and kids into a giant paint-by-number set. The double bathroom on the side had the same theme and colors.

There, on the top of this steep hill overlooking the river and the cornfields, safe from the frequent flooding, stood this green, brown, and sky-blue jungle school with birds and monkeys painted on the walls. Inside was melon-colored, a bright, cheerful contrast to the broken-down, dark, decayed adobe of the old school. The move was easy, just a handful of broken desks and a couple of boxes of school supplies. The beauty of having nothing was that there was nothing to move.

The inauguration followed some days afterwards. It was disappointing that Noémie could not make the long trip to attend the event, but we sent her photos. Everyone understood. It was such a long, expensive trip.

Marel and I showed up for the event in the late morning. We could hear the music and see the balloons as we approached. The kids were waiting for our arrival, and as we reached the slippery slope, we could see they were dressed in their best—albeit tattered—clothing. Berta, as always, looked stunning. Farmers also wore their best clothes.

As we reached the summit—and I was puffing from the climb—we were greeted by a giant hand-painted sign displayed by each child holding up one letter: *G R A C I A S*! Tears flooded my eyes. There were balloons everywhere: outside, inside, and even hanging from the bathroom. I tried to memorize everything so that I could fill Noémie in. We were in the middle of a hub of activity generated by this tiny community, with much talk and laughter, everyone congratulating, thanking us, and shaking our hands.

We brought a very special surprise gift for the villagers. I had taken pictures during the building process and made a large laminated mural of photos of the workers. Children and dads could see the progress of the entire project, a proud token to keep forever. As we hung it on the wall, folks rushed over to see if they could identify themselves or their friends and relatives in the photos, pointing, stomping their feet, and laughing with delight. Kids tried to find their fathers' pictures.

We drank Coca Cola and *atol* (a hot corn drink). Speeches were made. Most farmers were normally reticent, but that day—much to my surprise—flowing, poetic speeches were made as each leader stood up to speak. It was so touching to see this outpouring of joy and gratitude. I thought my heart would explode with joy.

I wanted to put my arm around Noémie and say, "Well done! Really remarkable!" but it would have to wait. Marel's speech came next, and finally mine, in broken Spanish, choking back tears of joy and gratitude for working with such wonderful people on such a worthy project made possible by such an amazing donor. A meal of chicken soup and tortillas followed, a tradition for special occasions. It was a momentous day and one of the most incredible experiences of my life.

The next morning, sleep deprived, I raced to my computer with coffee in hand and reported everything about the experience to Noémie. I forwarded her photos of the event, thanked her profusely, and told her I hoped she would come back one day soon and see the results of her absolutely amazing efforts. The villagers wanted to meet her and thank her in person.

We were thrilled that she was able to come back about a year later with her sister. We brought her to the school, where she received glowing thanks from the community. It was a lovely reunion. I told her how much this whole experience meant to me, how proud I was of her, and how inspired I was that one person could do so much to better the world. Here are Noémie's words:

> *In May and June 2011, I went back in Honduras but this time with my sister. We went to see the school. I was amaze by the beauty of the school. It was incredible to have the chance to see it. I was really happy to see that children could benefit of it. I use the occasion to tell you, Ellen, that you are the one who made this possible. You and everyone in the village. Also with the participation and donation of a lot persons. This is so great that people here wanted to help children in another country. Ellen you are amazing for everything you do everyday for all these people. I remember how you even take care of the dog! You had dog food in your pocket and when you saw a skinny dog you gave him food. The day after I went to buy dog food to do like you because I found it was amazing what you did. It is really touching me what you say about me but I don't feel to deserve it because you did all the work and still doing it today and years before. All these people are so lucky to have you!*

Because of one young girl's astonishing efforts, a transformation occurred, not just of a better, safer, lovely building, but also of an increase in the number of students who attended the school and, later, the formation of a small class for kindergartners. The teacher told us that the teaching and learning process was so much more fun, as well as more valued. She said the kids were happier, and everyone was delighted that the school had become a safe and healthy place where children could touch the walls.

One young teen made a huge difference.

Chapter 27

It was late afternoon when I heard the news. I was in my upstairs apartment overlooking the street. Everything seemed normal. Folks were going about their business, and I was listening to the radio as I washed dishes.

The news announcer suddenly interrupted the programming. There had been a coup. The announcer said that the Honduran army under the direction of Roberto Micheletti had ousted the current president, Manuel Zelaya. Soldiers had taken him out of his house in his pajamas in the middle of the night. That was all I got to hear. The electricity went out. The electricity often went out, but this time it seemed ominous. It added to the terror and uncertainty, and we had no way to get updates.

At this time, I was still living in the apartment above Elena. As I write this, I realize this chapter should've been written earlier, that this event happened pages ago. This is the problem with trauma; it throws off chronology. Big events happen outside of time and space. They break normal reality and play upon the memory. There was nothing linear about any of this, in my mind, or in the lives of the folks I lived around.

I went to talk with Elena to get her opinion. Was this true? Was this accurate? Although she was surprised and lost too, I found solace just being around her. She tried to make phone calls to her friends and family around Honduras, but the phone lines were jammed, so very little connection was available. When she was able to get through, no one seemed to know anything.

We heard bits of information through people who had arrived in Copán from Tegucigalpa, the capital. Endless questions crossed my mind. I had never experienced a coup before. *What does this mean? Are we in danger? What will happen to the country? What will happen to me? Am I in danger?*

Many people said it was supported or even initiated by American forces. (*"My" United States?*) I was able to use my cell phone and called a good friend in Canada. I reported what I knew and tried to find out if it had yet made international news. She said no, it hadn't. There I was, sort of feeling like Anderson Cooper, reporting from a country in the middle of a military takeover. *But in the middle of* what *exactly?*

The information that eventually came in was distorted, unclear. *Should I be scared?* Elena explained that there had been unrest for quite some time, a slow brewing of resentment against Zelaya by the opposing Nationalist Party. But this resentment was normal, a coup wasn't. There was always dissension and unrest no matter who was president, but Manuel Zelaya was relatively popular and viewed by many as a pretty good president and less corrupt than others. There were pieces of information in town, none of which supported the idea that the coup was initiated or even desired by the majority of citizens.

Micheletti did finally " explain" the reason for the coup, stating that Zelaya wanted to run a second consecutive term—he wanted to add an amendment and hold a vote. It was unconstitutional.

Clearly, Micheletti's explanation was a "presented reason" but not really what was going on. My personal suspicions were that Zelaya was starting to ally strongly with President Chavez of Venezuela and that scared people in North America, specifically in the White House. They wouldn't want socialism creeping up through their southern neighbors.

Within a day or so, the electricity came back and everyone was glued to their TVs. Since Spanish was my second language,

I struggled to understand what was going on. People were clearly upset in Copán, but riots and protests started to appear in the larger cities. Soldiers used gas and firearms, and beat protesters with clubs while most of us sat helpless in front of our TV screens, crying. It was horrendous to watch. Aside from the violence and emotional reactions were the practical new realities of living in Honduras. Daily life changed. Fear and uncertainty abounded.

The new acting president's first policy was to issue a countrywide curfew. The word *curfew* frightened me. Questions continued to flood my mind. *Is the situation that bad? Are we that much at risk? Is it the same risk in small towns as the cities?*

Then came exceptions, which contradicted the seriousness of the situation. For example, curfew hours on the nights of soccer matches were extended to midnight. We all had to be home by 6:00 p.m., except on Thursday nights. I was confused and admittedly amused. Amidst protests and violence we were still able to attend soccer games? Did this mean that folks could riot after 6:00 p.m. on Thursdays?

Foreigners left the country immediately. Shortly after, the Peace Corp pulled out, as well as CUSO, a Canadian aid organization. It seemed like I was one of the few North American individuals remaining in Copán. I had no intention of leaving. This was my home. I was with people I loved. When friends and neighbors asked me if I would be leaving, my answer was always no.

The US government posted a travel warning about Honduras. Tourism stopped. So did the tourism business. So did other businesses. As businesses failed, so did the economy, which was already in horrendous shape. Within a few weeks, our beautiful town turned into a ghost town, except for the dramatic presence of police and the battalions of young soldiers who were not yet old enough to shave.

Truckloads of both were everywhere. Patrolling what? This was a quiet little tourist town, recently emptied of tourists and replaced by a half-dozen soldiers on every corner in full combat uniforms with automatic weapons. I asked one soldier, who looked to be about fourteen years old and definitely not old enough to shave,

"Aren't you hot, dear, in all that heavy gear, standing in the sun?" I wanted to take him home for a meal. He told me he came from central Honduras and had never been away from his village and family; he missed them a lot.

No one, even after months, seemed to have a clear idea of what was going on or why, although there was quite a bit of speculation. Meanwhile, I proceeded as normal, doing projects in the communities, cooking my lunch, buying what few groceries were available, trying to help folks in the villages find at least temporary work. Most construction projects in town were suspended. Hospitality employees were laid off in scores. Shops closed. People didn't want to spend their money. Recession became depression.

I would go to our park, which had previously buzzed with activity, with tourists taking pictures, villagers meeting and talking, women selling their homemade wares. Now it was dead. No one was there but police and the regular starving street dogs, whom I continued to feed as the police watched me and laughed.

One day, I ran into my friend Leonides in the park. I loved this man. A true Christian, as many referred to him. He was a construction worker who did projects like building and repairing houses and hotels, or dealing with whatever needed fixing. (In Copán, everything needed fixing!) He was a strikingly handsome, strong man with a lovely, hard-working wife and nine children, one of whom was a newborn. He used to walk the hour into town every day to his job site, often carrying heavy materials or tools. He loved work and prided himself on the fact that he was a good, steady worker who did an excellent job. His average salary was about four dollars per day. He lived in a two-room adobe shack, with eight boys sleeping on the floor and the baby girl in the only bed, along with him and his wife. They also cultivated corn and beans. His eight boys helped in the fields after school. In spite of Leonides' poverty and his crushing workload, he would volunteer his time and expertise at the school in his village, doing repairs, building shelves, or helping with whatever was requested by the teachers.

I knew him and his family well. We had taken his twelve-year-old son to the hospital after an awful machete accident where he severed his fingers and some toes. We had taken his wife to the clinic the night she went into a complicated labor with her ninth child. (Her husband carried her halfway down the mountain in his arms where we finally met up with them.) We had helped his oldest son with grants so he could go to high school. I used to play soccer with his younger boys. I loved this family.

When I ran into him sitting on the park bench, his head was lowered. It occurred to me that I had never seen him sitting down before or without a beaming smile, and the sight disturbed me. After our standard handshake and greeting, I asked him how he was doing.

His head still hanging, he said, "I have lost my job. People don't want to hire anyone unless it is necessary, for fear of not having enough money to pay. I have been looking everywhere for even a small project."

I couldn't bear to see him this way. "How are you getting by with so many children and no work?"

"Beans are almost ready to be picked," he said, "and meanwhile we will eat tortillas and salt."

"I have a little work and need your help, but it will only be a few hours per week. I need help delivering, on foot, large quantities of beans and corn to schools." Since the government had stopped providing school lunches, I had decided to contribute what beans and corn I could to some of my favorite schools, and I needed transportation. I preferred using him to taking a tuk-tuk.

A few days a week, Leonides carried between fifty and seventy-five pounds of food staples up the mountain to deliver to each community school, and I paid him per trip. Sometimes his older son helped out. Both of them always appeared to be in a good mood and smiling. He must have thanked me on about ten different occasions for the work. The work helped some but didn't solve the problem. He needed ongoing work to support his whole family, as well as for his self-esteem as a provider, but at least there was some income for the basics.

In contrast to the desperation of local workers, there were the ridiculous effects of the takeover. In addition to the Thursday night game freedoms, we experienced other inconsistencies.

In the midst of national violence and local uncertainty, my friend Telma and I had birthdays that fell on the same date. We decided to hold a joint afternoon birthday party at her *posada* (hotel). A small group of us gathered to eat cake and drink beverages. As we enjoyed the late afternoon, we lost track of time and evening fell. We looked up to see, standing at the front entrance, five soldiers holding weapons. The leader said, " Excuse me, it is after curfew. You all must go home now."

"Of course," I said, "but first come have some cake."

The soldiers said eagerly, "Yes, thank you," and filed in. They sat and put their weapons aside as we brought each of them a big slice. Their formal demeanor changed as each one started wolfing down his cake.

The soldiers finished their tasty treats, but by then it was about 7:00 p.m., way after curfew. The leader said, "Sorry to break up the party, but you will have to leave and return to your homes."

I pointed out, "We can't leave because we'd be out past curfew and we'll get in trouble."

Everyone laughed. The leader decided that we would pair up. Each soldier would walk one of us home. (I was assigned the cutest one!)

"Thank you for the cake," the soldiers chimed. "Happy birthday to both of you!"

They escorted us down the deserted street. We paired up with our personal escorts and went our separate ways.

During this period of many months before the official election, there was a dramatic decline in prosperity. Since there was no tourism at that point, there was no commerce in our town or other tourist towns. There was an increase in crime, particularly robberies, which became bolder as time went on. They started to occur in the daytime on public streets, in spite of the heavy police presence. This mainly occurred, in my opinion, because the police drove around in pickup trucks with their automatic weapons—seven or eight officers to a truck—leaving many places unattended. Also, many robberies took place on the roads to the villages where police hardly ever went.

In the bigger cities, there were still ongoing protests and violence against the protesters. Every night we would watch the news, seeing the protesters being gassed and beaten by the police, and our hearts would sink. I remember sitting on Elena's sofa with her and some others, just feeling so helpless, with tears coming down our cheeks. Here I was, watching these people who I had come to love, people who I considered sweet, caring folks, suddenly at war among themselves.

In spite of constant protests and attacks by the police, the resistance continued. Within months, a new president was installed. Pepe Lobo. Everyone seemed to know that he was a major *narcotraficante* and that he was robbing the government coffers. It was obvious that the election was rigged, although it was supposedly monitored by the US and declared fair.

The protests, attacks, and murders continued under Lobo. Honduras spiraled downward. Teachers weren't paid; doctors and nurses weren't paid. Clinics were closing from lack of funds. Grocery shops were running out of certain types of food. Hamburger and Kleenex were not available and considered luxury items.

As I explained earlier in the book, in Honduras, there were separate voting places where the Nationalists would vote at one place, the Liberals at another. I passed many polling places on voting day. Men stood the required twenty-five yards away from the entrances of the Liberal voting areas with their hands on their holstered guns, staring down the people who entered. Some gave out whispered messages to the voters as they tried to go in.

Because of this voting system, everyone knew whom one another had voted for. Since many teachers were Liberals, they were all fired immediately from their jobs and replaced by Nationalists who were not necessarily teachers. They were housewives, salesgirls, and local people who really had no interest in teaching. Communities that resisted these changes were threatened with lack of government support or, worse, physical danger.

One of my favorite village leaders, Modesto, was the skinniest and quietest man I had ever met. When I first met him, he was fixing his roof. I was sure that because he was so skinny and his shirt was so oversized he would take off in the air like a kite. This man was so quiet and humble. My first impression was that he couldn't be an effective leader of a community. Why did they vote him in?

217

One day, without warning, four municipal government officials came to his community school in Malcote with two "teachers" (Nationalists, of course) to replace the two (Liberals) who had worked there for eight years. The students loved their teachers and so did the community. The officials tried to physically remove the instructors while the children screamed and cried; some of the little ones even tried to punch the officials to make them let go.

Modesto showed up within minutes of their arrival with an organized group from the community to push out the four intruders and block their re-entrance. Modesto told them he would not permit the removal of these teachers. Although furious, the officials left, but threatened to come back with force, if necessary.

My friend Suyapa was one of the teachers. She later told me that Modesto and the villagers told the authorities, "If you continue to insist on replacing our great teachers with these folks who have no experience, we will not send our children to school." Although attendance in school was required by law, it was never enforced.

The community won. The government temporarily backed off. The Liberal teachers ultimately finished their year with the children, but sadly the next year they were replaced by lethargic, unmotivated Nationalists with no experience. The students in Malcote all but lost their opportunity for education, as did an enormous amount of children elsewhere in Honduras.

* * *

Two years later, another president was elected, setting a national record of four presidents in six years. Each president blamed the problems and empty coffers on the previous president. No one believed them, and the country remained in chaos.

Chapter 28

amara, an excellent counselor in the United States, has been my friend and colleague for years. Many friends often told me I was giving them emotional whiplash when I reported on the extreme ups and downs of my daily life, and consequently I learned to spread my tales and my emotions among different people. This is an excerpt of a letter to her, and it explains a typical day for me in Copán:

Dear Tamara,

How are you doing? Thanks for asking again about my life here. In one word, unpredictable. Here's just a little description of my day yesterday.

I woke at 4:00 a.m. deciding to put Sparky to sleep today if I could. I think I told you about him; he was the dying, emaciated old dog that I saw in the street every day curled up in a tight ball. Lately he wasn't even eating the food I gave him, so I finally asked Tulio to help me bring him home to die at least safely and somewhat comfortably. Even though he is off the street now and safe at my house, I didn't realize how much he was suffering. I woke up early as usual and went outside to see him. He was way sicker yesterday morning, smelling of rotting flesh and street filth. When I saw him he was curled up in a ball, barely moving, so I thought okay, today's the day I put him to sleep, and crying, I thought about the hideous options. There is no vet here. When I approached him, he wagged his tail. That really threw me! How can I kill a dog who is wagging his tail at me? I decided to wait a while and do some work at home on the internet.

Marel called about an hour later, at 6:00 a.m., saying he was in the El Jaral clinic with a sick boy that he brought there who needed to get to the Guatemala hospital ASAP. He needed money for gas. It is a three-hour trip, but there was no hospital closer. I wrestled with this thought for a few minutes. The bank account was close to empty, but with some phone calls to local friends I managed to borrow some gas money, got it to Marel, and he was on his way. I tried to resume my work, but depression kept creeping into my thought process. Hard to try and raise money when depressed. The biggest factor is the continued grief and disgust from the slaying of the family in Nueva Estanzuela that I told you about. It was apparently some kind of revenge thing that is so common here. I have been working with this village for almost two years now and the people there are special to me. Anyway, the depression was starting to overcome me and my trying to work was useless, so I decided to walk into town for a break.

Ran into Augustin, a teacher who had lost his job due to the political system here. He told me that his wife was just taken to the emergency room in Guatemala, waiting for surgery. "Something internal," he said, looking down at his shoes. Men here never seem to know about women's issues. This conversation did not lift my depression, needless to say, and it left me feeling so helpless, but I carried on after we finished talking.

Within minutes, I ran into a high-school student who is on a grant with us. He came over to me in the street, telling me his studies were going well, but he needed a special calculator. I wanted to help out, but I just didn't have the fifteen dollars, and it would take time to contact his sponsors. I told him I'd do what I could do and would be in touch. Meanwhile, I asked him if he could borrow one from a classmate and then pitch in a bit towards the cost of the calculator. He said he could try. He is such a sweet, shy kid, and I know how hard it is for him to ask for anything extra.

I was thinking about Heber, you remember him, who was still in the hospital waiting for a tube that'd be inserted in his head before they could do surgery and how much more money would they need. And for him, it was probably a matter of life and death, so a calculator was less of a priority.

The sense of responsibility is crushing, Tamara. I know I can't solve everything, but how do I say no to small requests? Buenos Vecinos's budget is tapped out. We are always down to the wire, but I personally could help. I'm not rich but I do have credit cards, friends, and connections. I still wrestle with how much do I need to/have to do here. How and when do I set limits? It's agony sometimes to refuse a simple request.

To add to this feeling of overwhelm, yesterday I saw a box in the grocery store with info and a picture pleading for help for a darling eight-year-old boy in the hospital, his stomach and legs crushed by a falling tree. I walked away, obsessing about this little boy lying in the hospital while his family was frantically looking for donations. Having seen this beautiful boy's picture made it even more personal in my mind.

Buenos Vecinos's medical emergency fund didn't have the $625 for the surgery. That amount was way over our usual donation. I kept weighing in my mind, how could I afford this, asking myself what could I afford. I called *my assistant, Yarely, to call the aunt, who lived locally (the mom was with the boy in Guatemala), and found out that the family was frantically searching for help, including going to other municipalities begging for money. They had already collected a large part.*

Still wrestling with whether to help or how much to give, I became even more upset, depressed, anxious, and kept saying to myself, "Not my problem, I have enough on my plate." Yarely, who always has great advice, suggested that if I gave them fifty dollars, that would help further motivate the family. A good compromise, I thought. I decided that BV could afford that, borrowed a bit more money from a friend, and gave Yarely the money to give to the aunt.

At noon, I called the aunt myself and found out they had raised thousands more lempiras through their friend who was a host of the radio station. It was still not enough, but only lacked about fifty more dollars (in addition to our fifty dollars) to pay for the treatment. My friend Amy pitched in, and I personally pitched in a bit of my own cash and ran downtown to the radio station to meet up with the aunt.

The moment I saw her, I knew it was the right thing to do. I had doubts since we hadn't yet met in person, but I had an immediate gut feeling that she was sincere. She was a very small woman (Aunt Lucia) dressed very humbly in a black polyester skirt and shiny red polyester top. We hugged each other, thanking each other for valiant efforts, talking about the boy. I brought some toys and puzzles for the boy to play with. Hospitals here are pretty grim. I think this might have been the single most gratifying act I had done up to that point, completely inspired by the tremendous efforts of this family. We said our goodbyes and she promised to stay in touch. She wanted me to meet him.

In the meantime during all this, I was trying to remember that I needed to buy iced tea and get to the pharmacy to do a few more mundane tasks. How crazy is this big vs. small thing? And how powerful and how powerless I could feel all at the same time.

I came home exhausted. I dragged myself through my gate, and Tamara, there was Sparky standing up and walking towards me with his head erect for the first time, wagging his tail. I couldn't believe it! The joy was the perfect anti-dote for my weariness, but I felt like I had lived a month in this short time.

And it was only 1:30 in the afternoon!

* * *

I struggled often with the issue of power and powerlessness. Because I came from a childhood of privilege and relative safety, with a great education and a relatively steady income, I had so much available to me. I didn't want to squander the gifts I had been given in this lifetime. But days like this? How could I keep up? Did I just look the other way?

Honduras needed help. It had become a failed state. As a result, we had failed parents, failed business owners, failed students. The medical and educational system was failing.

I was failing.

Chapter 29

It always came down to the individual for me. I was working by then in more than eighty communities, dealing with the larger issues but always completely moved by the stories of the individuals. Especially relating to the children. It was getting to be an impossible balance dealing with the macro and micro issues that I witnessed.

Trini's early childhood was a blur. Unnoticed by most. Uncared for by his parents, he was always dressed in dirty rags and often shoeless. He was a handsome boy with piercing brown eyes that showed an entire range of emotion. He, however, was mostly silent. A smile was extremely rare.

He lived in an adobe and brick house that looked like it had been demolished in some kind of holocaust—broken pieces of brick everywhere, steps that were no longer steps, rubble. One had to jump up to enter the house. The only furniture was a broken bed with a torn piece of foam for a mattress. No blanket. It was dark inside. The walls were covered with soot from the cooking fire outside; smoke had entered through the only window, making it even darker.

His dad was mostly gone but would come home occasionally to drink beer using the food money and to beat his sons when he was drunk. His mother was hardly around. No one knew where she was.

There was never food in the house. Trini and his brothers did not eat every day.

Trini didn't go to school. Although extremely bright, he dropped out in the third grade, apparently because of behavior problems and lack of concentration. Malnutrition fogged his mind. Rage fueled his acting out. He went to the church for the children's food program twice a week, where he could have a meal, companionship, and spiritual support. His pastor took him under his wing, guided him, replaced some of his shabby clothes and shoes with those that his son had outgrown, and replaced his lack of values with moral direction.

Still, Trini struggled to survive. Too proud to ask for help, too desperate to refuse any, he sometimes allied with boys who were not good for him. Boys looking for trouble. In spite of this, Trini was always polite, thankful, and appreciative of those who bestowed a bit of support such as food, odd jobs, and second-hand clothing.

He longed for a mother and father and attached himself quickly to the pastor and his wife, and to anyone else who would notice him. Sometimes he sat on their porch waiting for them to wake up in the morning. Maybe he even slept there.

Although he was able to find short-term work doing odd jobs, there was nothing regular for him in his small town. There wasn't much work for anyone, but when he did receive a little money for a job, he would immediately run to the grocery store and buy food for his brother and himself.

He had a friend named Heber. Heber was younger by a couple of years and had the same family conditions, but Heber was also blind. He spent most of his days lying on the house bed, except when Trini would take him out. It was no easy task for a young boy to lead a younger blind boy through the rubble and trash of their *barrio*. Trini always had his arm around Heber's gaunt body and guided him to safety where they could sit on a rock and talk or eat a piece of food gifted by a neighbor.

Trini, with the help of the pastor, did find some employment in a restaurant when he was about thirteen. He worked there for many months until the restaurant closed due to lack of customers.

He was an eager worker and a quick learner. His demeanor changed upon employment, especially when he was able to buy some new clothes for the first time in his life. He was eating regularly. He was working and proud. He smiled.

Unfortunately, when the job ended, so did his joy, and he returned to walking the streets, kicking cans, and not eating every day.

The pastor and his wife did not give up on him, nor did a couple of other supportive adults in his life. These people became his parents. His life, however, was still a struggle; he did not always make good choices. Trini did go back to school, but not exactly by choice. When he turned fourteen, he was sent to juvenile detention because he was at the wrong place at the wrong time with the wrong kids. The judge eventually found him innocent, but during the nearly three years in detention, he at least received a decent education.

Upon leaving "juvie," he reconnected with the people who cared for him. His young life continues to be a struggle, but he has managed to finish grade school and to learn some healthy values. In spite of the challenging start of his life, he has found a temporary job and has become an appreciative young man who wants to grow and be a good person. There are a lot of challenges that continue for this young man. Hopefully he has the skills and opportunities to face them and succeed.

Chapter 30

I didn't know how to write this chapter. I still don't. It has been and continues to be a painful and hideous subject in Honduras. Flashbacks and nightmares haunt me. *Do I spare the reader the horrific details of what I've seen and experienced? Do I gloss over it with generalities?* I've decided to try to explain this situation limiting many graphic details but still showing the real picture.

Poverty, neglect, cruelty, and abandonment destroyed the lives of dogs in Honduras. In a society where there is severe poverty, oppression, depression, and repression it was not unusual to see the neglect and abuse of animals. In my years in Honduras, I saw more than my fair share and it weighed extremely heavily on my mind.

I saw endless numbers of dogs starving to the point of death, beaten, kicked, and run over without even an attempt to avoid them, left in the streets screaming in pain. I still have flashbacks and flinch every time I see a man with a machete near a dog or a car in the road approaching a dog. I still have nights when I don't sleep, haunted by all that I have witnessed.

Starving dogs came down from the villages into town in the hopes of finding food. Since families in the villages couldn't find enough food for their children, the dogs were not even on the priority list.

Spaying and neutering would be an obvious solution to the problem, but the municipality's response to controlling street dogs was and still is a monthly poisoning. They hire a couple of men to go around at night and throw meat laced with poison from a truck and then return a couple of hours later to collect the bodies. Since there was a bounty on each dead dog, many who were in their own yards or sitting on their own stoops were also poisoned. Many a time I had kids coming to my house sobbing, saying, "Doña Elena, they killed my dogs." The municipality denied any involvement in this, but everyone knew.

I was an early riser and would often be in the park just as the sun was coming up. One day, as I came down the hill and into the park, I saw a pile of about eight dead dogs. There was a dog near the pile that was having convulsions, foaming at the mouth, body jerking in the air, in the throes of death. I felt such horror and helplessness. There was nothing I could do. Sobbing, I ran back up the hill to my house and paced back and forth for quite a while, trying to get the vision out of my mind. It took days for me to only partially recover, and still to this day the vision remains burned into my mind.

Several of my own dogs were poisoned as well, bringing me tremendous heartbreak and fear. Even when dogs like mine were kept inside a gate, sometimes a malicious or annoyed neighbor would throw poisoned meat into the yard, maybe because the dog was barking too much or leaving the yard and relieving itself near a neighbor's house. Because the town officials did this, the average person didn't seem to give a second thought about also doing it.

I could not even count the number of dogs I witnessed being run over by a car, including some of my own—sights burned into my brain forever. There were occasions when I'd see a car coming and would run screaming to the driver, "Stop! Stop!" I'd be too late. I'd witness a dog being crushed or at least seriously injured, while their screams left indelible echoes in my mind. I couldn't integrate the casual indifference in my mind. People I loved. Animal treatment I detested.

Cruelty on the street towards dogs was something I would never get over. I remember incidents where, after witnessing a horror, I would take to my bed crying, depressed, or worse: numbed and paralyzed. I tried to rescue as many as possible, and at one point even had a small shelter for four or five at a time, but that was a drop in the bucket.

Fortunately, there were other dog lovers in town who also helped our canine friends in a major way, providing shelter, medicine, food and sometimes even a good home. Often they were foreigners.

Two of my nurse friends, who were a married couple, did an extraordinary job taking in emergency cases of illness or injury. They had a space on the top floor of their restaurant where dogs could receive medical care and lodge temporarily, and connecting with them helped keep me sane.

There was no sterilization opportunity in town, not even a veterinarian. There were a couple of places where one could buy dog food and basic medicines, but that was the limit of professional help. On occasion, a brigade from the city or from a foreign country would come to our aid to do sterilizations. It was often coordinated by my nurse friends and required an enormous amount of planning and work. It was extremely helpful but relied on outsiders who weren't always available. Most dogs had babies every six months, most of whom died via starvation, being run over, or through illness.

Since most people could not afford vaccinations, many dogs died of distemper. Seeing dogs in the streets with distemper or severe mange, knowing that they would have a slow, painful death, made me crazy. I did what I could but felt so helpless. I am a tremendous dog lover, and seeing them suffer in any way tore me apart. Also, during the blazing heat of summer seasons, dogs would desperately search for water, often with little luck. In addition to carrying food with me, I also brought along water bottles, pouring water into my hand. If the dog was brave enough, it would come forward and lap up a bit of liquid. Seeing dogs kicked was so painful. Often I would say something like, "Dogs, like humans, are creations of God." Since most people were religious, I was hoping that would have at least some impact on their thinking and behavior.

Seeing sick, starving puppies was the hardest for me to endure. Often I'd grab them and take them home, hoping to find a home for them. Sometimes I was lucky.

It was often comical, I'm sure, to see dogs following me in the street, usually in hopes for food. If a female in heat happened to be following me, she would be followed by all these "interested" males. This would lead to a virtual parade with me in the lead, followed by often as many as ten dogs.

I had a sweet, wiggly neighbor dog, Gaviota, a large white dog with brown patches who used to come for breakfast. She'd wait outside my gate early in the mornings until I woke up and would go crazy with excitement, jumping in circles and wagging her tail when she saw me. When I let her in, she would immediately bound to my back porch and wolf down the kibble and scraps of breakfast that I prepared, her tail wildly spinning.

She often came by during the day, as well. It wasn't always about food; it was also about safety, comfort, and—most of all—love. When she was inside my gate, she'd nestle onto my welcome mat, look at me, and wag her tail every time I passed by. When there were holidays, which always included firecrackers all day long, I'd let her into my yard. She'd bolt, tail tucked, to the back porch to spend the day and night. The next morning, I'd send her back home. The owners were grateful since they had no way to protect her, although in the mornings she wouldn't want to go home. I had to push her large body from behind, through my porch, across my yard, to the gate, and finally out. This annoying and sad effort would take about fifteen minutes. I would have loved to keep her. I loved her but couldn't keep someone else's dog. Even if I offered to buy her, they'd replace her with another dog who would be in the same sad situation.

She lived with a very poor family, parents and a teenage son who lived in a house made of pieces of tin and plastic. Although they loved her, her "shelter" was a tiny piece of rusted aluminum with holes in it, wedged onto the side of a muddy hill. She was always wet and shaking from the cold.

Gaviota had puppies every six months; most of them starved to death, were run over, or just disappeared. She had about forty-five puppies during the time I knew her (until she was also run over), but her family told me she'd had many litters before then. It was so upsetting to see her pregnant each time. I did my best to help the family find good homes for the pups, but not with much success. Occasionally I would find a home or two for some of a litter, but I had no idea what the outcome of these situations would be. I screened potential owners and did my best, and I hoped for successful placements.

We settled for a pattern where I became Gaviota's second mom, feeding her well, and giving her meds when needed and lots of love.

* * *

Pam was male; don't ask me how he got that name. He was a legend in town. Everyone knew him. We'd see him everywhere, showing up in a village and walking with a family towards town. We'd see him in a restaurant, usually being ushered out but sneaking back in again. We'd see him in the park with some foreigner who was treating him to a snack. He could "work the park" like no other dog, a great schmoozer.

Pam had a part-time job at our local health clinic. Or so he thought. He used to follow my friend Anne, who worked there, and would sit in the waiting room with patients or under a nurse's desk. He was continually ushered out, but the front door remained open, which seemed to indicate to Pam that he was welcome. Finally the staff gave up, and he was considered part of the team. He worked mornings.

I loved this dog. Little brown beagle mix. He'd follow me everywhere when he'd see me and wait for me when I went into stores or sit with me when I was at a restaurant. He even came to my Spanish classes with me. I thought he was more or less my dog. That is, until I found out that many people thought he was their dog. Pam got around!

He had his favorite restaurant where he often ate and slept. The owners also thought of him as their dog, and the staff loved and cared for him as well.

One day, I received an awful call from the owner of Pam's favorite restaurant. Pam had been run over. Hit and run. The staff heard the screams, rushed out to the street, and called the owners of the restaurant who fortunately were both nurses. They came immediately and were able to scoop him up, bring him inside, and give him pain meds.

He was in bad shape. His hind legs torn, crushed, bleeding, and rendered useless. Anne Marie called to get my thoughts about whether we should put him down or try to keep him alive and treat him as best we could. He most likely would never walk again. This was a horrible decision to have to make, and I wanted them to take it out of my hands. There wasn't much time to ponder this. He was suffering. If Pam had been "just a street dog" I would have said yes to putting him down, but since he was a legend in Copán and so many people loved him, I suggested they try and save him. Since he would most likely not be able to walk again, that meant no more living on the street. I had a house with a fenced-in yard and told them that I would take him if they could treat him.

For over a month, Pam was in their intensive care, living on the top floor of the restaurant. My friends changed his bandages regularly, fed him, loved him. The waitresses gave him love and nurturing, and I visited him twice a day. In spite of heavy pain medicine, he sometimes howled during the cold nights, and we questioned my decision to keep him alive.

He did get stronger, and eventually a veterinarian friend of the couple, who lived in Guatemala, came to see Pam. He checked for internal injury, but without access to X-rays, there was little he could do. There were no surgical or medical supplies in town, so he made a makeshift cast for one of the legs, with pieces of Kotex for inside padding, wire and a stick for a brace, and then wrapped it in bandages and a sock to cover it. We would have to wait to see if his leg would respond.

The other leg was extremely bent, and his lower joint was hanging. There was no hope for that one, but internally he seemed okay. He was stable but would probably not walk again.

A month later it became time for "the move." I'll never forget the scene of the four-by-four truck pulling up to my house and Pam being carried in by my friend as her husband brought out a suitcase filled with meds, pads, and other necessities. Prince Pam. The contrast to how other dogs were treated was hysterical. This little doggie had attendants waiting on him and moving him to his beautiful new home while I prepared his "space." The only dog in Honduras with a suitcase.

Pam was not an easy adjustment for me. He was willful and stubborn and didn't seem to know that he couldn't walk. He kept biting off the bandages at night, trying to get out the front gate when it was open by pulling with his front paws and dragging his hind legs. When he wasn't trying to go into the street, he would try to come into my house. He thought he was an indoor dog. The accident also left him incontinent, so I wasn't eager to have him inside for long periods of time. We had many power struggles, most of which he won. How did he get to be the alpha?

He became an indoor and outdoor dog, attending my house meetings with teachers and village leaders to request help. He would supervise workers who came to fix my oven or repair a window, keeping a steady eye until they finished. He always had work to do.

Often his social life was better than mine. Visitors from the restaurant and many other friends dropped by to see him. Although he remained badly crippled, he never seemed to know it. Even "lady dogs" would show interest. Pam was with me many years and lived a full life. He never knew he was handicapped.

* * *

Pam was one of the fortunate ones. Unfortunately, thousands and thousands of dogs had no care, living on the streets or in the woods of Honduras. Some cities had a spaying and neutering clinic, but the odds against receiving help were daunting.

It's my continual hope that the dogs and other animals living in Honduras receive medical attention, spaying and neutering, and good homes. Unfortunately, I am not optimistic due to the lack of funds, the lack of education about animals, and the lack of sponsored programs.

Chapter 31

I ran into my young friend Danilo in the park. I saw some of his family nearby, as well. "How are you doing, Danilo?" I asked.

"*Mas o menos* (so-so)," he answered.

The standard answer is usually, "Fine, thank you," no matter what the circumstance, so I knew something wasn't right. "What's the good part of *mas o menos*?" I asked.

"I'm glad to be with my family again after a long separation for my education."

I asked, "And what's the not-so-good part of *mas o menos*?"

"My brother was murdered yesterday," he said, his face blank.

"What??? What happened? Which brother?" I was trying to understand. This was regarded as "so-so"?

His mother was standing nearby, trying not to cry. At least there was emotion coming from her. I ran over with tears in my eyes, saying, "I'm so sorry. I'm so, so sorry." I had known this young family for years and naturally assumed they would be intact for many more.

Trauma was part of daily life in Hondurans. It wasn't hidden. People experienced losses, threats, animal cruelty, severe illness, injury, and premature death on almost a daily basis. Murder was not uncommon and rarely a shock when people heard about it or even experienced it with a close family member. People were sad, but there seemed to me an unnerving acceptance, a taking for granted of crime, of illness, of untimely death. Some parents lost as many as six children due to illness, starvation, accidents, or murder.

It was not uncommon to experience revenge murders, certainly within the drug world, but also between communities. I heard many Hatfield and McCoy stories where someone killed the father and revenge was taken out against the killer's children. Individual gravesites were scattered throughout the mountains. Tuk-tuk drivers would casually tell me a gruesome story as we'd pass a tiny pink or blue cross on top of a mound of dirt. Often it was a child's grave.

One day, Marel called to tell me there had been a truck passing through a mountain village and someone had wanted revenge on the driver who had "done something bad." Incidents were always explained with this kind of vagueness. Not only was the driver shot and killed, but all but one of the innocent passengers riding in the back, including a woman and her baby were also killed. The only survivor was Agripino, a young *campesino* (farmer), shot five times in the stomach but still alive.

We had been working quite a bit with his village and were acquainted with the people involved. We went up the next morning to meet with Agripino's wife, children, and mother. The head teacher from the community was waiting to help guide us through the brush since there was no path.

My first sight was Agripino's wife and three filthy children. She must have had some other kind of trauma because her affect was strange, almost robotic. Her eyes were glazed over as if she was staring at a fire. She didn't speak but had a haunting fake smile. Roxana told us that his wife had been "that way" for many years, but no one knew the cause.

We asked her if we could come up and talk with her and see how we could help. She didn't respond, but Agripino's mom came forward and yelled down yes. Roxana grabbed my hand to help me climb up the rocks and led us to the shack made of sticks and mud. I knew the mother and gave her a brief hug. The small children were playing recklessly around the campfire as I nervously watched in case I had to jump up and grab them if they fell.

I expected Agripino to be in the hospital, but, much to my surprise, he was home in his hammock with bloodstains on his old shirt. His eyes were glazed over, seeming to stare at nothing. Apparently, Roxana told us, the local doctor had removed only two of the bullets and left the other three lodged in his stomach because they were too delicately placed to remove in a doctor's office. The family didn't have money to take him to the hospital. I asked Agripino's mother what would happen if they didn't remove the bullets. She said, "He'll probably die." No affect.

We tried to talk with Agripino, but he mostly lay there staring and grimacing. Silent. I decided that we would leave things as they were for a day or two until we could get more information, but in the meantime we would send up food for the family. There was no food in the shack. No money.

Through the efforts of Marel, his father, and their churches, enough money was collected for treatment at the hospital. They continued to raise funds, and among us we were able to buy some food, clothing, and firewood during what would be a long recovery. Marel's dad was even able to get some toys donated for the small children. We pitched in with follow-up doctor visits, medicines, and food.

Agripino slipped into a serious depression and wouldn't talk. Every visit, we'd see him in the hammock (there was no bed). This went on for a couple of months. He had no will to talk or leave the hammock, and certainly not to work. This meant that his crop would die. Eventually, after several months and continued doctor visits, he was finally starting to get up and move around, and ultimately went back to the fields to work. Still, though, he was silent. I would see him in the fields from time to time on our visits, and he'd respond to my wave with a minimal hand gesture, but no more. We remained connected with his family, and so did the churches.

During all of this time, there was no outward expression of concern or emotion by any of his family members. I couldn't interpret this. Was it something they didn't feel or a manner of affect accumulated over years of sorrows, crises, and problems?

This story was not unusual, as I gradually experienced over my years in Honduras. There was a constant lack of affect regarding general crises from people that continually astounded me. *Don't they care? Are they just overwhelmed and numb?* I was appalled, frustrated, confused. There was poor communication, denial of feelings and thoughts, and a constant replacement of any emotion by quoting the bible. In fact, there was very little conversation that didn't include constant bible quotes. No one ever said words that I was used to: "How awful for you." "How are you doing?" "How can I help?" Rage was almost always pushed aside. Fear also. Often expressions of sadness were diminished too. *Why is this?* As a former psychotherapist who spent years helping people access their feelings, I tried to understand what caused so many people to shut down when it came down to expressions of deeper emotions.

I carried the energy, picking up their lack of reaction and feeling it myself—outrage, fear, hurt, disappointment, anger, shock, overwhelm, anxiety, grief. People must have thought I was crazy, the overemotional gringa, always emoting.

I learned that in Honduras lack of affect was normal for people who had experienced a lot of trauma, and since trauma was so common, most people responded this way. It was a kind of dissociation or disconnection from the self, a protection mechanism meant to shield a person from feelings that they were unable to process. Because I am a very sensitive person, it was easy for me take on other people's feelings. My energetic boundaries were not strong, and consequently I felt everything—things I wanted to let in and feel, but also things I didn't necessarily want to feel.

I once heard a story about a child who was chopped up with a machete, and the folks who told me about it were numb while I was screaming inside. They grew up with this. I did not. When I first started hearing about these kinds of stories, I flashed back to news that I'd hear in the US about drive-by shootings in the inner cities and then flash forward to the stories of mass shootings. These young schoolkids in the US lost their family members, neighbors, friends, and schoolmates. I would remember how horrified I used to be. I'd watch the news and feel so terrible for the survivors and so helpless. But I also remembered that they cried, screamed, expressed their grief. They had support from families or professional groups, teachers. In Honduras there was silence often followed by a bible quote, and private tears. Crime, death, pain, disaster, and crisis were the norm. It was too dangerous to speak out. Folks could get killed if someone didn't like what was said. Protesters and activists were murdered during demonstrations or later assassinated in their homes. *Narcos* or gang members would kill enemies, but also neighbors would kill neighbors. There was no safety, which meant that folks couldn't let themselves be vulnerable.

I noticed that as the years went on I also was becoming hardened to the accounts of misery and loss. My affect was changing, too. That frightened me. I heard myself calmly say things like, "He'll probably die." Eventually, I almost completely stopped crying. Crises often occurred back to back with no time to grieve. I also eventually stopped talking about these incidents to my Western friends. It was too much for them to bear, and they would be mad at me for not leaving Honduras and finding a safe, more comfortable place to live. I had nowhere to go with this energy. I certainly couldn't complain to Hondurans how hard this was for me. They lived this! They had no means of escape and they always lived in fear of retaliation.

Once, the streetlights and the windows were shot out of my neighbor's house and the glass crashed down on my tin roof. I was lying in my hammock on the back porch as pieces of glass fell onto me and the floor. No one came outside to investigate. No police showed up. We all hid in our houses that night. When I talked with the neighbors the next day, I was surprised that they didn't want to report it. Too dangerous. So, based on my cultural norm, I reported it to the police and mayor, thinking this would possibly lead to investigation and more protection. The mayor gave me two options: buy a gun and they'd teach me how to use it or leave the country.

As North Americans, we often think and take for granted that we can make a difference, that it's good to be in touch with our feelings. We think we are powerful and even immune to harm even when we are in other countries. This way of life contrasted with the realities in Honduras made me feel so powerless. What a wake-up call. Even though all my life I had worked in mental health or with poverty programs, I took my privilege and my ability to help make a difference for granted. I thought I had answers and that I could do something to change the situation. All I had to do was organize or seek help or go to the police. What incredible arrogance to think that I had some kind of power to help make meaningful change in a Third World country, a failed state.

Sure, I could slap up some schools and set up educational support, health support, but at times it felt like a drop of water in the sea of an overwhelming history of pain, suffering, and bloodshed. A country filled with people in crisis. I was becoming overwhelmed, angry, and confused and had bouts of depression and loss of faith. My perspective was becoming skewed. I didn't exactly know that I was shutting down, dissociating, pretending, and like so many people there, I denied my feelings and just kept going.

Chapter 32

This chapter chronicles the evolution of my personal journey in Honduras as a white North American woman of privilege living in a "developing country," as someone who was a donator of school supplies, a fixer of roofs and plumbing, a builder of schools and clinics, and a developer of education and health programs. It is about my evolution and partial understanding of what it means to be a "helper" and a neighbor in a land where I would always be one of the "haves" among a culture of "have-nots."

I was a part of the community, and I was outside of the community at times. I went from naive to someone desperate to help in any way I could, and then eventually to being an observer of how individuals, non-profit organizations, and other charitable groups operate, and how pity, ego-based aid, and lack of cultural understanding are part of a hierarchical construct that can hurt more than it helps. It is also about my psychological transition from a form of relative innocence to the resulting emotional effects of being a long-term aid worker living among people I cared for deeply, and how I witnessed the impact of extreme poverty, constant fear, tragedy, and crisis.

The following phases of my journey did not happen in a linear or chronological fashion. They overlapped, and often the issues and feelings returned with a feeling of depression and defeat, and other times there was laughter or some form of new, inspiring wisdom and transformation.

It was an emotional rollercoaster for me at times, especially in my last years there as the political situation worsened, as did greed, corruption, and the escalation of violence, but it was also a process of evolving that I will never regret.

Naivety and excitement. Shock and realization.

When I first arrived in Honduras and saw the tremendous poverty and need of the people living in mountain villages, I was stunned. I had seen all sorts of poverty in the United States, especially through my work in social services, but had never seen entire rural communities and schools in such a state of devastation and people in quiet desperation. I was overwhelmed. I couldn't bear the imbalance of my two worlds. It seemed so unfair. It was as if blinders were removed and the vision was almost more than I could take. My need to help out quickly turned into a passion for making a difference.

Overwhelm and Action

Being overwhelmed led me to do massive fundraising with passion. I started contacting my friends and the church that initially gave me cash for my trip. I sent photos of the harsh conditions, as well as of the beautiful children and their villages. I initially asked for any amount of cash that they could send.

I asked my friends to spread the word and was heartened to find that they and the church members who initially supported me responded positively, and many hundreds of dollars started to come in. At the time, this seemed like a huge amount of money. I worked twelve or more hours per day with pure joy, bustling around, making phone calls to the teachers, shopping, and arranging trips to the villages.

Feeling the thrill of support fueled me and led to even more optimism and encouragement; I had never expected such a positive response. I continued to write to people and send them photos of happy, beautiful children and thank-you notes from the excited teachers. We were able to expand our projects and programs and build schools, a library, and a six-room clinic. We were able to set

244

up an alternative school, for example, in a village for seventy-five children who could not attend regular school due to the work needs of their families. We expanded our milk program to include ten schools, and with the collaboration of villagers, we constructed about ten school bathrooms.

As the months went on, teachers and leaders from other villages who had heard of me started contacting me, asking if I could visit their schools. Word spread fast and exponentially. Coupled with all the joy and excitement, I began to feel overwhelmed by the need. I began to have thoughts and feel pressure about needing to do something more, something bigger. Overall, I felt optimistic. I could handle doing more, but I needed a vision and a plan to tackle the work on a bigger scale. I felt ready for this in terms of my enthusiasm, but I was lacking the experience and awareness as a base, and I also lacked someone in a position of supervision. A subtle internal shift was starting to take place that I was unaware of.

I started to fall into misguided thinking. Desire to help turned into wanting to rescue. This was dangerous thinking. I felt that I could fix the problems if I just found more money, more time, and more energy. At that time, I wasn't completely seeing it as a systemic problem. I didn't think much about analyzing the issues regarding the series of bad governments and long-term generational poverty. I just saw broken things and lack. I could help fix that.

I was a mature, educated, insightful woman and yet on some level so naive, as if all of my previous knowledge and experience with poverty, structural violence, and community activism had flown out the window.

My thinking set me up for frustration and failure. There were thousands of villages like this one. *Am I going to rescue or fix all of the villages in Honduras? In the world?*

If I was the rescuer, they had to be the victims. This was leading to a disrespectful, one-down position. We couldn't be equals if I was the rescuer.

I was also beginning to see situations through my Western value system. All of my previous insights about this were starting to be replaced with clouded thinking. I started to think I knew what was needed. Some things were obvious, like school supplies. I kept comparing these schools to North American schools, not the inner-city ones, but the suburban schools that were well equipped and money could be raised at any moment for repairs, field trips, and other activities. I wanted Honduran schools to have all this, or at least a bigger part of this. *Do I feel sorry for them? Pity? I didn't feel pity when I first started working here. Has burnout clouded my thinking?* They didn't seem to have options. Worse, they didn't seem to have hope. There was a lack of motivation among children and parents to struggle for their education. There was too much acceptance of the mindset, "This is the way it is."

Boundaries or Lack Thereof

I was aware and unaware at the same time of losing my boundaries. My staff were my friends. It was a small town and there was not a big pool to choose from when selecting staff. Everyone knew everything about everyone, and with the added gossip, my personal life and my professional life were an open book. I felt like I couldn't go out for an occasional beer without it becoming town news. This took away an outlet to relax. When I was buoyant and happily working, it was easy to connect and be seen. However, when I cried or felt anger, I was at home tucking myself away. Unfortunately, there were moments when I could not hide my feelings, like when I would see a dog run over by a driver who didn't even try to avoid it. I would go nuts, yelling at the driver, sobbing in public. Since people there seemed to hold in their thoughts and feelings, I often wondered what they thought of me, the crazy, emotional North American. I'd often get stares at these moments but rarely supportive comments.

The first couple of years, I tried to hold my emotions in, but that made me crazy. I always had been an emotional person and was never good at subduing or hiding my feelings, but given the difference in freedom of expression between our cultures, I worried that people would view me negatively. Eventually, I just couldn't hide my reactions.

This made it more difficult to work in the background. It was important to me to stay unknown and work with a low profile so that I would not get an onslaught of requests. I also didn't want to be put in danger from being seen as rich, which would make me an easier target for robberies and extortion. Still, my emotions often got the better of me, making me more visible. I stood out anyway, just being an older white woman. There weren't many of us, especially after the coup and the subsequent United States travel advisory.

It bothered me that we North Americans were often treated by locals as important, maybe even more important than they were. I could sense that they thought of us as smarter, better, and superior, so that almost anything we did was acceptable. Occasionally, people would even say things to me like, "I always thought Americans were smarter." It broke my heart. I'd always reply that we had more opportunities, better education, money, but we weren't smarter or better.

I knew people liked me, but I could also see a kind of reverence, at least at first meetings. It would show up in body language when they talked with me: a bowed head or lack of full eye contact. If I made a suggestion, for example, no one would ever disagree. If I asked for something, it was never denied. I remember once as a joke suggesting that a schoolroom be painted black. There was silence, but no one disagreed.

Part of the hook for me was that it made me feel special, which on some level I enjoyed. I wanted to be special, but not for my nationality or for what I did, but for who I was, and certainly not at the cost of diminishing someone else's self-esteem. The pitfall was that feeling special was sometimes connected to being treated as superior, which created a one-down relationship. I did my best to even things out, often through humor.

Hanging with the kids helped. It was just spontaneous play.

As the villagers and I got to know one another better, I could feel more of an equal standing. There was more directness in speech and eye contact, more laughter, an occasional slap on the back or hug. My name became Elenita. A sign of affection.

My house (and the park) was my office. As time went on and I became much better known, I wouldn't even look out my front window until after coffee, emails, and feeding the neighborhood dogs in an attempt to stop my internal pressure of taking care of everything immediately and skipping my basic needs for quiet. I had no time off work.

It was becoming increasingly impossible for me to set limits. Villagers came only when they could get transportation, so I didn't want to turn them away and tell them to come back another time or another day. They were leaving their farm work or families to come, and the trips were long and sometimes expensive.

Compassion Fatigue

Compassion fatigue is the cumulative physical, emotional, and psychological effect of exposure to traumatic stories or events when working in a helping capacity, combined with the strain and stress of everyday life. It's often associated with healthcare professionals, therapists, animal rights workers, and a myriad of other groups and individuals working on the front lines of service work.

Symptoms can include physical exhaustion, insomnia, hyper-vigilance, irritability, an exaggerated sense of responsibility, avoidance of work or clients, forgetfulness, and impairment of decision-making. In my final year or two, I had all of these to some extent. They would appear intermittently without predictability, so at times I thought I was relatively stable. As the years wore on, however, the symptoms increased and remained longer. My perspective of this problem became skewed. *It's not* so bad, I'd say to myself. *I'll take a vacation soon.* Or I would talk to a friend, feel better, and assume I'd dealt with the situation. I wasn't aware of how many times some obsessive thought or problem would be recurring unless someone pointed it out to me. Then I'd become aware. For moments only.

I cared deeply for the people there and felt so connected to them. In some ways this was a plus, feeling so much a part of people's lives, but it was also a challenge due to the quantity of people in my life and the number of crises they faced. A failed state brought desperation. I not only witnessed that, I *felt* it!

There were constant requests for meetings or for help when I walked down the street into town. It overwhelmed me and made me feel vulnerable, like I was a walking aid station. At times it was like getting on the loudspeaker at a sports event and asking if anyone had any needs. I'd often get two or three requests per day (not to mention my morning lineup). Sometimes I took a tuk-tuk for six blocks just to avoid requests. I understood why they would ask in the moment, especially since there was no office for them to go to or because they happened to be in town that morning. I would have done the same. Almost one hundred percent of the requests were valid: sick family members, school supplies needed for a child who otherwise would not be able to attend school, building projects and repairs. It was endless. My feeling of responsibility began to take an increasingly greater toll on me.

By my fifth or sixth year there, I became absolutely weighted down with grief. I worried more. I cried more. Turning to my North American friends, I burned them down more. I slept less. I cared for myself less. There wasn't much opportunity for diversion. It was not like I was able to even go window shopping. All the items were the same in each *tienda* (store), polyester that glowed in the dark. No movie theatre, no real recreation opportunities, little music and art, lousy TV. Most folks relaxed by sitting on the curbs in front of their houses. I loved joining them, but it wasn't enough stimulation or distraction for me, and it didn't supply the emotional support that I needed.

Vacations were not much of an option. It would mean a long, bumpy, smoke-belching trip to go anywhere and usually cost more than my minimum salary could afford. If I were to fly anywhere, it still required a four-hour trip to San Pedro Sula, declared as the second (and later first) most dangerous city in the world. Sometimes it meant an overnight stay.

There was no administrative support. I was the administrator. There had been no training for the onslaught of living in the middle of a desperate country, nor did I have training through my earlier education. There wasn't a day that went by when I wasn't approached by several people in extreme need asking for money or help. I would hear horror stories almost daily of accidents, murder, and hungry and sick kids. There were days where the problems of infrastructure were extremely challenging, such as no water, no electricity, and no internet to do my work. A road would be washed-out or caved in. Always obstacles to my work. This was their norm. It wasn't mine. My life was still way better than theirs. I had access to money for personal emergencies; I had good health and knowledge of how to keep it, and self-esteem, but above all, I could leave any time I wanted. The result of this comparison was that I couldn't share much of my thoughts, feelings, or needs with locals. I kept way too much inside myself.

Reaping huge rewards kept me going but would keep me stressed at the same time. It was gratifying to see a child become healthy, or finish repairing or building a school, or completing a furniture project. Sometimes it was a small gesture that gave me a lift. For example, if I felt helpless about something, I would simply go to the market where my villager friends sold their crops. I'd bring money that was not designated for a specific project and buy large quantities of produce from the vendors. We always needed food for our food bank, and this was a great way to support the vendors. I especially loved buying from Josefa, a mother of eight whose husband only worked part time due to illness. She'd get up at 3:00 a.m., make breakfast for the family, and by 6:00 a.m. would arrive in town with her squashes and corn and sit outside on the sidewalk. She'd wear the same homemade dress every day. No sweater in the cold weather. I would see her and tell her I needed twenty squash or thirty ears of corn and watch her try to hide her toothless smile. It was great for her, and it would buoy me up like a sugar high. Positive gestures towards me helped tremendously. I loved the hugs or the little gifts that people would hand me. I remember walking down the street with a four-year-old friend who had his arm around me.

Like sugar highs, these types of pick-me-ups weren't permanent. I'd be up for a while, but then came the crash. Rewards became the hook. If I received more rewards, I could work a little longer, harder, with energy, but the lows from the exhaustion and burnout that followed were becoming more difficult to deal with. I relied a lot on Marel and his family, but they too were burning out from the same overload. People were constantly at their doorstep asking for help, especially when he became pastor of his church. Everyone seemed to need everything.

We all had compassion exhaustion and didn't know how to deal with it given the limited options we had. Although they would often deny that they felt this, I wasn't of much help to him or to Zoila, other than as someone who could listen sympathetically. I would suggest they take a break (who was I to talk?) and they understood, but they had little money and, like me, couldn't just shut their door to folks in need.

There were hundreds of stories I didn't even remember until a trigger would remind me. Mostly, I just moved on to the next task. For example, since we had no veterinarian in town, we would often have to see an animal suffer. I remember one time having to put a special suffering dog down, and it broke my heart. He had been my buddy for almost a year, and I was devastated. I won't go into the process, but it was gruesome. Immediately afterwards, I received an emergency call about a boy who was electrocuted in a rainstorm when an electrical pole fell on him. He was in the hospital and his parents needed money for treatment. I rushed off to meet with the parents and temporarily forgot about the dog, but a dull, disconnected depression hung with me for quite a while. About two days later, I saw a dog just like him, same wiry fur, same whiskers, same color. The sudden recall of the dog's death hit me so hard I wasn't able to move. I just stood there in the street with tears pouring down my face and my hand over my heart.

During my second year in Copán, I started fundraising by writing a monthly newsletter that contained pictures and descriptions of the work we'd accomplished, as well as the projects we wanted to do. This opened the door to more support. Much of the support came in from the United States and Canada, but also from Europe and New Zealand. Folks would respond by sending me donations, of course, but they would also respond with encouragement, compliments, and kind words, and would refer other supporters to me. This meant a great deal to me, and often, in my mind, I pretended this was sufficient positive energy coming in, and that somehow I didn't need to have the other kinds of support, such as someone present to hold me while I cried.

I had fantastic long-distance friends with whom I connected by Skype or email. I'd always feel better after talking with them, but shortly afterwards I'd have to go it alone again, often feeling that I was being left behind at the train station. I had one friend in particular who was tremendously helpful. I called her my "most comprehensive friend" because over the many years of friendship, she was there for me in so many different ways. In this case, she was able to help me analyze situations and became my management consultant as well as my strong shoulder to cry on (long distance). I could talk to her about the joys, sadnesses, and absurdities of my life. After many years of extreme ups and downs, though, I began to burn her out. Up came the same old issue—she and other friends always ended up suggesting, "Get out of there! It's killing you!"

When I started to be in physical danger through extortion and increased threats, when my physical safety and even my life was on the line, my friends grew even more persistent, and even angry. They wanted me to get out and get out immediately. The messages from my friends became stronger and sometimes came with anger. It did make sense to me, but it was not an option for me. *How could I just step out and step away? This is my home. These people are my neighbors and friends and family. How could I live with myself if I just turned my back?*

All of this led to a separation with one of my closest, long-term friends. She could no longer witness my downhill slide. On some level, I understood, although it was really painful and further isolating for me. It would be enabling if she continued to help me survive there by listening to me complain and supporting my unhealthy decision to stay. It was as if I was in an abusive relationship and constantly saying, "Yes but …" a bit like saying, "He only beats me on Wednesdays."

During the final year, with threats to my life (which will be further explained towards the end of this book), I had to evaluate whether it was better to stay and possibly die with my loved ones there or break away. It may sound like an easy, no-brainer decision to most people, but I was literally considering both options.

Reawakening

I was reawakening to the issue that extreme poverty was not just local; it was all over Central America, and, of course, rampant in the world. I always knew this and always felt strongly compelled to do something about it, even if it was something small. I signed on to this spiritual commitment probably close to the age of five. In Copán, this started with seedlings of information and awareness during my first year. It continued as the months and years went by, and as I talked with more local people, as well as other humanitarian aid workers, and as I read more books, the awareness grew more intense. This was nothing I hadn't known about, and certainly I had worked all my life as a paid employee in the US in poverty programs and as a volunteer trying to make a difference, but the visuals, and being in the moment seeing all of this, hit me like small, and sometimes massive, strokes. At times my awakening was gradual, and at others it would be a full-blown, painful, sudden awareness. When people I knew were shot for protesting, for example, it was way more of a reality check than reading about someone dying in a newspaper.

I was living in it. These were my friends and neighbors, no longer an academic concept of poverty. I had taken so many things for granted. That clean water would come out of taps. That food was always accessible. That medicine or healthcare would be available, at least in some form, when needed. That the roof would stay on the house during a storm. The list went on and on.

I couldn't sleep. Ideas and thoughts raced through my head, not only about what I had been seeing but also what I could do to help, what was the best way to help, who could help, how could I raise funds, where to start. *Do I help many schools by donating a bit of supplies and furniture, or do I help only a few but more intensively? Do I buy medicine for sick kids? How many kids can I help?* The rate of malnutrition in children in the communities, although reported at an enormous sixty to seventy percent, was obviously almost 100 percent as evidenced by broken, decayed teeth; colorless hair (protein deficiency); emaciated bodies; glazed eyes; lack of energy; and the stories of children dying from related diseases such as dysentery. I was haunted by visions of emaciated dogs that could barely stand up, sick dogs with no fur and open bloody sores, their heads and tails hung low.

I was frustrated that answers didn't come quickly. Most didn't come at all. Urgency and enthusiasm were coupled with attempts to develop a longer-term plan of how I'd fit in. I talked to many folks, some in similar situations like my brilliant American friend who was head of a children's organization. She was also facing many of the similar challenges, such as a huge level of need and what actually could be accomplished. She also faced opposition, as well as threats. It gave me comfort and perspective to talk with her, and we often were able to find humor in our lives, as well.

I continued talking with my wise friends back in the States. I read as much as I could. Still no complete answers. Ideas, questions, trial answers abounded, but no solutions. My false thinking kept telling me there was one and I just hadn't found it yet. Was I naive to think that? Was I being arrogant to think that I could find a way in spite of all the analysis and efforts of generations before me?

Urgency and Lack of Understanding of the Big Picture

In the beginning, I rushed in without getting to know and understand the culture and without speaking the language fluently. With this lack of understanding, it was easy to make a lot of mistakes. I made assumptions about what people wanted. I made assumptions about what people needed. I made assumptions about how people would continue a plan of support without supervision. I assumed their culture was like mine, only poorer.

We collaborated with an organization that bought chickens for school program in order for the kids to learn both how to take care of the birds and how to set up an egg business. It was our job to build the chicken coops. I had worked with this marvelous coordinator many times with great success; we'd built a couple of schools together. This project, however, even with great planning and great intentions, had unexpected challenges. It was difficult to protect the chickens against disease, against robbery, against poor follow-through of feeding and care. It was difficult for the program creator to supervise from North America even though an excellent Honduran coordinator was hired. Communication between the coordinator and the funder was not always accessible due to failures of electricity and the internet. The project manager had other work, as well, and wasn't always available. There were holes in the procedure that would have been very hard to detect before starting. Sometimes it was impossible to know how a project would turn out until it was underway. We had to learn to expect the unexpected and to not attach too much hope or expectations to the final outcomes of similar projects.

As time passed, I tried not to make the same mistakes, but of course I did. For example, I tried to set up a program with a village school cultivating a school vegetable and sweet potato garden. People in the village were really struggling to survive economically. The soil was so bad there; hardly any crops grew well. This seemed like a wonderful partial solution to some of the hunger issues. The word *solution* was already a red flag that I hadn't realized at the time. However, I continued to work on this with a team of teachers, students, and parents.

With the help of an export farmer who grew sweet potatoes, our hope was to capitalize on this extremely nutritional food that grew easily and had few natural enemies. We decided to do a trial program where the exporter would donate sweet potato plants to the school, as well as the families. We donated fencing. The village fathers helped the children dig the rows, put up the fencing, and plant the seedlings, and we offered sweet potato plants to any person helping us with this project. I assumed, incorrectly, that the community leaders and teachers would manage the program and protect the potential crop. Within three months, just before the crop was going to be harvested by the students, the garden was broken into and the plants were taken, probably stolen at night or during a weekend when the school was closed. I wasn't sure that there was anything we could have done to protect them. Hiring a guard would have been too expensive. People living in extreme poverty often took such desperate measures to feed their families.

Almost nobody in the local community who had received seedlings had plants growing in their yard. When I asked the leader why this was, he shrugged and said he didn't know. The teacher had no answer either but suggested that local people seemed to prefer to stick to their meager crops of corn and beans. Here was a community in desperate need, and therefore I had made the assumption that they would capitalize on this offer to help. That is what *I* would have done. I was frustrated and once again forced to re-evaluate what the recipients considered helpful. They hadn't asked for the sweet potato plants. I offered and they said yes, but this didn't mean that they necessarily wanted them or would take responsibility of them.

Going forward, I evaluated even more carefully any potential project, especially those that were "long-term-results based," like educational training programs. I was thinking more about going back to our original plan of just giving out school supplies and teaching materials or doing small repair projects in the schools. There were always plenty of roofs to repair or bathrooms to fix. They were useful short-term projects that didn't require a lot of supervision or angst. Most local folks knew how to do these repairs or installations, and teachers could always use educational materials.

I started using crowdfunding internet sites such as Go Fund Me to raise money for specific projects like building school bathrooms, or smaller projects such as building a water tank and tubing, or funding school supplies. I would post pictures of the project, write a description, and set a financial goal. Support came easily.

Projects, however, did not always move quickly. I am a quick-moving sort of person and pride myself on completing tasks efficiently, but excitement and eagerness would turn into a sense of urgency coupled with backup plans. It wasn't easy to move ahead on a project in a country where there were always delays. I was trying to learn to combine efficiency and patience and have a plan B, C, and D. It never really worked. Lumberyards often were out of lumber, building stores out of supplies, school supply stores out of school supplies. It always seemed like I had to plan way ahead, but in the land of crises, there were always delays, changes of plans, and superseding emergencies.

A storm might blow off a school roof. A water system would fail. A wall would be in danger of falling down if not supported immediately. Decades of neglect due to lack of funds and little government support caused havoc. I felt I needed to respond to these emergencies on the spot, like a person who spins multiple plates on sticks and has to keep going back to maintain the spin on the first plates while adding more. I want to mention again here that the violence and danger caused continual disruption as well as excruciating pain.

Two times our head builders were murdered, one by two drugged-up men in the night who entered his house and opened fire while his children ran out screaming for help and the youngest hid under the bed. The other was shot in the back in the street by *narcotraficantes*. How does one put the horrid contingency of that into a proposal? In addition, there were accidents, injuries, and major health issues. There was no time to do long-term planning, and not many resources to help me see a bigger picture.

Since I was pretty much on my own, with only Marel to help figure things out, I felt like I was putting out fire after fire. I didn't know where to look for more help. I didn't even know how to help myself or what that would look like. Feelings of being overwhelmed continued to cloud my thinking.

Privilege Guilt and Responsibility

Privilege, as defined by Oxford dictionary, is a "special right, advantage, or immunity granted or available to a particular person or group of people." It is often referred to in the context of being white in a society that discriminates against people of color or the discrimination of women by a dominant male culture. Essentially, one gets positive responses simply for being born with certain traits. Often this is taken for granted until we see the contrast in the lives of the less fortunate.

I think that many of us are becoming aware of just how much privilege we have, coming from the West. When we are willing to see this in contrast to how little many of the other parts of the world have, it compels us to want to share some of what we have. Sharing can be a natural phenomenon, a beautiful, spontaneous act when we see a lack, however, something happens when we feel we have been given too much, when it feels like more than we deserve. The natural desire to share goes overboard. We grant extra favors. We are extra nice. We "help" too much.

Once in graduate school in a class on rehabilitation, we had to assume the identity and the handicap of another person. I put on dark glasses and used a cane for the day. When we went out and met people, most spoke to my friend who accompanied me, not directly to me. When they did speak to me, their voices were softer and higher. I had the feeling that, although they were sympathetic, there was a tone of caring condescension.

Stepping off a plane into a land of abject poverty compels us to "help." We have so much more than they do. Sometimes the potential recipients don't feel the lack until they see the expressions, actions, and words of a donor. If enough people give out that same message to the same individual or group, the receiver starts to see their own lack whether it's real or not.

Privilege and lack was something I learned about at an early age. In the lower-class immigrant neighborhood where I grew up, I didn't know we were poor since everyone in my neighborhood had the same material items or lack thereof. I didn't feel poor until we moved to a middle-class neighborhood and heard boys and girls talk (sometimes whine) about what they didn't have. It was usually about something I didn't even know I was missing.

In my early days working in Honduras, I was eager to share, but the more economic disparity and tragedy I saw, the more I became compelled to help out. It was not just an issue of compassion, fairness, and balance; it was also guilt.

By the time I moved to Honduras in my sixties, I had decades of education and experience regarding guilt, privilege, and balance of power. I knew it was an issue internationally and intranationally, yet still I didn't initially identify the tremendous impact these issues had on individuals in Honduras and how they both subtly and outwardly affected the entire nation.

Within the country itself, there were issues with privilege. The lighter the skin, the more privilege and opportunities one could receive. There was prejudice by the Latinos in the city against the Garifunas, who were of Caribbean descent. The Garifunas were seen as lazy, wild, less than. This was also common towards the Maya Ch'orti', who were seen by the mainstream population as inferior. They were way poorer than most villagers. Their level of education, malnutrition, and mortality rate, job training, and work opportunities were way below the national standard for these people. They were darker in color.

The disparity in privilege between the Western visitors and the locals was obvious. As a white person, I felt favored, but it was difficult to discern whether it came from being a North American, or if it was because I helped out with a huge amount of local projects, or if it was simply the color of my skin.

* * *

I learned quickly that the best way for me to diffuse my feeling of inequality was through humor. Once, I received a donation of a truckload of giant squash and brought it to a community school where the local women came to pick up the delicacy. They sat down with me in a classroom, maybe a group of thirty-five. I asked them how they cooked it and described how we often prepared it at home. They were mostly quiet as they usually were when I was in their presence, until I took one squash that had formed a shape of a handle and suggested that they could also use it to bop their husbands on the head when they misbehaved. Then they could quickly eat the evidence. The room was filled with laughter. After that day, the women would come up to me and laugh and joke and touch my arm.

It was impossible to experience laughter and guilt at the same time. I knew in my heart that guilt did not help anyone, so the more aware I became of it, the harder I worked to conquer it. I'd check in with myself constantly about what I was saying or doing, trying to monitor if it was coming from guilt or caring or maybe both at the same time.

With foreign visitors, one could see the disparity with the locals in wealth not only by how folks dressed but also in their interactions. It was easy to see who had the most confidence.

I was encouraged when visitors came, maybe not with the knowledge, but with the desire to be culturally sensitive. Often they would ask me if I thought it was okay if they did something or offered something. I really appreciated their sensitivity and willingness and was pleased to discover that most people were tactful and excited to learn.

On occasion, however, foreigners would confide in me about their negative opinions about "those people," as if I was not one of them, the Hondurans, but one of "us," the visitors. It was all I could do to hold back my anger; often it got the better of me and I would get visibly angry. I always dreamed of being the kind of person that spoke always with kindness and patience, but I didn't always succeed at it. My patience was far greater with locals.

Aside from the privilege guilt, I do believe that we have a responsibility to help each other as brothers and sisters. I've often had it said to me that God will repay me tenfold for my work. I didn't do this for points. I did this because my heart wanted me to and because I believe that taking care of one another is a healthy, normal condition. I also believe that everyone has something to offer regardless of limitations, and that relating and helping out is a two-way street.

Many Honduras helped me too, offering friendship, support, protection, sometimes a place to stay when I was away from Copán. People taught me unconditional love, patience, acceptance. They showed me how to be resourceful in a country that had so little. On a practical level, I was often brought gifts of fruits, vegetables, and plants for my garden; local medicinal products; and, as I mentioned earlier, even live chickens. Children would bring pictures that they drew for me.

As a caring person, I find it difficult to just walk away from a situation where I could pitch in. My issue was that when I lived in the middle of such need, what were the limits? *Can I walk away from a child who needs medicine? If there are no other organizations or people to help with some specific problem, will it be up to me?* I almost always felt it would. *When I see an abandoned litter of puppies in the woods, what is my call? There are no animal protection groups. Should I just walk away and leave the puppies to starve and die a slow death?*

I continually wrestled with how much responsibility to take. *Could I live with myself if I didn't do anything?* There were many haunting nights where I wrestled with an action that I might have taken and didn't. Often this meant returning the next day, reversing my decision, and starting to look for ways to raise funds to help.

As the years went on, I started to realize that there were additional ways I could help without continuing to work on the front lines. I could utilize my perspective and experience of privilege to communicate the disparity to others, not just to educate but maybe also to expand the help redistributing some of the resources of the world. I could raise funds, provide discussions and lectures, and write about what life was like for the people in Honduras.

At first my thoughts were about giving myself less, allowing myself less luxury, less pampering. If I lived in a house that was more humble, if I didn't have better-quality clothes, or if I didn't buy "luxury foods and household items" such as hamburger or Kleenex, maybe I'd feel more on the same par. It would reduce my privilege guilt.

Maybe if folks saw I was more like them, I would feel like our relationship was more balanced. Guilt stopped me from taking in more for myself. Guilt can be a great motivator or a crippling force. I couldn't distinguish very well at first. Friends in the States would sometimes send me money just for me, as I've explained earlier, but I had great guilt about receiving these funds. I once bought a beaded necklace with a gift of money. I wore it under my shirt for about a month until I felt comfortable showing it on the outside.

Another time, I saw a little stuffed animal—a lion. It was being sold on the street for the equivalent of about one dollar. I loved that lion, with its big floppy paws and lots of neck fur. I thought, *This is great! I want this for me!*

A little boy in rags was standing next to me, maybe four years old; he looked at the lion and joyously screamed to his mother, "*Un leon, Mami!*" You guessed it. I gave him the lion and watched him skip away with his mom, examining and playing with it. His older brother joined in with the joy, laughing and holding it as well.

I kept asking myself for things, telling myself I deserved them but then would turn myself down. Guilt somehow seeks punishment. Depriving myself, however, led to burning down. That was another lesson I needed to learn: how to refuel and that it was necessary. Although I began to incorporate this new thinking into my work, behavior change was another matter altogether. I could take in only a bit at a time, and, of course, a crumb is not a meal. I thought it was.

Survivor Guilt

Survivor guilt is a mental condition that occurs when a person perceives themselves to have done wrong by surviving a traumatic event when others haven't. This was a serious issue that also severely haunted me.

People were starving everywhere; people were being killed, robbed, threatened. Their children were dying. I'd had my own threats and robberies, but I'd also had the luxury of stepping in or out of any situation at my will. It was like going to a movie. I could leave my seat at any time. If life became too tough, I could buy a plane ticket. I could ask my friends for a loan. I could use my credit card to buy a bus ticket, and in a matter of a few hours I could be out of any given dangerous situation. Folks there didn't have that luxury. They were stuck. That was their life and only option, and it ate me up inside. I couldn't protect them. It was tortuous to think that these people, my friends, these precious children and their families would not be able to make the choices they needed to succeed and realize their dreams, or even just be safe. It tore me apart to think someone's child would die because they didn't have the $150 for a life-saving operation. It was agony to hear stories about the preventable deaths, illnesses, loss of fetuses all because of lack of what seemed like pennies to us in North America. It was tragic and horrifying that parents so desperate would send their children unaccompanied to the border to try to get into the US. When I thought about these beautiful kids all alone and scared, away from home for the first time in a hostile world, I'd go crazy.

I didn't want to be a fountain of money, but poverty was such a core part of many people's issues. How could I say I couldn't find the money? Just a bit harder work, some longer hours, and I could have success. It wasn't just about protection from disease; I couldn't protect them from death, from gangs, from *narcotraficantes*, or from street crime. I couldn't buy them a visa to leave the country.

I was spurred on to raise more money, to try harder. This was not the solution. The more people I could help, the more I was sought out. I was in a cycle that I couldn't stop even if I wanted to. Of course, this guilt-ridden cycle led to a downward spiral of exhaustion, worry, and feelings of being overwhelmed. Receiving donations and being able to sponsor a new program or help out some families, however positive and temporarily exciting in the moment, led to higher expectations. And bigger crashes when I failed. I started having more highs and lows. The highs became higher, and the lows, lower. On the good days, I could work for fourteen hours with encouraging success, but the lows were nearly incapacitating, and the mental strain was intense. I would often isolate myself and obsess or cry. I would go to bed as soon as it was dark, with my trusted dog Pam at my side.

It was not just an issue of aid frustration. As the danger level in town began to skyrocket a few years after my arrival, I began to sleep in my clothes with my shoes at the bedside, a phone under my pillow, and a can of Raid as my only weapon. I didn't know this at the time, but Marel's wife told me later that he also slept with his phone under his pillow and checked it every few hours in case he missed my call. My fear of the dark gradually became more intense as I experienced or heard about so many things happening in the night. Sometimes my neighbors' windows or streetlights were shot out, leaving me even more fearful. My young friend and neighbor Juanita was murdered just a couple of blocks from my house.

Gunshots in the night became a regular occurrence, sometimes as many as two or three times a week. Twice I found dead bodies in the early morning. Altogether, I lost twenty friends, neighbors, and colleagues to murder. Once, right at my gate. It was awful, but I still could step out of the situation any time I wanted to. My neighbors couldn't.

I started to have more flashbacks. The tiny children's graves that I had seen haunted me. Loud noises made me jump. My sleep cycle became disrupted; I was lucky to have four or five hours per night. Making a meal was exhausting. Most of these symptoms I kept to myself. I didn't want my donors to know about this for fear of them pulling away their support, so I would continue to present a positive, upbeat image. I did have a lot of positive information to report regarding our projects, so I just presented those which I felt were helpful to hear about. This, however, increased my separation and loneliness. I was living two lives.

I withheld lots of stories of traumas from my friends. I started to lie about how I felt, or I'd make up excuses why I couldn't talk with them. Too busy. Out of town. Internet not working. I was desperate to talk with them but afraid to make the call for fear of the same rebuke: "Leave! Get the hell outta there!" As painful and challenging as all this was, I still had a back door.

If I went back to the US and lived a normal life, it would have been completely empty. I would have thought about my kids, my friends, and I would have felt like a deserter. Still, it was an alternative that no one I knew had.

Locals would beg me for letters of invitation to the US to help them travel there for work. I knew these letters would be useless since I had no work to provide them there. Often they would ask me for money to pay for coyotes (human smugglers) to help them illegally cross the border, usually the sum of six thousand American dollars. Every time I said no, a little part of me died watching a moment of hope come crashing down on them again.

Cognitive Dissonance

I'd talk to visitors from the Western world, and they would complain about their privileged lives. One person complained about how they needed to have their driveway widened because their two cars didn't fit. I would think of the teacher who had told me about a boy in her community who had dysentery and died in the night. His last words were, "*Papa, caca*," referring to his diaper filling again, only this time with blood. I felt like I was going crazy. At times, I served as a link between two worlds. Other times, I was torn to pieces straddling the line.

Once I was listening to a tourist complain about how a local restaurant didn't have good meat. She joked that she would starve to death if she lived in Honduras. Her comment sent me into an immediate flashback of a devastating episode I'd witnessed with a father and child. She was talking while I was trying to push back the tears. What had happened a year earlier was that Zoila, Marel's wife, called me with an emergency. A man from a village a couple of hours away had called her and asked if we could help get his small boy to the hospital. He added that his older son had died last week (I assumed it was related to starvation) and he was hoping to help this child before the same thing happened. The mother had died in childbirth earlier that year, along with another baby, and since then he didn't know how to care for his boys.

Zoila, always compassionate, told him to come down and we would find a way to get the child to the hospital. She tried to call me, but I wasn't immediately available. A couple of hours later, I received the message and rushed over. I opened the front door without knocking and saw one of the worst, most indelible visions of my life. Everyone was seated, barely moving, silent with pale faces. There was horrendous agony in the eyes of the crying father who was gaunt, weathered-looking, and unkempt. He held his lifeless child in a brown, dirty, torn blanket. I came in without saying a word. I touched the tip of the blanket as I went to sit down, too afraid to open the blanket and look at the child. Zoila confirmed what I already knew, the first to speak among us, saying when the father arrived she had opened the blanket to look at the son, and he was already dead.

I don't remember much after that. Marel told me he would "take care of things," and I left some money for his expenses and some with the father—I don't remember how much. I tried several times to tell the father that I was so sorry, but every time I opened my mouth, words just didn't come out. I felt so bad that I couldn't even say "I'm sorry." After nodding goodbye to the man while my own eyes flooded with tears, and hugging Zoila on the front porch, I staggered home, alone, not knowing what else to do.

I still remember the blanket, the father's eyes, and the boy's lifeless body. I didn't know him, and yet I knew him and loved him. Does that even make sense? I remember the horribly pained eyes of his father. I knew I would be haunted by it for the rest of my life.

Meanwhile, the woman in the restaurant was still complaining about the sub-par meat on the menu.

I struggled with how to inform people in North America about life in Honduras without repulsing them with the stories or putting them off with my anger. Fundraising was confusing. Should I tell the hard stories or the "happy results" stories, or maybe mix them together? The longer I worked in these communities, the more I was invited in to listen and really understand on a deeper level what their lives were like. I usually tried to convey a blend without graphic details. I felt a lot of pain and sympathy for their situation and their exhausting struggles, their concerns and their lack of hope. I learned what it was like to live in fear. Fear of losing a loved one to sickness. Fear of speaking their truths. Fear of retaliation for saying bad things about an individual or the government. Fear of being robbed of what little they had, such as their chickens.

I myself had been robbed more times than I could count. There would be break ins at my house, or thefts of items that were left in a truck bed for a matter of moments. Sometimes people would take money out of my purse if I left it unattended for fifteen minutes. There was fear of gangs coming into town, fear of street crime, fear of *narcotraficantes* and their revenge. Threats, extortion, and violence were abundant both in town, in the cities, and in the villages. There was no escaping this. Everyone had a story or two to tell. Everyone seemed to have a least one family member dead from violence. I had seen dead bodies in the street in the early mornings. I had friends who were murdered for their beliefs, actions, or simply by a jealous lover.

Adan was a pastor at Marel's church, which was situated on the edge of town. Most of the parishioners came from the area and from the nearby mountain villages. It was the most impoverished area of town. Adan was a sweet, quiet man, very religious, who always carried his bible. He was too poor to own a car but did have an old motorcycle that kept breaking down, which gave us frequent opportunities to chat in the street while he repaired it. As our friendship grew, we talked about wanting to do a project together in conjunction with his church. His parishioners had so many needs.

He very much wanted a children's food program since these kids did not eat every day and were extremely malnourished. After much discussion and planning, we decided to set up a lunch program for the kids, whether or not they were members of his church. His goal was to start with about twenty-five or thirty children from his neighborhood and provide them with beans, tortillas, vegetables, and a healthy drink, and hopefully vary the menu as donations came in. He was excited about this project and so happy to finally have partial funding from us. The rest of the funding came from various businesses in town. He essentially went door to door, asking if they would help donate food, plates, cookware, or cash. He talked with the women in his church about volunteering as cooks. The response overall was incredibly positive.

After a few weeks of solicitations and planning on both Adan's and my part, Marel called me and said he was coming over. He needed to talk with me. When he arrived, I saw a very rare sight: his ashen face, holding back tears. No greeting.

"Adan was murdered," he blurted. "The police found his body hanging by the neck in his house. It was made to look like a suicide, but I know it wasn't. He would never do such a thing. He was a strong Christian and it's against the bible."

I sat down, weak from shock and grief. Marel filled me in with what little information he had. The immediate investigation determined that he had hung himself in despair of his wife leaving him, but there was much evidence of a struggle. Furniture was broken, the room was in disarray, and there were bruises all over his body. We believed that the police had been paid off to look the other way and call it a closed case. Although we didn't know why this happened with Adan, we had seen this kind of thing many times before. Impunity existed on a grand scale, and bribery and corruption were common.

The funeral was huge. It seemed as if half the town was there, mostly quiet with prayers. I tried to hold back my sobs. It was the loss of a friend, the loss of a good man, and the loss of a worthy project.

Marel and I were despondent for many days, but in typical Marel fashion, he decided he would take over the project. He was appointed temporary pastor of the church, and his first task other than helping parishioners grieve, was to connect with me on the food program. We would set it up after all, in Adan's name.

Within a month or two, we set up a temporary outdoor kitchen on the side of the church and informed the community to send any of their children who wanted to come. We organized the women into cooking teams, three or four women making each lunch. Marel borrowed plastic chairs and set up long boards on bricks as tables.

When we served our first meal, thirty-five children showed up the first week. We gave out balloons and marbles. The kids had a great time, some of them shoving spaghetti and beans into their mouths as fast as they could. Bigger kids helped little kids by carrying their plates to the table, bringing them juice, or even feeding the tiniest ones. Within a few months, we were serving well over 150 kids. Pastor Adan was not forgotten and received much appreciation posthumously.

In contrast, I remember once talking with a visitor who mentioned there was a restaurant for dogs in Los Angeles. I kept thinking about what I could do with such a dog owner's spare change. It was so hard to get my head around the level of the disparity. Gradually I started communicating less with local visitors from other countries. The disparity hurt me so badly. I always wondered if these stories hurt the Hondurans as much as they hurt me.

Secondary Trauma

There was another kind of trauma that was taking place for me during these years: the continuous witnessing of suffering. Exposed to other people's losses, disasters, deaths, pain, and other forms of suffering, I began to internalize the feelings. I would go to the hospitals, to the homes, and to the funerals. I would hear relentless stories of horrible occurrences, violence, and victimization—stories around the ramifications of poverty such as starvation, illness, and desperate crimes. I witnessed what was referred to by many as "structural violence," in which the social structure kills people slowly by preventing them from meeting their basic needs.

It took the form of institutions that were not working or that had been destroyed, classism, racism, domination by the government, or terrorism by local gangs and *narcotraficantes*. There was inequality and oppression of groups, like the Indigenous peoples of Honduras, and denial of services for them. When this happens, the soul starts to wither. Folks give up.

People lived in pain and suffering, and I was absorbing that pain. It affected my work, as well as my personal life.

Sympathy Shifting to Admiration

At first, it seemed like Hondurans had so little, but that was because I was focusing on a material level. Gradually, my eyes opened, and I saw that they had positive energies in their lives. They had united, large, loving families. They had communities that pulled together. They had a strong connection to God and the church. They lived on gorgeous land and were very connected to Mother Earth. Their lives didn't have the competition, stress, and anxiety that we had in North America. They smiled and laughed more. How was that possible given their circumstances?

As visitors and aid groups came down, I noticed their pity and oftentimes their sense of superiority more. "We are here to help."

"We are here to convert." "We are here to save." "We have come to teach." "We have come to build." I didn't remember ever hearing a group state that they had come to learn.

I started to feel caught in the middle of visitors and locals. The visitors would often compensate for their sympathy by overindulging a local with gifts that were considered too expensive. I saw a man give twenty dollars to a child standing on a corner. It was meant as an act of caring and generosity, but this was equivalent to a week's salary. What message did that give? How would the father react after working a long, hot day in the fields and making the equivalent of three dollars? Would the child think it was better to wait on corners than to go to school? Should I have said something to the man? Should I have told him that free money helps perpetuate the welfare mentality? I also had to question if and how much I was overindulging others. And in what ways?

I was an outsider and an insider. I wasn't native to Honduras, but I also was no longer a visitor. I was included in family, village, and church events. I was becoming more Honduran than North American. I was slowing down. I could lie in my hammock without feeling like I should be doing something. I was smiling more (which changed, of course, during the last couple of years). I was hanging out on the curbs with my neighbors or taking the time to sit on a tree stump with folks in the villages. Even though I had work pressure, I would still see the contrast with the urgency of the foreigners. They were on timelines, trying to fit "help" into their short week's stay.

My priorities in life were shifting. My values and beliefs were being reassessed. The first few years I was there, on a good day, I felt like I could fit into both worlds. On a bad day, I felt I fit nowhere, although I was more "home" in Honduras than I had ever been in the US. I had come to know an enormous number of people, from the villages and from town—neighbors, teachers, co-workers. Although I always felt sympathy for their struggles, any pity I felt disappeared. I felt protective of them; I wanted to shield them from the onslaught of pity and personal agendas of many of the visitors.

Most people who came to visit were wonderful. They were open and wanted to learn and share. Sometimes, however, visitors would act like I was one of "them," a Westerner, separate from the people of Honduras. (*Am I one of them?*) They would make comments about the locals: "These people can't do it correctly." "These people wouldn't understand." "They are lazy." They thought that I would agree. Hondurans were often seen as incapable, helpless, and needing rescue. Although I spoke out each time about these insensitive and often racist remarks, I began to grow wary and suspicious of the aid groups that came to visit.

I was becoming polarized, often defensive and ready for a fight. I didn't like this in myself, but I didn't like seeing the people I love belittled. I was mixed in my feelings. I was cheery and positive, although constantly questioning my role. *How can I be useful but not "the woman in charge"?* This question mixed with admiration and with sadness, overwhelm, anger, frustration. I could sit happily one moment with friends in the park, and then talk with someone ten minutes later who sparked my rage.

Reaction to Political Upheaval

With the coup of 2009, when the current president was taken away from his house in his pajamas, the resulting chaos, anger, and uncertainty changed the tide of Honduras once again. They were used to this on some level; I was not. The temporary replacement president would blame all of the current problems on the past president. The next president blamed past presidents, and so on. Four presidents in six years, each giving an excuse of why there would be no help for health, education, or any other important area of Honduran life. More programs were cut. School lunches stopped arriving. In many cases, children lost their only meal in a day. I felt compelled to set up more milk programs for the mountain schools or find donations to be able to deliver one-hundred-pound bags of beans and corn. Unpaid teachers began to quit, leaving villages without education.

I felt I needed to work harder to help compensate. I had learned this growing up; when there were challenges at home, I just had to take on more responsibility. A "hook" for me was that I was a successful fundraiser. The more success I had, the more I felt responsible to keep going, to work more, to do more.

I didn't want to take the place of the government's role, though, by paying teachers or even giving them an incentive. I knew that if I supported them financially, even minimally, the Hondurans would not pressure their government to change. Doctors, nurses, and many others also were not paid for months—eventually even years. The money I could've given them was not enough. Crumbs would have just kept them in their places.

Again, the ongoing issue was, how could I help without being crippled by overwhelmment, and how could I help without hurting the people I wanted to help? How could I avoid injuring their self-esteem? How could I stay separate and still be a part? How could I be compassionate without being hardened? How could I work without feeling survivor guilt and privilege guilt? How could I witness without being overcome with horror? How could I see the bigger picture and still be a part of the details?

Compassion fatigue books and books about burnout and trauma talk about self-care. They discuss getting a support group, setting boundaries between work and home life, doing nice things for yourself. Much of my support group were murdered or left the country. As for support from a work group, this just did not exist for me. Boundaries were impossible when I lived in the area where I worked. I wasn't able to set work hours because folks in need were also my neighbors. Gunshots and murders happened all the time. There was no way to separate this.

Nice things for myself? I didn't have access to a bathtub or even hot water. Sometimes there was no water at all. Special food items were limited and usually required a long trip to the nearest and highly dangerous city. There was no movie theater or concert hall. Going for a walk, especially alone, was dangerous. It was always noisy at night, with dogs barking, roosters crowing, yelling in the streets, gunshots. I developed a huge fear of the dark. Roads were often closed due to weather issues such as mudslides, falling rocks, floods. Going anywhere in a bus would always carry a risk of being robbed. Many people just outside the town limits were assaulted.

When I tried to reach out to friends in other countries, the infrastructure—or lack thereof—often interfered. There would be no phone service or electricity. I'd be waiting for a Skype date with a friend, and suddenly we'd lose power. I would be left with overwhelming feelings and nowhere to go.

Above all, I had no training to prepare me for this. Life, university, and special courses never addressed working in structural violence and living in a war zone, or management skills under challenging situations. I couldn't find many books that addressed trauma management in a foreign country.

Spiritual Evolution: The Beginning of Some Perspective

There came a point when I knew that, spiritually, it was time for me to leave. I tried to deny that the life there was hurting me emotionally and mentally, but also that it was important for me to keep growing, to have new positive experiences. My soul was begging me to change. My heart kept saying no. I couldn't face the fact that it would be healthy to leave people who I loved and who loved me.

I had an identity there. I was the friend/neighbor/helper, and I loved being all three. I thought that maybe it would be better to wither and even die there than to abandon people I loved. The metaphysical message was to go. I thought it would be good to no one if I were killed, and yet the pain of leaving was so great that I wrestled with the choice for way too long.

Perspective

Eventually, I was forced to make the choice to leave. It was the hardest decision of my life. That first year away was about the worst in my life, an excruciating separation. Keep reading; I tell the whole story later in this book. After I left, I missed my friends and my loved ones terribly. I missed my work there and my role. I missed my life.

As I set up a new life in another Central American country, I started to get some distance, both physically and mentally. New thought patterns gradually started to form. Sadly, I still didn't (and don't) have answers. I know a lot about what doesn't work, but I still wrestle with what form of humanitarian aid, if any, could work.

The guilt of having left still haunts me to this day, even though I know it was a matter of survival. I cry at the drop of a hat when this conversation comes up. The guilt of being so privileged also haunts me. The anger is still very much a part of me: the anger at what is so unjust, the unbalanced distribution of resources. Anger at folks who have the ability and means to make a difference but don't care or won't pitch in.

Pity has shifted. The need to rescue is diminishing. Acceptance is creeping in. I will never accept injustice and cruelty, but the acceptance is telling me that it's okay if I don't work full throttle every minute. It's an acceptance that I can't do as much as I would like, and maybe that's okay. It's also an acceptance that I need to take better care of myself, and that may mean pulling out from the direct line of service. I am doing more administrative work these days, planning, and creating, and now writing; I'm letting others go into the front lines.

I long for the day when my perspective becomes more enlightened, when I can sort out even more of what I've been through, what I have witnessed, visually and emotionally. Maybe it will never come, but I keep trying.

Chapter 33

This is an excerpt of a letter that I wrote to a friend during my final days in Honduras. As some of it is repetitive, I debated on whether to include it. I decided to do so because it shows the immediacy and rawness of my feelings, and I decided the new information it does include is best told in the form of a letter:

Are you tired of me and my emails? You are always so helpful and comforting, and I again need your support.

Something very bad has been happening here. I know we've been talking about this situation for a while, but it's getting worse. Teachers on strike, doctors on strike, clinics closing, schools closing. Increased violence. Stores running out of certain food and supplies. It's our fourth president in six years. It's crazy here.

Decreased government programs are causing even more problems. For example, they just stopped supplying school lunches in most rural areas, maybe in the cities too, I don't know. This means near starvation for many rural kids. There's no food in the homes; school lunch was their opportunity for a bit of nutrition. These are kids whom I have known and loved for many years. I can't bear it.

Honduras was in bad shape when I came, but this down-hill slide is awful to watch.

My huge dilemma is that I don't want to pick up where the government fails. It's not my place, and it would be enabling. If we offer to give teachers incentives, they may stop pressuring the government. If we don't, they will likely just quit. If teachers protest, they are often met with physical aggression and sometimes murder. Same thing with environmental activists. Protesters are getting murdered or they "disappear" suddenly. Folks are trying to stand up to the mining companies or the creation of a dam that will endanger the environment. These brave people risk their lives daily. There is an incredible activist here named Berta Carceres. She's been jailed many times and keeps on fighting, but I so fear for her life. I have this sickening feeling that is only a matter of short time before they get her too. [Note to reader: Carceras was assassinated in her home by armed intruders in 2014. A total of twelve environmental activists were murdered that year, making Honduras the most dangerous place for environmental activists in the world, relative to its size, according to the research organization Global Witness. Two more activists would be murdered within the month.]

My debate of how to help replays constantly in my head, searching for answers or even ideas. Regarding the supposed school lunch program, food rarely arrives at the schools, and often when it does, it's rancid or filled with bugs. If we supply or even supplement the lunches, teachers and parents will back off and governments, both local and federal, will not receive any pressure to do their part. Yet I don't want kids to starve. It's a horrible dilemma for me, and I don't see any positive options. These are my kids. I've known most of them for many years and care about them very much. What do I say to these kids? "Sorry you're hungry, but I won't do anything to help because it's the politically correct thing to do?"

*People are out of work and tourism has completely shut
down since the coup, so businesses such as hotels, transportation companies, and restaurants are going belly-up. I'm
watching my friends lose their incomes. People are angry
all the time. I see hard-working folks, many who have
giant families, now just sitting in the park. I watch people
like Jose, the ice cream man, who made a pittance before
this downward spiral, and now on some days doesn't even
sell one ice cream cone. He pushes his cart all day in the
blazing sun and still smiles, but it's different now, less
genuine now, and more for show.*

*There are thirty-five NGOs in the Copán area, not to
mention service clubs, missionaries, churches, and individual aid workers. Many of them are enabling the locals,
treating them as pitiful charity cases. When I talk to them
about my views on this, most don't even seem interested in
dialogue. I believe everyone is a capable person with something to offer, and I know people here don't want charity,
they want work, and yet I see them developing into the
dependent, sad people that the aid workers think they are.
Worse yet, I see them turning to crime.*

*I see nasty people reaping the advantages from donors. The
injustice infuriates me. I see organizations and churches
skimming the donations. Very few funds or products get
to the people who need it, sometimes none at all. The
skimming is at the national level, local government level,
as well as within organizations and even churches. This
trickles down to individuals. I'm hearing more and more
from folks that it's useless and even detrimental to maintain their values against a tide of corruption. They are
developing attitudes that say, "Well, the hell with it then.
I'm going to get mine." I'm watching people give up. It's
breaking my heart. I love these people. I care so much for
these children.*

*I'm not sure what is right to do any more in terms of
"aid." I thought I knew. I thought I had a useful plan,*

*but now I am constantly assessing if what I do is help-
ing or enabling. I don't want to see kids go hungry, and I
can't stand by and do nothing while I see more and more
programs canceled here and more groups stepping in to rescue rather than set up self-sustaining programs. This isn't
healthy. I can't bear seeing or hearing about folks dying
needlessly in hospital waiting rooms or in hospital beds
because there is no medicine or no doctor. Can I do more?
Should I?*

*My initial reaction to this recent decline was to work
harder. Raise more funds. Do more projects. But now,
after a couple of years of this, I know in my heart that
it only speeds up my burnout, and I'm not sure it is even
useful. Maybe Honduras has to hit rock bottom before it
rises. I thought it was already at the bottom, but things
keep getting worse. It's a failed state, and, frankly, now
I'm not sure it is even capable of rising. Maybe I need to
get out and let Honduras deal with Honduras. I just don't
know anymore.*

I'm so tired. And confused. And sad.

*This is a country that has been struggling for centuries,
from its birth even. My friend Adin so aptly told me that
Latin America is a history of blood and tears. And now,
the coup here has just turned what little there was to
ashes.*

*I'm mad all the time now. Well, not all the time. I'm also
sad, depressed, overwhelmed, lost, and afraid. I thought
I had caught the burnout in time, but now I know I
haven't. Although I still have a lot of good moments and
still think I can do worthwhile projects, the violence, corruption, and extortion here is so high I can't even think
straight.*

*My house was robbed again a couple of days ago, in
front of many witnesses who were afraid to come forward
because the robber is a gang member. I'd seen him kick a*

sick, emaciated dog. Something in me snapped and I ran after him like a madwoman, calling him a bully and a coward. I didn't know he was a gang member, and I was so blinded by rage I couldn't stop myself. (My rage was way more than just about the dog. It was about the loss of humanity.) He retaliated by breaking into my house, and now he is also stalking me, giving me intense, menacing stares on the street. Now I have to get a restraining order, which will probably be useless. This was the thirteenth or fourteenth time I've been robbed in some form, but this guy is really scary.

I can't count how many times I've been extorted. A couple of them really scared me. One I actually paid off because they threatened to harm a dear friend if I didn't pay. And as far as murders—I can't even count how many friends, workers, neighbors have been murdered by police, by an angered person, by narcotraficantes, by gang members. I barely cry anymore.

My neighbor had her head cut off with a machete in broad daylight on a main street. The police didn't find her attacker. Police never "find" anyone.
One of the worst scenarios that keeps haunting me is the murder of Odilio. He was the kind and respected leader of a mountain village where we built a small school. He had just finished building the school when, in the middle of the night, two crazy men high on drugs forced their way into his house and shot him point blank while his kids hid under the bed. The children are still traumatized, as well as all of the members of his community. They have now all dispersed, leaving the village empty. This kind of violence can and does happen anywhere and at any time. My friend's son was murdered in a restaurant. We all live in fear.

I had never experienced personal terror and hyper-vigilance before, and I often think of folks in ghettos in the US where this is their norm. My heart goes out to them.

One night, I heard gunshots and called the police. They never showed up. In the morning, at about 5:00 a.m., I found a dead body at my gate, full of bullet holes, dried blood everywhere. He was a young fellow I knew. No motive found. No murderer found. What's worse is this wasn't the only time I had found a dead body, and I live in a supposedly quiet tourist town. San Pedro Sula, our largest city, a few hours from here, is now considered the most dangerous city in the world due to gang violence.

But where do I go? What do I do? This is my home. I love a lot of people here. I still love my work despite the challenges. North American people say, "Why don't you leave?" It's just not that easy. I'm nearly seventy years old and I expected that Honduras would be my forever home. And how could I just walk away when folks here are trapped? Survivor guilt would haunt me forever. And where would I go? I keep making deals with myself. Ride this through. Or don't go out as much and don't answer the phone. I can keep playing piano for solace and a bit of joy, keep reading books and invite my friends over—but not at night. My friends don't want to go out at night either. We are becoming prisoners in our houses here.

What am I supposed to be learning here? Whatever it is, it's a huge lesson. It's more and more of a strain staying connected with my North American friends. Our realities are so different. There are only a few who I can turn to, and I feel I'm burning them out as well. And their comfortable lives make me angry sometimes. Not so much angry at them, but angry at the imbalance. I hear complaints from visitors about the food here; it's not good quality. I hear complaints about the lodging, subpar. It makes my mind explode to see the contrast and waste of money when so many folks I love need just the basics. If each person who talked with me could give up a month' of lattes we could build schools, get kids to doctors, support orphanages. I can't go back to the US. It's too awful for me to witness the disparity.

We have grants for education, and we help these kids succeed in school, but then what? Only for them to go back to
work in the fields? There are no jobs, especially for Indigenous folks. Did you know that often starving kids here
won't eat when I offer them food? I don't know why. Eating disorders for not having the right to have food when
their siblings don't have any? Does long-term starvation
kill their appetites? Do the parasites hurt them so badly
when they have food in their stomach that it's better to not
eat?

In the United States, North Americans throw out food,
leave restaurant food on their plates, or complain about
food. There are aisles and aisles of potato chips and other
snacks on supermarket shelves. How could I go back to
that?

I need help. Sometimes I feel so alone. I keep looking for
books on philosophy of international aid or any info or
insights on the subject, and they are usually so heady and
boring I can't get through them. Any you might recom-
mend?

Not all days are this bad. Things can turn around on a
dime. Someone gets a job. We get a nice donation; I play
with kids in the park and do fun things like buy them an
ice cream cone, making both the vendor happy, as well
as the children. My work is still satisfying in many ways;
it's gratifying to see a school improve, a clinic have more
equipment, or to help improve the health of a child. So of
course, the good moments are a hook.

Some folks have asked me if I'm in physical danger. I say
no. Am I being naive? It's a crapshoot here. Anyone can get
killed or hurt at any given time. They can be a target or
just collateral damage. Why should I think I'm invincible?
I know you'll think this is strange when I say this: I'm not
afraid of dying, but I am afraid of dying by machete. Do
"normal" people debate their preferences for dying? So, am

I personally in danger? No, I don't think so. But my mind and health are now at risk. I wish I knew what to do.

I'm so lost. So torn. I don't want to leave but don't know any longer how to survive. How to be healthy. How to protect myself. How to do the work I do, or even if I should be doing it.

Any ideas, perceptions, insights? Most folks would tell me to get out of Dodge. But I have nowhere to go. This is my home.

Chapter 34

"**H**ay gente que no le gusta lo que esta haciendo. (There are some people who are not happy with what you are doing)."

I was leaving a community. Nearby, a man was leaning against a red truck, staring at me, watching me. I'd seen him from time to time when I visited schools, always standing at a distance, always leaning against the truck, always staring. This time, he walked towards me slowly and deliberately, and when I turned and smiled to say hello, his eyes fixed on mine. "There are some people who are not happy with what you are doing."

I didn't understand. He said it in a way that was terrifying. What did this mean? What didn't people like that I was doing? And what was it that I was doing? I didn't know if he was warning me against others, or threatening me.

Spanish was my second language, and when I was emotional, it became even harder to understand. I wasn't sure if I understood correctly. I was not in the position to say, "Excuse me, could you repeat that?"

"This is our territory, not yours," he said, still fixing me with his stare.

I didn't understand. What territory? Did territory mean a village or certain villages? Honduras? I wasn't trying to make it my territory. I was just bringing a helping hand to villagers. He turned away. He didn't stick around for follow-up questions. I turned and walked to our truck, shaken.

Time dulled the anxiety. Maybe I misunderstood. After all, it was in Spanish. Maybe some community was envious that we weren't helping them? I dropped my worry level a bit. There were always threats in Honduras, and more often than not, folks ignored them. However, a few days later, I had a meeting by Skype with a healer friend, Donna, in the US, who had been helping me with all the stress, trauma, and secondary trauma. I was crying constantly, sometimes over something tiny like the internet not working, other times over another death. I was no longer able to distinguish between large and small issues. Running out of milk could reduce me to tears.

Donna was helping me learn techniques to relax. I always had concerns about death. I had lost so many friends and neighbors to violence, and so many children to illness, that I had a heightened awareness of my own mortality, as well. There were good days when the issue didn't come to mind, and other days where I was obsessive. In between periods of denial, I had started preparing for my possible death. I needed my orphan family to receive whatever there was in the bank. I made Isaias the beneficiary. I cleaned up my house thoroughly, not wanting people to clean up any mess "afterwards." I wrote emails of appreciation to my friends, without alluding to any danger, but just casual, friendly words of love.

I'd had several sessions by Skype over the years with Donna, who was an excellent healer, and these meetings always helped me tremendously. I was a strong believer in metaphysical and alternative medicine and always had excellent results with Donna's spiritual readings and practices. I always experienced more peace, clarity, and perspective on my current experience. Donna was also gifted psychically and always accurate in her descriptions and predictions. I always had confidence in her work and guidance.

We had set up a meeting to work on my stress issues. I made the Skype call and her face appeared on the screen. It was not the warm, peaceful face I had been accustomed to. She was stressed and teary-eyed, trying to stop her tears. I thought something had happened to her just before our session and was concerned for her. Much to my shock, she was finally able to speak and looked at me with tears streaming down her face, choking out the words, "You are in grave danger. You are on a hit list."

"*What?* A hit list? How could this be?" I was stunned. This sounded like a bad TV series. It didn't make sense. I was a seventy-year-old woman bringing aid to villages. All I was doing was building schools, helping folks with medical issues, and bringing milk to children. "How could this be?" I asked again, with partial disbelief and partial panic. "Who would want to do this and why?"

It just didn't seem real, and it didn't make sense. And if it were true, what would I need to do? Where would I go? And when? This was my home. And then the chilling question, how would they do it? Questions continued to swamp my mind. Then in an instant, my mind went numb. I stared out the window in disbelief. I watched the birds in my bushes. How could there be danger if birds were chirping and the sun was shining? Finally, I mustered up the nerve to ask Donna what she meant.

"Can you give me details?"

"Not much. Just that dangerous people do not want you around. Something about 'their territory.'"

I had not told Donna what the man in the red truck had said. She used his same words. Territory. *Narcotraficantes?* They were the only people I knew who had "territory."

People in Honduras were always being threatened or extorted—some of it real, some not. Murder was the norm. *Should I take this seriously?* My head was flooded with racing thoughts, then more denial, then practicalities. I even considered staying there and letting them get me. I would have rather been dead than run away to nowhere. I had nowhere to go. How could I just walk away from the people, the work, and the land I loved? My sweet house, and garden, and doggie. My neighborhood kids. And how could I simply run away when my friends were stuck there? It would be cowardly, disloyal, and selfish.

After processing this with Donna, we agreed to be in touch later in the week. (I wondered if I had that amount of time still available. She seemed to think so, but couldn't give me more specific information.) I decided to stay. Maybe nothing would happen.

As the hours became days, further internal arguments possessed me. *What use would I be as a friend or worker if I were dead? What would my friends and loved ones want for me?* I wrestled with options and had no one to talk to about this. I didn't want to scare my friends or endanger local folks. I held it in, waiting to talk with Donna again, hoping for more information and advice next time. I knew that my North American friends would want me to "come home." But the US wasn't my home. It never was. It was a place I had lived, but it hadn't been home since I had left my immigrant neighborhood when I was seven.

More realities entered my mind. Honduras had been changing dramatically. After the coup, the violence had been increasing at a tremendous rate. My friend's son had just been murdered in a restaurant at dinner time. He was sitting with friends when a young man walked in, walked over to him, took out a gun, shot him point-blank, and walked away. This kind of brazen act was happening more frequently. It seemed that most folks were involved in some way, more or less, with narcotics trafficking.

Tourists and locals were getting shot in open crossfire in the streets. Robberies had increased. Extortion had increased. Gang violence had increased in the cities. I spent two days considering the situation and options, walking around like a zombie, wondering if I even had the luxury of a couple of days. Something could happen at any given minute. I couldn't make decisions, but my deepest instincts told me that Donna's words were true, that I was in serious danger. I couldn't discuss this with anyone locally for fear of putting them in jeopardy, so I was pretty much isolated and devastated. Still, a part of me was in denial. *How can this be happening to me?* I was just an ordinary person, not a "hit list type."

The semi-denial and panic continued. Two days later, I went to the bank. I had to withdraw my money if I were to be "on the run." Again, the words *on the run* didn't make sense. This wasn't my life. This wasn't me, but I would have to prepare in case this were a reality. And if I were on the run, would they follow me?

It was early morning and the bank hadn't opened yet, but the line was forming. I took my place behind a couple of women, and others gathered behind me. Something felt strange. I had a creepy feeling that I was being watched. I casually looked around and spotted a man across the street staring at me. His body was facing me, motionless. He didn't dress like most of the local people there who were working people and farmers casually dressed in work clothes. He wore a new cowboy hat, had polished boots, and was neatly dressed in a clean shirt and pants. I tried to casually turn back to look ahead at the bank doors, but I could feel his eyes on me even from across the street.

I looked again and saw that he was crossing over towards me, walking slowly. He came to about a foot away from me and stared into my eyes. I gave him a "friendly" hi, trying to diffuse the tension and looked away.

He continued staring. "So you're the gringa."

I responded as lightly as I could. "Yes, I'm one of many here." Again, I turned away.

He continued to stare. Without saying another word, he cut into the line behind me, nudging a woman out of his way. His energy was palpable. I turned a bit as if to get comfortable, while placing my grocery bags in between us. It took an effort not to shake visibly. My heart was pounding.

The bank doors opened and we walked in and separated into teller lines. All of us except for this man. I looked around, and he was gone. I walked up to my regular teller and tried to pull out a withdrawal slip, but my hands were shaking badly. He asked if I was okay. I couldn't respond. He suggested that I sit down for a while, but I said no thanks, left the bank, rushed into a tuk-tuk, and went home.

Once inside, I felt paralyzed and stood in my living room. After a few minutes, I sat on the floor with my dog, Pam, and started to cry.

I didn't see that man again, but I did realize at that point that I had to tell someone. *Who? How? What the hell do I say?*

In spite of my reluctance to involve Marel, I decided I needed to call him. It was looking like I'd really have to leave Honduras, and he needed to know. There were just too many clues to avoid or to deny.

Marel came over. I asked him to sit on the sofa. For us, that usually meant something big, since we normally met at my kitchen table. He kept looking at me while I searched for words. I could not imagine what my face looked like: panic, fear, desolation. I tried not to cry.

I explained while he listened quietly. He didn't seem to be shocked, probably because these kinds of things happened so often there, but he was clearly extremely distressed. He kept repeating, "I don't want you to go." I asked him to keep this secret. He told me he would "investigate safely" and get back to me. I told him no, that this was way too dangerous. He said had confidential connections and contacts that could help us get to the bottom of things. I begged him not to, again repeating that it was too dangerous for him, as well as for me. He didn't respond. He asked me to move in with his family and I declined. How could I put his family at risk? A stray bullet or a fight could only invite more disaster. He told me he'd keep his phone by his bedside and would ask church members and his father to walk by my house regularly during the night. I said no again, not wanting to jeopardize anyone. I was sure he would go ahead with his plan anyway. There was no way to change his mind.

We said a reluctant good night. He told me he'd be over first thing in the morning. He gave me a long, giant hug and left. Once again, I was alone and paralyzed. That night, I remained home, imprisoned, scared, and completely obsessive, pacing the floor with deep unrest. Every sound made me panic. Finally, I got into bed with my clothes still on. I pulled Pam onto the bed with me and watched him continually for any signals of intruders. I had my hand on top of his body the whole night to feel a possible head or tail movement. I slept very little.

For the next day or so, I couldn't move. *Should I pack? Should I work? Should I visit friends? Should I buy groceries? Would I even need groceries if I was going to die? What does one do when they are on a hit list? And what is a hit list? Do people murder in order of the list? Am I at the top of the list or maybe way at the bottom? How much time do I have?*

Marel had done some investigating in spite of my pleas and the next day came back to me with some information. We sat down on my couch and he filled me in as much as he could. He said it was true. Again, something vague about territory and a man with a red truck came up. That man was a well-known *narco* member. These were absolutely the worst words I could have possibly heard. Marel had always protected me against all kinds of danger. He could always arrange things, fix things, organize things. He had spoken with his two hundred church members and they organized a "block watch." My block only. My house only.

I didn't notice this at first, but after my conversation with Marel, I periodically saw men walking by my house in pairs, especially in the evening. This frightened me terribly at first. They appeared to be reading. This made no sense. Why would folks be reading? When I asked Marel, he told me that he hadn't wanted to worry me, so he hadn't mentioned anything. These men were from his church, many of whom I had helped over the years in one way or another, with food baskets, emergency medical help, house repairs, and school supplies. And yes, they were in fact reading. Bibles. They were walking around my house in two-hour shifts. When Marel told me this, I didn't know whether to laugh or cry. I was so touched. These men were protecting me in shifts, two at a time, two bibles at a time, praying, monitoring, their cell phones at the ready.

Marel went to investigate some more, again against my insistent protests. I knew that I had to start packing or at least organizing for a possible sudden departure. I went to the kitchen and looked around to tackle the task. I picked up my favorite frying pan and then instantly realized I would probably not need a frying pan since I wouldn't have a home.

I went to the bedroom and looked at my clothing drawer. *Warm weather or cold weather? What does one wear when on the run? Where would I even go and how do I prepare?* I was frozen and couldn't make any decisions. I kept looking at Pam and wondering if I could take an old, incontinent, toothless dog with two broken back legs with me. *How could I leave him and not even explain?* My heart broke again each time the thought crossed my mind.

About a day later came the final blow. Marel came over with tears in his eyes. "I'm sorry, Ellen, there is nothing I can do to protect you." I had never heard the word *can't* from Marel before. He always had a solution. My heart sank. The worst moment and worst words of my entire life.

My mind kept spinning. *Where to go? When? For how long? Why? Who can I trust? Can I even say goodbye to folks? Do I need to keep this a secret? Do I even want to stay alive if I am going to lose so much? On the other hand, do I want the bad guys to win?* The thought of dying wasn't nearly as scary as the thought of exile.

There was a continual yet futile search for more information. As I came to understand it, the *narcotraficantes* didn't like that we were working in "their communities." The more we empowered the communities with schools, or a clinic, or a bakery to make them self-sufficient, the less power and control the *narcos* would have to extort from the villagers. I still didn't get it completely, but I was in no position to try and figure it out. I had to leave if I wanted to stay alive. *What do I do with my house and dog? Do I cancel the electricity? Do I buy a gun? Do I make supper?*

Returning to metaphysical support, I called my friends with psychic abilities. Each told me the same thing: "Go immediately. Pack a bag and go! It will be extremely dangerous if you stay."

I knew it made sense to my North American friends to just "come home," but the US was no longer my home. I couldn't go back to a country filled with ignorance about these issues, with so many people there living such a sheltered life. So many folks there were self-centered and self-important. Even if I did want to go back, I couldn't afford to live there. I had very little savings. At sixty-eight, how would I even make enough money to cover the cost of living? Most of all, I wanted to be as close as possible to Honduras. The US was so far away from home.

After much deliberation, I called my friend Anne who worked with me off and on in Copán for years, doing mostly medical outreach and support in the clinic. Although she lived in Chattanooga, Tennessee, she came down for months at a time, and we would work together doing projects or going into the communities to help out children and the elderly. We were great friends and could laugh easily together while still having much respect for the local people. The call took everything I had to make. I didn't know how to explain what was going on or how to ask for help. It seemed so surreal, and I was worried she would not take it seriously.

To my tremendous relief, she understood immediately, having heard about so many experiences like this in Honduras. She immediately invited me to come to her house in Chattanooga for a couple of weeks until I could come up with a plan. Her words were so comforting that the relief sent me crashing onto the sofa.

This I could do. Anne had first-hand experience, much of it the same as mine, and understood the danger, the violence, the desperation of people, the political situation, and the poverty. Going to her house was the only decent option. Otherwise, I'd go to another country somewhere in Central America and stay alone in a hotel … a horrid option. I felt an incredible sense of relief and at the same time the worst isolation and desolation I had ever experienced in my life.

Relief quickly turned to urgency and panic. *Will there be enough time? Will "they" get to me before I leave?* Another sleepless night. Every sound terrorized me.

I spent the next day trying to pack up, wondering if I was taking too much time. I arranged for Marel's family to take care of Pam. I canceled the water, electricity, and internet (I remember my internet guy asking if I was changing companies because he hated to lose me as a customer. I burst into tears), all the while worrying about my time frame. *Maybe I should leave immediately.* I was doing practical tasks like arranging dog care and taking care of all the necessities of moving, while at the same time sobbing all day long. I closed bank accounts and arranged for money to be given to my three kids should I "not be available." I spent most of my time with Marel and his family. Finally, sobbing, I told Elena. She understood immediately. It was not her first experience with this type of thing. She suggested I wait it out. Often threats were just that, not something to be taken too seriously.

My emotions changed from minute to minute. I was riddled with guilt. Survival guilt. Privilege guilt. Life was tough and scary, but I could walk away. My North American friends could send me money to help. I had a credit card. I thought of all my local friends, colleagues, and neighbors that couldn't run for their lives. There was nowhere for them to go.

To make matters even more painful and guilt-ridden, I couldn't tell anyone what was happening. I didn't want to endanger anyone. Only Marel, Zoila, and Elena knew my secret. I was sneaking out of town like a criminal.

In my last few hours, I rushed up to Llanetios to tell my orphan family in person that I had to leave because something important was pressing. I knew it was a risk staying a bit longer and making a trip up into the mountains, but I couldn't just abandon them without words. They had been abandoned so many times already.

Marel took me up there while I sobbed all the way. The moment the truck pulled up to the house, I saw their smiling, young faces and felt like my heart would literally just give out. I didn't have much time to talk and asked them to sit down, that I needed to talk with them about something very important. They pulled up a couple of broken plastic chairs and a log

"I have to leave Honduras," I said, trying to control my voice and my tears. "It's urgent." I didn't want to scare them with the truth.

Maria gasped so loud it was nearly a scream. The boys were stunned. Their shock turned to tears. "Oh no, Ellen. No!" Then came the inevitable question: "Why?"

"I can't explain right now. I'm sorry."

It felt so feeble and inadequate to answer so minimally. I felt like a traitor. Their parents died, their grandparents died, and now their surrogate mom was moving away suddenly and without giving them a reason. It was agony for me to not be able to explain.

Maria took it the worst, or at least in her emotional expression. She screamed and sobbed and threw her arms around my neck and begged me not to go. Sobbing, she said, "You'll never come back! You'll never come back! People never come back!"

As I was holding her, I looked behind her at Isaias, who was doing everything he could to hold back the tears but not succeeding.

I went to him next. He gave me a bone-crushing hug. "You can't go! I don't want you to go! You'll never come back!"

Alex, the youngest, sat down on the ground facing a tree. He wouldn't let me hug him. I tried to give him some time.

Questions kept flying, but mostly, "Why?"

I kept saying, "I'm so sorry. I have no choice. I love you all so much!"

Finally came the question everyone in Honduras ultimately asked when someone talked about leaving: "Are you in danger?"

I said reluctantly, "Possibly."

Then there was silence and a shift in their energy. This answer they could understand. It happened all the time. Better that I was safe and alive than dead.

I wasn't so sure, myself. "I will continue to be in touch and support you. You know that I love you very much and wouldn't make this choice unless it was absolutely necessary. We'll be in touch by phone and through Marel and Zoila. You can visit them anytime, and they will help us stay in contact."

My attempt at reassurance wasn't much comfort to any of us. They continued to sob. I continued to sob. Hugs continued. Horrible, sad silences. Tear-filled eye contact. And then came the moment. That horrible, horrible moment when I had to go. Tearing myself away from them was absolutely excruciating. I literally thought that I would die right then from heartbreak.

Marel gave them hugs and promised to stay in touch with them as we turned away and walked down the muddy incline to the truck. I turned back and saw them standing in a row with the saddest faces imaginable. I sobbed all the way back into town. We headed down the road that I had climbed on foot, rode on horseback, and scooted by tuk-tuk so many times. *Will I ever see these neighboring houses and these kids and smell these wonderful pine trees ever again?* In that moment, my death wish to "get it over with" was replaced by the need to survive for their sakes.

Back in town, I told a few others that I needed to leave, but without giving reasons. This was not how I did terminations. I always took pride in the fact that I could try to explain and understand and process what was happening and help others process, as well. This felt like running away. It *was* running away. I felt like a coward and hated myself. I continued to wrestle with other options. When things were tough for Hondurans, they had no options. They couldn't run away. I felt so completely spoiled and privileged. The guilt was as bad as any I had felt in my life. At least if I stayed and they killed me, I would have felt loyal. The mental debate continued frequently about staying and letting them kill me. I wouldn't have a life if I left anyway, and the horrible feeling of guilt was crippling. I was a refugee with a credit card. Never before had I seen the contrast of lifestyles so vividly. Most North Americans don't know how fortunate they are. This made me furious, bitter, and resentful. My issue was a common, normal occurrence for much of the world, and this seemed so painfully unfair.

I thought about the murder weapons after I arrived home. *Would they shoot me or cut my head off with a machete?* Those were the most common murder options. I thought of my preference of a gun. Machetes terrified me. If I died, I'd be no good to anyone. If I lived, my life would be hideous, filled with loneliness, guilt, depression; I'd be disconnected and without an identity. I had never felt so powerless in my entire life or faced consequences so grave. Sleep was not an option. *Might they come at night?* I was wired. I tried lying down and cuddling with my incontinent dog. I would miss him so much.

The next day, I called my extremely intuitive friend. She cried, "Go now. Pack a bag and *go*! Run!" It was going to happen right away. That day even. It was a reality. No more denial. No more bargaining.

I stuffed a few things into a small duffel bag. *Should I bring warm clothes, summer clothes? What kind of shoes? My camera? My laptop?* My heart was pounding; I'm not sure if it was grief or fear.

I called Marel and within an hour he pulled up with his big blue truck filled with a few friends. *For protection?* He walked into to the house deliberately and grabbed my bag. I stayed behind for a moment and looked at my pretty yellow house and then at my beautiful flower garden that took so many years to develop. I locked the door, walked over to him, and with trembling hands, gave him the keys. The walk to the truck was the most depressing twenty feet I had ever walked. It felt like death row. A dark cloud hung over me. It was the end of life as I knew it.

Marel and other loved ones took me to the airport that afternoon, a four-hour trip. I was sobbing all the way. They were silent. A bitter numbness replaced the grief. As we drove, I said goodbye to the town, to the houses and shops of friends, and the park that I had come to love. Then onto the highway, the potholed road that was never in good repair.

Along the way, we passed the women selling corn roasted on barbecues, ten cents each. Broken shacks. Beautiful green fields and mountains, farms of corn growing high. I'd miss all of it. Eventually came the hideous sight of the airport. Cement and airplanes.

I dragged my body out of the truck, along with a small bag of clothes, leaving my entire life behind. I felt so small, so scared, so alone. There we were, surrounded by families saying hello or goodbye to their relatives, but with joy and hugs. I was a refugee holding a one-way ticket. Absolute desolation, a crushing depression, and terrified of what was ahead.

Chapter 35

Thank God for Anne. There she was, upon my arrival, taking me in with smiles and affection. She whisked me away in her car. It was a whole car, not a vehicle pieced together by parts. It was in working order. It was new and clean. The seats were comfortable, and everything worked. I could open the window by pressing a button. We were on a highway, not a rutted piece of road. I saw houses that were new and clean with driveways, and manicured lawns, and neatly painted fences. Dogs were fat and healthy. Kids were wearing clothing that wasn't ripped or dirty. There were stoplights that people obeyed. There were advertisements on billboards that presented luxury and options. The models were all happy and white. It was like landing in Oz.

She took me to her home. Comfortable furniture, potable water right from the sink. You could see right through it. Electricity. Good lighting. All kinds of food options in the fridge. She showed me my room. It was safe. I couldn't remember the last time I had felt safe. There were window screens, so no bugs. No spiders on the walls. No noise at night, no one shooting, no one killing anyone, no piercing screams of dogfights. No roosters crowing at 3:00 a.m. I slept in pajamas for the first time in many months. No telephone beneath my pillow. No weapons on the night table. I cried myself to sleep.

My laptop was my lifeline. Most US folks didn't believe what I was telling them. I think even Anne had doubts that it was real, and at moments even I doubted it. It was a consequence of my friends and I living in such different realities. It made me crazy, and I felt even lonelier. Some friends abandoned me. It was too painful for them to experience feeling so helpless. I tried to understand, but losses piled on top of losses and it was just too much to bear. I went into denial about the pain of their loss. I couldn't deal with that too.

A giant piece of good fortune did smile upon me during that period. While I was in my last months in Honduras, I had found an amazing therapist online, and we had been working together through Skype if and when we had electricity and internet. Linda was my lifeline. Before the issue of imminent danger occurred, we had started working together on issues of secondary trauma. She asked me once if I was in danger. I thought, "What an odd question." *Why would she ask that?* I'd said no, I didn't think so. Then, I remember telling her a week or so later, that yes, I thought I was. Up until then I hadn't considered that I was in danger. My awareness of the seriousness of my situation was growing.

Linda and I continued to work together though all of this weekly during my refugee time. We worked on untangling the tentacles of co-dependence that I had with Honduras, a slow process of letting go that began before my escape and continued throughout my recovery. She most likely saved my life.

I was hungry for information, mostly from Marel, but little came. *Could I go back? When would I go back?* I couldn't stay at Anne's house forever. Linda kept encouraging me to just do "normal things" for a while. *Normal? Normal for North America? Go out to breakfast with an array of all possible goodies to eat?* Beans and tortillas were normal. *Chairs undamaged that are not made of plastic?* Suddenly I was living the high life. Some people at the restaurants actually left food on their plates and walked away. I wanted to grab a bag and take it all home to folks who didn't eat. But then, I wasn't home, was I?

Anne's friends were intelligent and worldly, and I liked them. It certainly helped to connect with them and see another part of life. At the same time, I felt so different, so alone, and so incredibly homesick.

The chilling news came a couple of days after my arrival at Anne's. My neighbors had called Marel. He called me. The night I left, three armed men came to my house looking for me. My neighbor said they circled the house for hours in their fancy, brand new Hilux truck. These men asked where I was, my neighbor told me through Marel. Bad folks, she said. No one seemed to know. Rumors abounded. Sick parents, dead parents, sick brother, I was sick. I was in the United States. I was in Europe. I was in El Salvador. My favorite rumor was that I had beaten up a young tuk-tuk driver and fled afterwards. It was my first chuckle in months. Yes, a seventy-year-old woman beat up a young stud. I liked that one.

I would come to find out that these men continued to circle my house every day for the next month. *What if I had stayed a few more hours in Honduras?* On the other hand, I was in so much pain, I kept thinking that at least it would have been over. Then my thoughts turned to my kids. They loved and needed me. I loved them.

Staying with Anne was so helpful. I played with all the luxuries in her house. I flushed the toilet just because I could. She had pretty little soaps. My first bathtub in years! I was in Wonderland. She listened to me sob and helped me try to work out a plan, at least for the next step. Lots of friends invited me to come and stay with them. I couldn't accept. All I wanted was to be as close to Honduras as possible. I wanted to go home! I felt like a lost little girl. I just wanted to go home.

Over the years, it had become increasingly harder to relate to the lifestyles of my Western friends. Our lives had become so different. It was hard to listen to their descriptions of dinner parties or vacations. I could still relate when we talked about personal issues and politics and philosophy, but I had become so wrapped up in a different culture and lifestyle that I was not always the best listener. I was almost obsessed with my work and the issues at hand. I needed them and needed the support badly, but I couldn't enter their world without pain. Pain from the contrast. Pain from the relative ease and safety of their lives. Pain from the tremendous discrepancy of resources between countries. I was caught between two worlds. I'd never be fully Honduran, and I was no longer North American. I was sorry for the people I had let down, on both ends. I felt that I had deserted the people I loved in both countries, in different ways.

For the first couple of weeks, I tried to pretend I was on vacation. It worked occasionally. I ate bagels, was treated to performances, laughed at American TV, and even bought new clothes. That was definitely a lift, finally having clothes that fit, that were new and not ripped or stained, that were my style. It was hard at times, treating myself, and yet at other times, it felt so good to have some of the "good life." I was torn between staying in the comfort and safety of my friends and the nice people I was meeting, and the need to get back home.

I loved that Anne and I could talk about Honduran life and she would get it. She could understand me, and the culture, and the situation. However, it was time to leave. I toyed with the idea of staying and finding an apartment for a few months, but that was just a fleeting option. I was compelled to at least be back in Central America, even if it wasn't Honduras. I hated to leave her, knowing I would feel so lonely without her, and yet I couldn't stay. I couldn't stay anywhere, really.

Life was like sitting on a hot stove. I was in so much pain that nothing would feel comfortable, and so overwhelmed that nothing felt clear. I thought that maybe exploring Central America would help educate me and open new possibilities. This meant spending more money from my little savings, but then if I was saving for a rainy day, this period was surely "it."

I bought a ticket to Nicaragua. I traveled around a bit. I met some nice people, but it was too far away from my kids, and I missed them terribly. Loneliness and desolation followed me relentlessly. Even though I was able to talk on the phone with folks in Honduras, the signal and connections were terrible, and there was not much to say. I regularly called my kids in Llanetios. The same question kept coming up: "When are you coming home?" I had no answers. It broke my heart each time I had to say I didn't know. My friend Yarely helped me transfer some emergency money to them. They were always in dire straights, and I hoped this would let them know in a concrete way that I was still there for them. I always included a loving note.

They didn't understand. I couldn't tell them. I just sent words of love and caring, saying that I would do what I could. I remembered an old movie where a couple talked about being apart but they would look at the moon and know that it was the same moon, and the thought would help them feel closer. I told Isai this. Whenever he looked at the moon, he would think of me looking at the moon and thinking of him. He told me that gave him tremendous comfort.

Nicaragua was comforting. At least I was back in Central America. But a life there? I couldn't see it. An option came to me, vague, but at least it was an option. I remembered someone had told me about a wonderful experience they had in Guatemala with the Mayan people. I thought about this. Mayan people were generally so sweet and peaceful, connected to the land and their culture. Maybe this was worth investigation. Guatemala would also be closer to the western part of Honduras where I used to live. My kids at least could come and see me. I could pay for their trips. And at least I'd be in gorgeous territory with kind people. That could be the start of some healing. With some financial help from a friend, I flew to Guatemala.

* * *

I have now been living in Guatemala for three years. It is peaceful here. I am surrounded by incredible natural beauty and lovely people. The Honduran government has since caught and imprisoned the men who threatened my life. Nevertheless, I will not return to Honduras to live due to the extent of need there and due to the constant threat of violence from gangs, local desperate people in need, and the continuation of major drug trafficking throughout that area. Although I am doing projects here in Guatemala, I am so happy that I am now able to visit Honduras more safely (for short periods of time). We continue to do projects there, as well. I love these visits!

My first return trip was mind-blowing and revealing. It was so incredibly love-filled! I was home again! Tremendous feelings of gratitude were accompanied by awareness of what I had lost. As the visits continued every few months, my perspective grew. I could see the hooks. They were almost palpable and definitely visceral.

Hindsight is an amazing gift. I have a much broader global perspective now, as well as new insights into my own personal issues and the traps that they can cause. There is a kind of hero or saint stereotype that attaches to people who do this kind of work. People often have referred to me as one or the other, and I think often this is because our work is so public. We send out newsletters with our accomplishments, or visitors are able to visibly see what we do. We sometimes face enormous challenges and sacrifice quite a bit to do what we do, therefore we can appear "heroic." It's easy to get seduced by that and start believing some of it. I've learned so much about myself and my ego.

I also think of all the folks who fight less publicly every day, supporting the preservation of the environment and public safety, or working as political activists. There are endless examples of committed people who are improving the situation of the downtrodden. Their work is often less publicly seen or acknowledged but requires enormous commitment, energy, and often self-sacrifice.

I did what I did, and I do what I do, because I truly love helping out. I always have. I haven't always fit the model I would have liked to be ... that is, the ever-patient, spiritually based helper, but this is an ongoing process and I hope I have the opportunity to keep growing. I am continuing to learn about myself and about the *art* of helping out without self-damage and damage to others.

I am still in the process of healing from the tremendous grief and fear I experienced over the course of eleven years in Central America, and I am still learning, *poco a poco* (little by little), how to reopen my heart.

Epilogue

You've got to be kidding! Write a book? Do you know how hard that is? When folks suggested that I write down my stories about my life in Honduras, it was something that I could never imagine. *Easy to suggest,* I thought. *No way I'd put myself through something like that.* And yet, these messages chipped away at my resistance.

Things started to reach a climax where I actually considered doing it. At first, it seemed like an overwhelming task, like hearing in the initial meeting with a therapist that this process would take several years. I had so much to say and didn't know how to begin. I also had a number of fears and concerns.

For the first couple of years after I had left Honduras, I was afraid to talk. Afraid to endanger anyone. Afraid of the immense flood that would pour out of me if I broke down the dam. I was new and on my own in Guatemala, with no local support. *What can I do to stabilize myself during this process?*

I was also afraid of burdening my friends who were already tired of hearing about my experiences, mostly of my crises. My emotional needs were just too great. I wasn't afraid of releasing the joy, laughter, and love that was also inside, but the predominant feelings of sadness, horror, anguish, would overcome me if I pursued writing a book.

My other concern was that I didn't have any experience as a writer except for writing my thesis in graduate school. The learning curve would be too steep. I was not a writer and didn't want to be.

And yet, I had to get this out of me! It was burdensome to carry this load alone. I often thought about the PTSD that veterans faced coming home from a war and the emotional cargo they brought with them without adequate opportunities to unload.

I stuffed this desire for years, until a sudden encounter set up the possibility. A friend of mine was visiting Guatemala with a group of university staff and asked if I would meet with them and talk about my projects here in Central America. Always loving to talk about my work, I invited them to my house. We sat on my giant porch with coffee and cake, overlooking my lush garden, and I talked about our projects, about some past stories of my work, and about the complicated issue of humanitarian aid. Most folks eagerly participated, and among the group was a professor of cultural psychology who particularly stood out.

He spoke to me afterwards and said that I absolutely had to write a book, that these experiences were so colorful and informative. I told him that I had thought about this many times, but it was just too big of a project and explained my reservations. He offered a surprising new twist to the process. He told me I could dictate to him, and he would record and write the stories down. I was intrigued by this idea and his sincere offer to help. I told him I'd be open to discussing it further. We met a couple more times before he left. Each time he took notes and offered ideas on how to organize the writing.

I loved being listened to, heard, and supported. I had so much I wanted to say and eagerly awaited each meeting. His trip came to an end, and we agreed to keep meeting through Skype when he got home. We set up a process where we'd meet regularly, once a week, through Skype. I would dictate, he would record, and the transcript would be printed out before the next session. It was fabulous to talk. It was my favorite subject. It felt so releasing to put my thoughts and opinions out there.

At first, it all came out in a rush of words, rants, stories, opinions, insights, and complaints. I talked about my experiences, my fears, and my thoughts on humanitarian aid. I felt like I could talk for weeks nonstop. This rush of words, however, came out all over the map. When a dam breaks, you get everything all at once. This oral process was a fabulous release, but I wasn't able to organize a system in my brain without first writing down what I needed to say. I was continually overwhelmed and scattered, pelted with memories, feelings, thoughts.

Although it was cathartic, I was still holding myself back emotionally. I couldn't talk to a stranger about my deepest feelings and needs, and this book was about being an emotional witness to very intense experiences. Although I loved the idea of working this way and having a great and willing writing partner to help, I realized I really did need to actually write down what I wanted to say, look at it, think about it, and organize and edit it on my own. He said he understood, but I was concerned about letting him down. However, I knew I had to do it myself. Again, I felt overwhelmed by such a daunting task. *How can I do all this by myself? What the hell have I started?*

A dear friend, Caroline Allen, who runs a book-coaching business called Art of Storytelling, had encouraged me from the beginning to write my stories. She kept encouraging me as I wrote. As time went on she, offered her help as a writing coach and editor. She has decades of experience. She has been an international journalist and is now a published novelist. After some deliberation and months of working on my own, I hired her as my coach and editor. Much to my shock and delight, she donated the first three months of coaching for the good of the cause.

We went to work. She was incredibly positive and encouraging, with amazing ideas. She was well organized. She also had great insights about me, having known me so well for so many years. She helped me tap into emotions that I had been burying and kept encouraging me to go further, to go deeper. As a world traveler and international journalist, she also understood deeply the imbalance of the patriarchal, privileged world versus the world of the have-nots. It was a good match creatively, politically, and personally, and that moved me forward. She was very sensitive, and it was important to me to not feel criticized personally by the feedback but be given the information I needed in a constructive way. I decided to go further with her. In my head, however, I kept the back door open. If this got too hard, I would bolt!

My commitment was to write two or three hours per day, six days per week. Caroline's commitment was to send back written feedback and discuss the work biweekly via Skype. I sent her my stories for review a few days before our meeting. Finding topics was never a problem for me; ideas kept exploding out of my brain. I couldn't wait to sit down each morning to write.

Caroline's feedback was always extremely helpful, interesting, and exciting, and I was eager to learn about how to express myself through the written word. I was not so eager, however, to learn about computer programs like Google Docs, MS Word, or how to organize things on my computer, having no experience or much comfort with technology. Inner tantrums abounded, coupled with external complaints that this was all too much!

Consequently, there were two barriers: breaking through the fear of the mechanics of writing, and the fear of allowing myself to speak about what would be very emotionally challenging subjects. The computer-skill barrier, after a short time, started to dissipate (but only to a point).

At first, the stories came out of me like a flood. So many memories, so many emotions, so many ideas, and I was so eager to communicate. I would sit in my tiny Guatemalan house in my "writing room," which was really a closet with an ugly, broken, blue tile floor, walls painted a hideous shade of electric lime-green. Each morning I would get up at 4:00, get my coffee, go to the "room," and do a spider check to see what crawling visitors might have arrived in the night. I would kill the dangerous ones and let the others stay. (I had a favorite one in the corner I named Charlotte.) It was quiet at that time, except for the roosters, so the flow was uninterrupted. I loved that peaceful, special time all to myself. After a couple of hours, the birds would start chirping and the sun would start to come up, indicating it was time to start my workday. It was disappointing to pull myself away, but I had a sense of satisfaction and eagerness to return.

I didn't tell many people that I was writing. It seemed like such a pretentious thing to say. Who was I to think that I had something people would want to read about? My work? My life? My thoughts?

My long-time, trusted friend Dan, who lives in Canada, was the only person I was actually comfortable mentioning my writing to. He kept encouraging me. He had great writing skills and a great sense of humor, so his encouragement meant a great deal. I would send him an occasional paragraph, not to edit, but just to tell him about an incident I had remembered. A few shaky times when I was ready to quit this nonsense, he was solidly there, telling me absolutely not to stop. During our thirty-five years of friendship, he rarely told me what to do, so this statement had quite an impact on me.

I wrote about the Honduran people I knew and loved, and some of the comical incidents. These topics were emotionally safer. No pain, just positive memories. It was comforting and healing. It was a mental trip home. I was starting to remember things besides tragedy and fear. Caroline continued by my side during this process, not as a therapist, but nevertheless it was extremely therapeutic. She would encourage me to "talk more" and to go into more detail, a process that had never been strongly encouraged in my life. She told me not to edit my thoughts or feelings, just let it come out on paper in whatever way it wanted to. We would edit later. This made the process much less daunting. It was so releasing and fun! I could say things without having to be polite or politically correct. No holds barred. I could tell my secrets, spew venom, or be sarcastic—whatever I wanted.

The more difficult chapters started to come within a couple of months. I was slowly becoming ready to talk about some of the painful experiences. Some of the previously forgotten, horrific, haunting memories started to come out. So would the tears and the agony. There were stories about children's deaths; abused, neglected, and poisoned animals; mothers dying in labor; murders. For days I would cry over some of these, and afterwards sit on my porch and stare out to nowhere for hours at a time.

One story that particularly challenged me was of the father carrying his final remaining living child into town and the child dying in the blanket. Every time I reread and rewrote this episode, my heart broke in unimaginable ways. I hadn't experienced the full impact of my emotion at the time of the event. It had been too painful to let it sink in. It completely enveloped me to write it. I revised it over and over, sometimes only adding a word. It didn't matter. I just wanted to be with them. I cried on and off for weeks. I finally got to cry!

The process was hugely cathartic but drained every ounce of energy out of me. Some days, I could barely go to work. I didn't want to leave this story and move to another chapter. More than anything else, I wanted to stay with that tiny boy and his father and grieve. Although extremely painful, the good news was that after seven years in Honduras of suppressing my feelings and thoughts, I finally had a vehicle that allowed me to express myself, and I wanted to stay with my emotions.

This brought an additional challenge: how to stop the rush of feelings from overcoming me each time. I would write down memories and thoughts and refer back to add more thoughts and more details. This made events more real and concrete. I could pick up that page and reread my stories anytime I wanted.

One astonishing effect of this was that I could see just how many incidents there were of pain and misery. I'd had no idea until then the extent of the pain and grief that I had been experiencing during all those years. It was enormous. Without the writing process, I didn't have the perspective. At the time of the actual events, new crises would curtail the reactions to older crises. During those years, I just kept keeping on.

On one chapter, as I was exploring the myriad number of deaths that I had experienced, I was trying to recall all of my friends, co-workers, and neighbors who were killed. I was afraid that if I didn't keep their names in my head or the count of deaths, I'd forget them, and their deaths would therefore somehow be in vain. I was their witness and their voice.

At first, I only had vague thoughts and memories of a number of deaths. I kept it in my head—something like twenty people that I knew had died—almost like a newspaper headline. I could not remember specifics. It is difficult to write well without specifics. I remember meeting with Caroline about this. I told her I couldn't remember all of the deaths and had a feeling of panic that I had forgotten them. Or maybe I was making some of this up, or exaggerating.

Caroline suggested that maybe this was the effect of trauma, that the more time I spent on the chapter, the more likely the names and faces would come back to me. I tried to relax, stay calm, and move on with our conversation. In an instant, like a thick rubber band snapping, the flood of faces passed through my mind and I remembered with horror the people, their families, and the violent incidents that caused their deaths. It was horrific. It was like I was experiencing it for the first time, but this time with an emotional impact that had me reeling. I started to sob. Not just with sadness and horror, but also with overwhelming guilt. I wanted to apologize profusely for temporarily forgetting them and diminishing their importance. For years I had been trying to memorize them so as not to lose them, and consequently this process circled in my brain endlessly. And still I had forgotten so many. Writing it all down, telling the stories, took the pain away from obsession and into healing.

Although excruciating at times, this process of telling my stories reduced my obsessive memories almost immediately, and as I moved into the heavier stories, I was able to take them on, knowing that I would ultimately feel better. Therapy.

I was also fortunate to be working with my incredible therapist, Linda. She helped me enormously. She had the social and political awareness to not treat what I was going through as a mental health issue. She helped me become aware that what I was experiencing was a normal reaction to an unhealthy situation. We also looked at my early family dynamics, which resulted in me making some decisions that were not always for the best. I had learned to stay in unhealthy situations regardless of my emotional damage.

With Linda, Caroline, and Dan, I had a great team of support. They gave me strength, insights, and encouragement, and I was able to continue to write and looked forward to it each day. Now, even the pain couldn't stop me. There were times when I was emotionally exhausted, and the fears of writing, and the fears of facing "the uglies" came up, but I could deal with that. Caroline and Linda helped me set limits and find ways to care for myself in this process. I needed to learn to not only be aware of when it was too much, but also how to take a break. I needed to titrate some of these experiences, sometimes only writing a bit and then going to a more upbeat story, or just taking a break from writing.

At one point, I couldn't go any further. My overwhelming feelings of sadness, pain, and rage were too much. I just had to stop. Caroline suggested that I write a "gratitude chapter," not necessarily to put in the book, but to help me move along, to revisit the good that had come out of my experience. I liked the idea but wasn't sure I could get to that point at the time. I sat down a couple of times. Nothing. I wasn't feeling gratitude. I was feeling pain, fury, and low-grade depression. After two or three days of frustration, I decided to write the chapter in form of a "love letter to Honduras." My heart opened and all the love started flowing out. I was grateful for my experience and the opportunity to learn what Honduras had to teach me. I was grateful for all the people I loved. I was grateful to have the privilege to be in the position of neighbor, helper, and emotional witness. Loving faces kept flashing before me. First, Isaias, my Honduran son; and Maria and Alexander, who I love so much; and then a series of beautiful people: Elena, Marel, Zoila, Yarely, and a myriad of others. My heart just started to open again and joy started seeping into my being as I thought about all of the children that I loved so much, and the special teachers and community leaders. As I wrote this piece, I started to rediscover other ways to nurture myself during this process.

Music helped. I often put on music afterwards to break the cloud of emotion that was enveloping me. Sometimes I'd go to my piano and bang away, or play something sensitive and classical. Music has always been my release.

Caroline's gratitude idea worked! My mind was freed up again. I was delighted to have pushed through this hurdle and went back to work, naively thinking I was mostly done with the writing challenges.

However, then came a whole new one: I needed to write chapters where I talked more intellectually about the subjects of international aid, guilt, and secondary trauma. I was not an academic writer. I had much that I wanted to say about these subjects, but I couldn't seem to put this down in writing the way I wanted. Words and ideas came out disorganized and unclear. It was a mess. I whined constantly about having to organize my thoughts and write. This was not my best skill, although whining indeed was.

Caroline seemed nonplussed. *Oh no, not more! I don't want to!* My main phrase almost became a mantra: *I'm not a writer.* I just wanted to tell my stories and thoughts! I had always pictured writers as stoically sitting in front of their computers with calm persistence, and here I was, acting like a six-year-old. My constant internal complaint was, *Now what do you want?!*

I always expected Caroline to tell me to "shut up, grow up, and just do it," but she always helped me find a way to tackle the next hurdle. Almost always, I signed off from our meetings with encouraged excitement. *I can do this!* To my relief, this process moved along nicely for many months. It had a good rhythm.

After almost a year in Guatemala, I was told that it was safe to go back to visit Honduras. Including the first months of wandering, it had been well over a year and a half of agony, of banishment from people I loved and cared about. I was told that they had captured the group of *narcotraficantes* who were after me and that it was safe to go back. I wasn't certain I believed that. The consequences could be grave if we were wrong, but I was desperate to come home.

I decided to go for a visit, but not to move back there. I planned the visit cautiously and was committed to return to Guatemala if I felt even a twinge of fear about my safety. I would go for only four or five days. I was worried about the street violence. My sweet town had become so dangerous. However, I was so lonely and cut off from folks who I wanted to be with, and for me it was worth the risk.

Excitedly, I made my plans. The day for departure arrived. I could barely breathe, I was so excited. My two-day trip was by shuttle van; I would have to spend a night in a hotel and transfer to another shuttle service the next day, a total travel time of about twenty-four hours. As we rode closer to the Honduran border, I recognized familiar places such as the hospital in Chiquimula where we took so many children and pregnant women. Flooding memories, the heat, the familiar plants and trees, the watermelon patches for miles. As we edged closer, I noticed that the other passengers were asleep or quietly talking among themselves. In contrast, I was doing everything possible to hold back tears of joy. I laughed at the thought of losing complete control and standing up, turning, and announcing to the other passengers, "I AM GOING HOME!" As we pulled up to the border crossing, my heart was pounding. Joy, fear, anticipation, and desire. I could barely breathe.

My re-entry turned out to be way more mind-blowing than I even had anticipated. As I crossed the border, scared, excited, and hopeful, I entered the immigration station and immediately ran into people I knew. Upon seeing them, my heart almost leapt out of its cavity. They showered me with handshakes, smiles, even hugs, telling me how much they missed me. It delighted me to no end. I would have cleared immigration in a matter of minutes had it not been for the greetings of so many folks, passers by, money changers, immigration and customs staff, and even the bridge-raising guy. Folks asked me where I had been, what had I been doing? Was I coming back to stay? Why did I leave?

I answered with the truth: *amenazas* (threats). Everyone immediately knew what that meant. It was common that folks fled because of threats, extortion, murder, or revenge. Not one person asked for details. Everyone knew not to ask for details. Too dangerous. I said my *hasta luego*s as our bus reloaded, and we took off for the *pueblo* that was only a ten-minute ride away, excitement building as we closed in on our destination.

At the edge of town, I transferred to a tuk-tuk. Inside was Marvin, one of my favorite drivers, handsome, strong, and always polite and respectful. I remembered the time he literally picked me up out of the tuk-tuk and carried me across a giant, flooding road. I felt like Katherine Hepburn in *African Queen*. Here he was again giving me a big laugh and smile along with a huge hug. Same questions. Same answers. He grabbed my bag, threw it in the tuk-

tuk, and we were off, chatting and laughing. He told me how people were wondering about me and how much they missed me. It was so gratifying.

Entering through town, I felt like a returning queen. As the tuk-tuk puttered through the roads, I saw the shock and smiles on people's faces. They waved enthusiastically as I passed by. I just as enthusiastically waved back, almost falling out of the tuk-tuk with such joy. I saw the familiar sights and smells of Copán. I was home! Tears of joy kept pouring out of my eyes as the journey went on. Passing Central Park, I saw more familiar faces. I recognized some of my street dogs and was so glad that they were still alive. As we ascended the hill where I used to live, I saw my beloved yellow house from a distance. I passed familiar neighbors, kids, and dogs.

We finally pulled up to Elena's house, where I'd be staying. People came running from the neighboring houses and the streets, hurrying towards me with open arms. Kids ran at full speed, and—most wonderfully—Marel, Zoila, and their family were there. Giant hugs ensued. And there was my *Mami* Elena, my trusted friend. It was so good to be home! I couldn't stop crying. I had missed them all so terribly. Telling Marel that I'd see him in a little while, Elena took me in and gave me a great meal, joined by Elena's *posada* (guest house) staff and local workers. I was once again eating the best beans and tortillas of my life.

We started catching up. She filled me in on town happenings and the state of safety there, what I needed to do or not do, where I shouldn't go alone, what politicians were still in office, and who I might want to avoid. After a couple of hours, and with a full stomach, I ventured out cautiously, still unsure of my safety. Just to stand on the cobblestone road again meant so much to me. To my amazement and pure joy, I couldn't walk five feet without a greeting, a hug, or kids running up and slamming their little bodies into mine.

Same questions: *Where have you been? Why did you leave?* Same answer: *amenazas*. I needed to tell the truth this time. Although I hadn't said anything when I first left except to a couple of people, word got around. Also, some folks had already assumed I had been threatened, since this was a common exit situation. I wanted them to know that I hadn't thoughtlessly abandoned them. I had run for my life. Everyone knew and understood. I felt I had been released from my imprisoning thoughts of abandoning my loved ones. Redemption.

That day and the five days of my visit were one big lovefest, with folks surrounding me at all times, like nothing I had ever experienced. I was finally released from banishment and the guilt of leaving. Through all of this, my mind periodically referred to my book. Yes, I was starting to call it "my book." I also felt at that time that I would be able to write more easily when I got home and add more happy chapters. I had new emotions to add.

I can't say I didn't have moments of terror when a "*narco* car," a brand new Toyota Hilux with lots of bling, appeared. *Do they know about me? Are they friends of my potential assassins? Should I discontinue my visit and rush back to Guatemala?* The pull to stay was too strong.

Meanwhile, I was taking everything in, I imagined, like a "real" writer. I was observing, seeing things I hadn't really noticed before, and looking at my own reactions, as well. The greens seemed greener and the smell of the dusty roads wafted up, the aroma of the river, and the smell of heat rose up from the ground. I noticed people's faces differently. I looked at their eyes more intensely, looked at their creviced skin, took in the beauty of farmer skin. I also paid more attention to the emotional feelings that were expressed in people's faces and the subtleties of the words that they spoke or didn't speak. Everything became more vivid.

I left on my planned day, heartbroken to say goodbye again, especially to my three kids in Llanetios who had already had so many goodbyes in their lives, but I also knew I could now begin regular visits. I was also excited about getting back to writing. My stories would be refreshed by new visuals and new perspectives. Leaving would be different this time. Sad, but also hopeful. I saw a future, and I saw a further connection through writing. I saw why I had to leave and why I had to come back. New eyes.

A pattern began of visiting about every three months, each time with so much joy, lessening fears, and new revelations and insights about my past life and work there. Often I felt like someone meeting up with an-ex husband and remembering all the things I loved, hated, or was annoyed by. *Did I always feel this way? Did I always react this way? How many times did "this" happen? Was there always so much garbage in the river?* I didn't remember being so popular, being so loved and so cared about. I began to see the hooks that kept me co-dependently tied to people who needed help, and how my need to fix things used to take over, and how unhealthy this was for me. This all fueled my motivation to write. I was compelled to share what I was learning.

Then, to my surprise, came a sort of mission with my writing. A shift. I no longer wanted to write stories just about my feelings and experiences. There was also a need to inform people in the Western world about inequities brought on by extreme poverty, about privilege, about patriarchal systems, about the inadequacy of international aid. It became less about me and more about the needs of the world and the gigantic imbalance of resources.

Most books I had read about workers in foreign countries dealt with such inequities but glossed over the internal process of the person experiencing the situation. Many read like hero stories, where the main character was nearly flawless and never lost hope or questioned themselves. If I were to do this differently, if I were to be more self-disclosing in my writing, I knew it could mean opening myself up to a flood of reaction, and my fear of rejection or criticism started to worry me. Initially when I started to write, it was in a way to protect myself, but it wasn't gut writing. I was being tactful and careful, self-conscious. I needed to confront this.

Caroline had said all along that the real me wasn't completely coming through, but I didn't understand her at first. I realized ultimately that being over seventy made me a tough ol' bird who could withstand the confrontations and feedback. Consequently, I started getting a little bolder in what I wanted to say and how I wanted to say it. And I could always pull the plug if I wanted to.

I put my worry away and spoke more from my gut. As Caroline often said, we can cut parts out later if I needed to, but we needed to speak our truth fully first, and not self-edit. That is where the power of storytelling lies. It was comforting to know that I could say everything I believed, and also that I could revisit it later and decide how much I was willing to expose.

What was my motivation for writing? Of course it was an opportunity to undergo catharsis and to process all that had happened, but the motivation became more complex as time went on. It was fun sharing my stories and experiences, but I also wanted people to see what it was like and to have an experience out of their comfort zones, even if it was secondhand. I wanted folks to wake up. I wanted to help make changes in the world where more people would participate in taking care of our brothers and sisters, maybe through financial support of good organizations, or through self-education. I also wanted to show my gratitude to the wonderful supporters throughout the years, and for them to have a clearer, deeper picture of what I really went though and what Hondurans faced daily, thereby connecting all of us even more intimately.

I also wanted to write this to apologize and explain to those who wanted more of my love, my time, and my energy that although I love them very much, I was, and still am, compelled to do this exhausting, time- and energy-consuming but fulfilling work.

I would love to see a bigger push to help develop international aid in healthy ways and not accept the limiting traditions of charity. Most of all, I hope that this book can help folks transform the world a little bit more, bringing more consciousness and efforts to balance resource distribution. Finally, I would love to see more openness and acceptance of one another, and for people to become kinder and more loving to those who are different from themselves.

This book has become the outcome of all that I have processed over the years. Love, pain, and joy all bring transformation. Being away from that life has given me way more perspective. I feel like I am coming full circle in this experience of living and working and witnessing that which is Honduras.

About the Author

Ellen Finn is a former counselor and social worker. She became a jazz bassist and composer at age fifty. At nearly sixty, she fell in love with the people of Honduras, sold most of her belongings, and moved to Copán. She set up an informal organization, *Buenos Vecinos*, to provide aid to people living in extreme poverty. During her years in Honduras, as well as in her current life, Ellen spends a great deal of time rescuing, treating, and finding homes for street dogs. She plays jazz piano.

Ellen currently lives in Guatemala and continues her work in both countries. She has just completed the construction of her twentieth school. Contact Ellen through *Buenos Vecinos* at www.buenosvecinos.org or at Ellenlfinn@hotmail.com.

All earnings from this book will go to *Buenos Vecinos*. Donations are always very much appreciated!

Accomplishments

with the Help of our Great Donors

Communities Served

Guatemala: 10 Honduras: 80

Construction

- 21 schools and classrooms

- 2 school playgrounds

- 2 bridges so children could access the schools from their homes

- 1 community medical clinic

- 1 cooperative bakery

- 11 water projects, small and large

- 1 library serving 7 villages

- 16 school bathrooms and wash sinks

- 30 villages received school repairs and renovations

- 60 schools received shelves, desks, and blackboards

- 11 clinics received furniture

Programs

- Ongoing nutrition and health programs for schools include vitamin supplements, milk programs, medical visits, and health and hygiene workshops

- Recycling for soaps project: recycled cans and bottles can be traded at the schools for various kinds of soap

- Shoes for more than 2,000 kids

- Emergency medical support and transport for kids and pregnant women

- Christmas baskets containing clothing, food, toys, and miscellaneous items for more than 250 families yearly

Student Support

- School supplies for students in 80 communities

- Teaching materials for more than 100 classrooms

- Donated textbooks and storybooks for more than 100 schools

Scholarship Program

- Supplemental financial support to hundreds of grade-school students

- Grants for high-school kids

Medical Support

- Equipment, medical supplies, furniture, and medicines to 11 rural clinics

- Emergency transportation to doctors' offices, clinics, or hospitals

- Visits to children in local hospitals and donations of stuffed animals

Relief Work

- Emergency relief for floods, hurricanes, and community displacement

- Emergency food banks and clothing banks

Further Reading

Anderson, Mary B., Dayna Brown, and Isabella Jean. *Time to Listen: Hearing People on the Receiving End of International Aid*. Cambridge: CDA Collaborative Learning Projects, 2012.

Corbett, Steve, and Brian Fikkert. *When Helping Hurts: How to Alleviate Poverty without Hurting the Poor ... and Yourself*. Chicago: Moody Publishers, 2009.

Kidder, Tracy. *Mountains Beyond Mountains: The Quest of Dr. Paul Farmer, A Man Who Would Cure the World*. New York: Random House, 2003.

Lanier, Sarah A. *Foreign to Familiar: A Guide to Understanding Hot and Cold Climate Cultures*. Hagerstown: McDougal Publishing, 2000.

Lupton, Robert D. *Toxic Charity: How Churches Hurt Those They Help (and How to Reverse It)*. San Francisco: HarperOne, 2012.

Newton, Connie, and Fran Early. *Doing Good ... Says Who?* Minneapolis: Two Harbors Press, 2015.

Van Dernoot Lipsky, Laura, and Connie Burk. *Trauma Stewardship: An Everyday Guide to Caring for Self While Caring for Others*. Oakland: Berrett-Koehler, Publishers Inc., 2009.

55512208R00203

Made in the USA
Middletown, DE
10 December 2017